WAY
BOOK SERIES

XML  **es,**

2nd Edition

P9-EDI-659

Cheat Sheet

DTDs in ⌐

The following in

- A DTD is a set of rules defining what tags can appear in a given XML document and how they must nest within each other.

- You use the DTD to declare ⌐ but have to be transmitted o

- DTDs are not necessary in e by themselves, without need

- A DTD specifies the set of re

- A document's DTD specifies

...xt that can appear many times

...l-formed documents can stand

...attributes) for documents.

...which they may be combined.

Rules for Creating Elements

You can create many rules in your DTD that govern how elements can be used in an XML document.

Symbol	Meaning	Example
#PCDATA	Contains parsed character data or text	`<element (#PCDATA)>`
#PCDATA, element-name	Contains text and another element; #PCDATA is always listed first in a rule	`<element (#PCDATA, child)*>`
, (comma)	Must use in this order	`<element (child1, child2, child3)>`
I (bar)	Use only one element of the choices provided	`<element (child1 | child2 | child3)>`
name (by itself)	Use one time only	`<element (child)>`
name?	Use either once or not at all	`<element (child1, child2?, child3?)>`
name+	Use either once or many times	`<element (child1+, child2?, child3)>`
name*	Use once, many times, or not at all	`<element (child1*, child2+, child3)>`
( )	Indicates groups; may be nested	`<element (#PCDATA | child)*>` or `<element ((child1*, child2+, child3)*	child4)>`

XML™ For Dummies, 2nd Edition

Cheat Sheet

Common Reserved Characters

XML has certain reserved characters that can't appear directly in an XML document's content — unless they're part of a CDATA section. To use these reserved characters, you must replace them with their character references in your content, as shown in the following table.

Character	Reference
<	<
>	>
&	&
'	'
"	"

XML Rules

Opening and closing parts of a tag set must always contain the same name in the same case: `<tag>...</tag>` or `<TAG>...</TAG>`, but not `<tag>...</TAG>`.

Empty elements must be written in an abbreviated form. The tag for a break, for example, is `<br/>`.

If you include an opening tag for an element type, you must not omit its closing tag: `<tag>...</tag>` or `<tag/>` is valid.

All tags must be nested correctly: `<tag><element>...</element></tag>` but not `<tag><element>...</tag></element>`.

All attribute values must be enclosed in single or double quotation marks: `<element id="value">` or `<element id='value'>`.

Validating versus Nonvalidating Parsers

Validating parsers:

- ✔ Must check for well-formedness
- ✔ Must read the entire DTD and check that the document meets those constraints
- ✔ Must replace all entity references with the value stated in the DTD
- ✔ Must support all validity constraints and report errors when those constraints are violated

Nonvalidating parsers:

- ✔ Must check for well-formedness
- ✔ Must read the internal DTD subset
- ✔ May read the external DTD subset and external entity values
- ✔ Must replace all entity references if they read a corresponding value in the DTD
- ✔ Do not check the document structure against the constraints specified in the DTD

The First (and Last) Word on Valid versus Well-Formed

A *valid document* must conform to the rules in its DTD, which define what tags can appear in the document and how those tags may nest within one another. A *well-formed* document must have these characteristics:

- ✔ All beginning and ending tags match up
- ✔ Empty tags follow the special XML syntax
- ✔ All attribute values are contained within single or double quotation marks
- ✔ All entities are declared

For Dummies®: Bestselling Book Series for Beginners

XML™

FOR

DUMMIES®

2ND EDITION

XML™
FOR
DUMMIES®
2ND EDITION

by Ed Tittel and Frank Boumphrey

Hungry Minds™

Best-Selling Books • Digital Downloads • e-Books • Answer Networks • e-Newsletters • Branded Web Sites • e-Learning

New York, NY ◆ Cleveland, OH ◆ Indianapolis, IN

XML™ For Dummies,® 2nd Edition

Published by
Hungry Minds, Inc.
909 Third Avenue
New York, NY 10022
www.hungryminds.com
www.dummies.com

Library of Congress Catalog Card No.: 99-69388

ISBN: 0-7645-0692-7

Printed in the United States of America

10 9 8 7 6 5

2B/SR/QW/QR/IN

Distributed in the United States by Hungry Minds, Inc.

Distributed by CDG Books Canada Inc. for Canada; by Transworld Publishers Limited in the United Kingdom; by IDG Norge Books for Norway; by IDG Sweden Books for Sweden; by IDG Books Australia Publishing Corporation Pty. Ltd. for Australia and New Zealand; by TransQuest Publishers Pte Ltd. for Singapore, Malaysia, Thailand, Indonesia, and Hong Kong; by Gotop Information Inc. for Taiwan; by ICG Muse, Inc. for Japan; by Intersoft for South Africa; by Eyrolles for France; by International Thomson Publishing for Germany, Austria and Switzerland; by Distribuidora Cuspide for Argentina; by LR International for Brazil; by Galileo Libros for Chile; by Ediciones ZETA S.C.R. Ltda. for Peru; by WS Computer Publishing Corporation, Inc., for the Philippines; by Contemporanea de Ediciones for Venezuela; by Express Computer Distributors for the Caribbean and West Indies; by Micronesia Media Distributor, Inc. for Micronesia; by Chips Computadoras S.A. de C.V. for Mexico; by Editorial Norma de Panama S.A. for Panama; by American Bookshops for Finland.

For general information on Hungry Minds' products and services please contact our Customer Care Department within the U.S. at 800-762-2974, outside the U.S. at 317-572-3993 or fax 317-572-4002.

For sales inquiries and reseller information, including discounts, premium and bulk quantity sales, and foreign-language translations, please contact our Customer Care Department at 800-434-3422, fax 317-572-4002, or write to Hungry Minds, Inc., Attn: Customer Care Department, 10475 Crosspoint Boulevard, Indianapolis, IN 46256.

For information on licensing foreign or domestic rights, please contact our Sub-Rights Customer Care Department at 212-884-5000.

For information on using Hungry Minds' products and services in the classroom or for ordering examination copies, please contact our Educational Sales Department at 800-434-2086 or fax 317-572-4005.

For press review copies, author interviews, or other publicity information, please contact our Public Relations Department at 317-572-3168 or fax 317-572-4168.

For authorization to photocopy items for corporate, personal, or educational use, please contact Copyright Clearance Center, 222 Rosewood Drive, Danvers, MA 01923, or fax 978-750-4470.

Hungry Minds™ is a trademark of Hungry Minds, Inc

About the Authors

Ed Tittel is a 19-year veteran of the computing industry. After spending his first seven years in harness writing code, Ed switched to the softer side of the business as a trainer and a talking head. A freelance writer since 1986, Ed has written hundreds of magazine articles and worked on more than 100 computer books, including seven different ...*For Dummies* titles on subjects that include Windows 2000, Windows NT, NetWare, HTML, and XML.

Ed still teaches on computer subjects for Austin Community College, the NetWorld + Interop trade show, and the Internet Security Conference (TISC). In his spare time, Ed likes to shoot pool, cook, and hang with his Labrador retriever, Blackie. Contact Ed at etittel@lanw.com.

Frank Boumphrey is new to the ...*For Dummies* team but not new to XML. His rather disreputable career has included punch-card programming, jumping out of airplanes and hoping he didn't get shot on the way down (or when he landed), and spells as a Doctor of Medicine and, more recently, as a medical document consultant.

His most recent crimes include helping to usher XHTML into the world as an editor of the XHTML recommendation, (the namespace police are still trying to locate his whereabouts) and attempting to foist classical literature marked up as XML on the world. He is perpetuating this latest crime under the alias of Director of the HTML Writers Guild Project Gutenberg Markup initiative. He is also a vice-president of the HTML Writers Guild.

Dedication

To the unsung heroes of the W3C, and the many XML working groups, who have made the world (or the Web, at least) a better place through their tireless efforts.

Authors' Acknowledgments

Writing a book is like making a movie — when it come time to thank the contributors there are always more people involved than you might think! So, please, don't think I'm not grateful if you worked on this project and your name doesn't appear here. . .

To begin with, I'd like to thank my colleagues and co-workers who also contributed to the book: Frank Boumphrey, who's got more on the ball than I would ever have imagined; Chelsea Valentine, my Webmaster and local markup wizard, and Natanya Pitts, who's seen this content go through more gyrations than a top! Thanks also to Mary Burmeister, a truly amazing woman with wonderful eyesight!

Next, I'd like to thank the team at IDG who gave us a welcome second try at this book — particularly Sherri Morningstar, our acquisitions editor; Susan Pink, our project editor; and Simon St. Laurent, XML expert and tech editor extraordinaire. Thanks for adding so much to this book! Finally, thanks to Carole McClendon, my truly wonderful agent from Waterside Productions, for making this and so many other good books possible.

On a personal note, I'd like to thank Monica McCrory for finding her way back into my life. Thanks also to Mom and Dad for providing the love and support that made my present life possible. It's been a great ride!

— Ed Tittel

First, I would like to thank my wife, Rona, who reminds me from time to time that there is a life other than the virtual one; second, my 18-year-old cat, Hergie, who likes to sleep on my keyboard but who deigned to get off a sufficient number of occasions to allow me to complete this project; and last but not least, Mary Burmeister, who made working on this project a positive pleasure!

I would also like to take this opportunity to pay my respects to Michael Hart, the founder and Inspiration behind Project Gutenberg. Michael, what you have done is a gift to future generations that will resound down the centuries!

— Frank Boumphrey

Publisher's Acknowledgments

We're proud of this book; please register your comments through our Online Registration Form located at www.dummies.com.

Some of the people who helped bring this book to market include the following:

Acquisitions, Editorial, and Media Development

Project Editor: Susan Pink

Acquisitions Editor: Sherri Morningstar

Proof Editor: Teresa Artman

Technical Editor: Simon St. Laurent

Media Development Specialist: Megan Decraene

Permissions Editor: Carmen Krikorian

Senior Editor, Freelance: Constance Carlisle

Media Development Manager: Heather Heath Dismore

Editorial Assistants: Beth Parlon and Candace Nicholson

Production

Project Coordinator: Regina Synder

Layout and Graphics: Amy Adrian, Brent Savage, Brian Torwelle, Dan Whetstine

Proofreaders: Laura Albert, Corey Bowen, Charles Spencer, York Production Services, Inc.

Indexer: York Production Services, Inc.

General and Administrative

Hungry Minds, Inc.: John Kilcullen, CEO; Bill Barry, President and COO; John Ball, Executive VP, Operations & Administration; John Harris, CFO

Hungry Minds Technology Publishing Group: Richard Swadley, Senior Vice President and Publisher; Mary Bednarek, Vice President and Publisher, Networking and Certification; Walter R. Bruce III, Vice President and Publisher, General User and Design Professional; Joseph Wikert, Vice President and Publisher, Programming; Mary C. Corder, Editorial Director, Branded Technology Editorial; Andy Cummings, Publishing Director, General User and Design Professional; Barry Pruett, Publishing Director, Visual

Hungry Minds Manufacturing: Ivor Parker, Vice President, Manufacturing

Hungry Minds Marketing: John Helmus, Assistant Vice President, Director of Marketing

Hungry Minds Production for Branded Press: Debbie Stailey, Production Director

Hungry Minds Sales: Roland Elgey, Senior Vice President, Sales and Marketing; Michael Violano, Vice President, International Sales and Sub Rights

◆

The publisher would like to give special thanks to Patrick J. McGovern, without whom this book would not have been possible.

◆

Contents at a Glance

Cartoons at a Glance

By Rich Tennant

page 9

page 329

page 51

page 251

page 93

page 313

page 139

page 207

Fax: 978-546-7747

E-mail: richtennant@the5thwave.com

World Wide Web: www.the5thwave.com

Table of Contents

Introduction

*W*elcome to the latest frontier of Web technology. In *XML For Dummies,* 2nd Edition, we introduce you to the mysteries of Extensible Markup Language (XML). XML is helping developers add all kinds of cool applications to the Web's already formidable foundation, which is built on Hypertext Markup Language (HTML).

If you've tried to build complex Web pages that integrate multiple sources of data, require active and dynamic behaviors, and need lots of programming and tweaking to accommodate your special needs, XML may be able to come to your rescue. If you know HTML, you'll probably find it less of a stretch to add XML to your arsenal than you might believe. (No kidding!)

We take a straightforward approach to telling you about XML and what it can do for your online publishing efforts. We keep the amount of technobabble to a minimum and stick to plain English as much as possible. Besides plain talk about hypertext, XML, and the many special-purpose applications that XML supports for chemists, mathematicians, document authors, and many other online constituencies, we include lots of sample code to help you put XML to work on your Web site.

We also include a peachy CD that contains all the XML examples in usable form and a number of other interesting widgets for your own documents. The *XML For Dummies* CD has numerous XML authoring tools, parsers, development kits, and other goodies that we hope you'll find helpful for your own projects!

About This Book

Think of this book as your friendly, approachable guide to using XML to extend your presence on the Web. Using XML is a bit more challenging than using HTML, but this book is organized to make it easier to grapple with XML's fundamentals and then use them well. We also document voluminous additional sources of information, both online and offline. Here are some of the topics we include:

- ✔ An overview of XML's capabilities, terminology, and technologies
- ✔ A comparison of XML to its junior partner HTML and its senior partner SGML

✔ Information on designing, building, and using XML's extensible characteristics

✔ Reviews of a slew of XML applications — special-purpose markup definitions that support chemical and mathematical notation, push publishers, resource delivery, dynamic interfaces, multimedia, and other domains that require more functionality than plain-vanilla HTML can deliver

Although you might think that using XML requires years of training and advanced technical wizardry, we don't think that's true. If you can tell someone how to drive across town, you can certainly use XML to build documents that do what you want them to. The purpose of this book isn't to turn you into a true-blue geek, complete with a pocket protector. Rather, *XML For Dummies,* 2nd Edition shows you which design and technical elements you need so that you can understand what XML is and how it works and gain the know-how and confidence to use it to good effect!

Conventions Used in This Book

Throughout this book, you see lots and lots of code. All XML code appears in monospace type, like this:

```
<Greeting>Hello, world!</Greeting>. . .
```

When you type XML tags or other related information, be sure to copy the information exactly as you see it between the angle brackets (< and >) because that's part of the magic that makes XML work. Other than that, we tell you how to marshal and manage the content that makes your pages special, and we tell you exactly what you need to do to mix the elements of XML with your own work.

Because of the margins in this book, some long lines of XML markup or designations for Web sites (called URLs, for Uniform Resource Locators) wrap to the next line. On your computer, though, these wrapped lines would appear as a single line of XML or as a single URL — so don't insert a hard return when you see one of these lines wrap in the book. Here's an example of a wrapped line of code:

```
www.infomagic.austin.com/nexus/plexus/lexus/praxis/this_is_de
         liberately_long.html
```

XML is sensitive to how tag text is entered: It requires that you use uppercase, lowercase, or mixed characters exactly as they appear in the book (or more importantly, as they're defined in the Document Type Definition, or DTD, that governs any well-formed, valid XML document). To make your work look like ours as much as possible, enter all tag text exactly as it appears in this book. Better yet, copy it from the CD!

Foolish Assumptions

Someone once said that making assumptions makes a fool out of the person who makes them and the person who is their subject. Even so, we're going to make a few assumptions about you, our gentle reader:

- ✔ You're already familiar with HTML and Web pages.
- ✔ You have a working connection to the Internet.
- ✔ You understand the difference between a Web browser and a Web server.
- ✔ You know what a plug-in is and why plug-ins are needed for so much Web-related work.
- ✔ You want to build your own XML documents for fun, for profit, or because it's part of your job.

In addition, we assume that you have a modern Web browser — one that can support XML directly. As we write this, Internet Explorer 5.0 (and higher) is the only widely distributed browser with this capability, but the alpha Version 1.1 Milestone 13 release of Mozilla also shows promising XML capabilities. Don't worry, though, if you don't have such a browser. Part of what you find in these pages (and on the CD) is a collection of pointers that will help you obtain the tools you need to work directly with XML on your own computer. You don't need to be a master logician or a programming wizard to work with XML; all you need is the time required to discover its ins and outs and the determination to understand its intricacies and capabilities.

If you can write a sentence and you know the difference between a heading and a paragraph, you'll be able to build and publish your own XML documents on the Web. If you have an imagination and the ability to communicate what's important to you in an organized manner, you've already mastered the ingredients necessary to build useful, attractive XML documents. The rest is details, and we help you with those!

How This Book Is Organized

This book contains eight major parts and each part contains two or more chapters. Anytime you need help or information, pick up the book and start anywhere you like, or use the table of contents and index to locate specific topics or keywords. This section gives a breakdown of the eight parts and what you'll find in each one.

Part I: Why XML Is "eXtreMely cooL"

Part I sets the stage. It begins with an overview of XML's special capabilities and discusses the design goals and motivations that led to its creation and specification. We also discuss the relationship between XML and HTML and explain why you can convert HTML to XML and why it's probably not a good idea to try to convert XML to HTML. We also briefly explain the relationship between XML and SGML (Standard Generalized Markup Language), which represents a true subset-superset relationship. We conclude Part I with an overview of the contents and notation that make XML what it is today!

Part II: Structuring XML Documents

XML mixes ordinary text with special strings of characters, called markup, that tell XML processors how to display XML-based documents. In Part II, you find out about how XML documents must be structured and about the difference between a well-formed XML document and a valid XML document. Next we launch into a couple of chapters that explain the purpose and functions that Document Type Definitions, or DTDs, play in XML documents and explain what's involved in building your own DTDs.

Part III: Building XML Documents

In Part III, we use a DTD to teach you about the XML markup that it enables. To begin, we explain how to create attributes for the tag definitions that appear in a DTD. Next, we explain how to put a DTD to work. After that, we explain how you can combine DTDs or even build modular DTDs to give yourself a mix-and-match set of building blocks for document markup. We conclude Part III by exploring the character sets and related entities that XML depends on to represent content and explain how to use them in your documents. The four chapters in this part represent some of the most important nuts and bolts in the entire book.

Part IV: The Sense of Style for XML

In Part IV, we tackle the notion of creating document style sheets for XML documents, in terms of both current capabilities and the powerful but not yet complete Extensible Stylesheet Language (also known as XSL). After exploring the capabilities of standard CSS (Cascading Style Sheets), which works with both HTML and XML documents, we jump into the ins and outs of XSL itself. After that, we explain the details involved in applying styles to XML documents and talk about the best ways to use styles to make such documents more presentable.

Part V: XML's Lovely Linking Languages

XML supports some serious enhancements to the simple unidirectional hyperlinks you might know from HTML. In Part V, we explore XML Linking Language (XLink), which you can use to create many kinds of complex hyperlinks. We also investigate XML Path Language (XPath), which is so helpful when pointing from one location on the Web to another, be it within a site or from one site to another. This part concludes with an exploration of XML Pointer Language (XPointer), which you may use to refer to anchors and targets in XML documents.

Part VI: Sampling XML Applications

Part VI takes all the elements covered in prior parts of the book and puts them together to show you the special-purpose XML markup languages, which we call XML applications, that others have created. One way of looking at Part VI is as a short list of several of the more than 100 applications that have been — or are currently being — defined using XML. These include the Channel Definition Format (CDF) language, the Mathematical Markup Language (MathML), and the DocBook DTD, developed for book-length documentation projects.

But aside from assembling a formidable collection of acronyms and their underlying technologies, we created a tour-de-force demonstration of how you can use XML to create compact, powerful markup languages that can meet just about any kind of document-handling or information-delivery needs. These XML applications also demonstrate what's possible within XML.

Part VII: Cool XML Technologies Rule!

In the short but sweet Part VII, we explore a small yet select collection of XML editing, authoring, and validation tools that you might find helpful should you decide to try your hand at this XML game. In addition, we also provide a fine list of pointers to online resources for XML in the hopes that it can lead you closer to XML enlightenment. Enjoy!

Part VIII: The Part of Tens

In Part VIII, you have a chance to observe some of the best and brightest uses of XML, to consider how tag extensions can extend your capabilities, and to understand how attributes can augment your documents' contents. In Chapter 25, you can read about some of the most compelling XML applications known to man (and woman).

Appendix: About the CD

The materials on the *XML For Dummies* CD are organized into separate modules that reflect the layout of the book itself. The CD is designed to help you match up the code and examples that appear within the pages of the book to their electronic counterparts on the CD itself. Given the option, we thought you'd want to take advantage of our research and let our fingers do the walking, so to speak; therefore, you can find on the CD numerous examples and elements that might plug nicely into your own XML documents.

The remainder of the CD is devoted to as comprehensive a collection of tools and programs for XML as we were able to gather for your delectation and use.

Glossary

In the glossary, you can find definitions for all those terms that make you go, "Huh?" We did our best to choose the ones that really need an explanation and defined them in a way that's easy to understand.

Icons Used in This Book

This icon signals technical details that are informative and interesting but not critical to writing XML. Skip these if you want (but please, come back and read them later).

This icon flags useful information that makes XML markup, Web-page design, or other important stuff even less complicated than you feared it might be.

This icon points out information that you shouldn't pass by — don't overlook these gentle reminders (the life you save could be your own).

 Be cautious when you see this icon. It warns you of things you shouldn't do; the bomb emphasizes that the consequences of ignoring these bits of wisdom can be severe.

 When you see this spiderweb symbol, it flags the presence of Web-based resources that you can go out and investigate further. You can also find all these references on the "Jump Pages" on the *XML For Dummies* CD!

 When you see this symbol, it indicates a resource, a tool, or a pointer to resources that you can find on the *XML For Dummies* CD that comes with this book.

To keep up with the latest version of these references, please visit the related "XML For Dummies Update" site on the authors' Web site at `www.lanw.com/XML4Dum2e/`. Here, you find the results of our best efforts to keep the information in the book current and a list of errata to straighten out any of the mistakes, boo-boos, or gotchas that we weren't able to root out before the book went to publication. We hope you find this a convincing demonstration that our hearts are in the right place.

Please share your feedback with us about the book. We can't claim that we'll follow every suggestion or react to every comment, but you can be pretty certain that suggestions that occur repeatedly or that add demonstrable value to the book will find a place in the next edition!

Where to Go from Here

This is where you choose a direction and hit the road! *XML For Dummies,* 2nd Edition is a lot like a recipe for goulash; you begin by tasting the final dish, proceed to assembling the ingredients necessary for your own "document stew," and then get to work on cooking up what you need for yourself (or your organization). A certain amount of studying will be involved, along with lots of Web surfing and investigation of our software and materials — not to mention the galaxy of stuff available online. To the untutored eye, it might even look as though you're fooling around — but we know that you're about to embark on a voyage of discovery that could change the Web as you (and we) know it. Good luck on your journey, and don't forget to keep your eyes on the information highway along the way.

Enjoy!

Part I

Why XML is "eXtreMely cooL"

The 5th Wave   By Rich Tennant

"OK, I think I forgot to mention this, but we now have a Web management function that automatically alerts us when there's a broken link on The Aquarium's Web site."

In this part. . .

Here, you get a gentle but formal introduction to the Extensible Markup Language, also known as XML. Starting in Chapter 1, you find out about XML's history and its parentage. You also ponder the basics of XML markup and the many technologies it can support. In Chapter 2, you explore XML's relationship to HTML and examine the methods available for building XML documents of your own. Finally, in Chapter 3, you have a chance to jump into some technical details as you peruse the rules that make XML markup work, build a simple XML document of your own, and explore the roles that Document Type Definitions (DTDs) and style sheets can play in XML documents.

Chapter 1

What Is XML and Why Should You Care?

In This Chapter

▶ Attending a short history course

▶ Introducing XML's many uses

▶ Exploring the similarities between XML and HTML

▶ Examining XML's syntax and rules

▶ Looking at XML's element types and attributes

*T*he Extensible Markup Language (XML) is pretty hot stuff. Have you ever wanted to extend the Hypertext Markup Language (HTML) beyond its limitations? Have you ever wanted to define your own markup language? Have you ever wanted a document format that you could use to exchange data across the Internet?

Well, XML may be just the solution for your problems. Although XML hasn't been around for very long, it's already employed in various software products in many different industries.

Is it hard to get started with XML? No! Just check out this chapter, and you'll find out more about what XML is, what you can use XML to do, how HTML and XML compare, and what types of XML applications exist — waiting for you to take advantage of them.

A Wee Bit of Background

To understand new technology, it's useful to know a bit about its history and the people behind the phenomenon. So here's a short history of XML. Soon, many folks will know and talk about XML; reading more about this will certainly set you apart from others.

XML was developed by a working group under the umbrella of the World Wide Web Consortium (W3C). This working group includes researchers and experts from many parts of the computer industry: Internet and intranet technologies, the publishing industry, and markup language construction.

The goal of this merry band of technologists, known officially as the W3C XML Working Group, was to bring the Standard Generalized Markup Language (SGML) to the Web. SGML is a powerful *metalanguage* (a language designed for talking about other languages); its primary job is to create markup languages, such as HTML and XML. SGML is a parent to both HTML and XML, among many other markup languages.

XML's design was driven by examining SGML's strengths and weaknesses. The result was a standard for markup languages that contains all the power of SGML without dragging along every complex or seldom-used feature of SGML. (SGML is a "kitchen sink" metalanguage, in that it includes facilities and capabilities solely to make it as complete as possible. These extra bells and whistles make SGML software difficult to implement and slow and unwieldy to run.) XML is a faster, slimmed-down version of SGML designed from the get-go for use on the World Wide Web.

XML made its first public appearance in 1996 when SGML celebrated its 10th anniversary. The first official specification — known in W3C terms as a *W3C Recommendation* — was published in February 1998.

XML has enjoyed wide success and has received plenty of attention from analysts, reporters, and the developer community. XML is already in use or is being introduced in many different applications on the Web today.

XML Suits Many Applications

If you take a close look at today's Internet industry and at the many different research and development initiatives underway, you soon recognize that pinning down a single function for XML is nearly impossible. Case studies of XML never fail to mention new and exciting possibilities in which XML adds value to existing environments or solves what were intractable problems. Nonetheless, many key XML implementations fall into one of two categories:

- Complex document creation
- Data exchange and database connectivity

Each of these is covered in the following sections.

ON THE WEB

The XML Files and other XML phenomena

Those in the W3C's XML Working Group keep most of their materials, including text for speeches, presentations, and technical specifications, freely available on their Web server. Visit their site to find out what you need when you need it most — that is, when you're slaving over some hot XML markup. The address is

```
www.w3.org/XML
```

Not only have these XML gods declared their collective wills, but they've also started a regular e-zine called — you guessed it! — *The XML Files*. The figure shows what the home page looks like. Keep up with the latest and greatest information on XML and its development by visiting

```
www.gca.org/whats_xml/whats_xml
_xmlfiles.htm
```

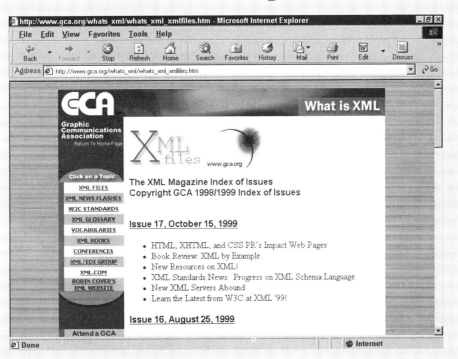

In addition, you might want to visit www.xml.com and click the <u>Annotated XML</u> <u>1.0</u> link to take a peek at Tim Bray's annotated version of the specification.

XML for documents

Nowadays, more and more folks are switching to XML when creating documents. XML is similar to HTML for document creation — except XML supports a richer set of document elements and applies better to various publishing media.

XML for data exchange

Suppose you want to exchange database information across the Internet. In particular, suppose you want to use a browser to send information on a user questionnaire back to the server. This and many other examples require a document format that's extensible — one that can be tailored for some specific application — open, and non-proprietary (see Figure 1-1).

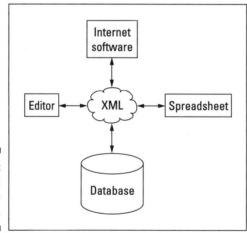

Figure 1-1:
Data
exchange
using XML.

XML is the solution for this kind of problem and will become more important for data exchange over the Internet in the future. The time for import/export filters for thousands of interchange formats is fading fast. In some cases, XML can provide a single platform for data interchange between multiple applications.

It's always difficult to find an interchange format suitable for data transfer between databases from different vendors on different operating systems. One of XML's most important applications is to define such independent formats.

If You Know HTML, You Know XML

Take a look at the following chunk of code:

```
<p>
Superficially, XML markup is the same as HTML markup.
Therefore, you can start writing XML <em>right away</em>.
</p>
```

If you know HTML, you're probably saying, "Sure, that looks like part of an HTML document." You're absolutely right. This excerpt is something that could have been taken from a Web page. However, it could also be part of an XML document. So which statement is correct?

The truth is, both statements are correct. Indeed, XML documents don't look all that different from HTML documents. XML documents use a syntax that has all the same bits and pieces that you know from traditional HTML pages.

An XML document consists of a set of tags, including, for example, the `<p>` and `</p>` and `<em>` and `</em>` tags from HTML. Like HTML, XML also allows you to use attributes and attribute values. Therefore, this next bit of code could also be seen as a piece of XML as well as HTML:

```
<p>
Both the HTML and the XML specification reside on
the Web at the <a href="http://www.w3.org/">World
Wide Web Consortium</a>
</p>
```

Marking Up Is Hard to Do — Not!

You might wonder whether it's hard to get started using XML to create your documents. It isn't.

To create your own XML documents, you don't need anything more than a plain old text editor. If you plan to use XML more often than once in a while or for a lot of pages, however, think about getting an XML editor. (See Chapter 21 for some suggestions on good XML editors.) This special-purpose software can make your job easier and help keep those creative juices flowing! (We all know that tracking tags and cleaning up structures can interrupt, and sometimes completely destroy, the creative train of thought.)

Break out that text editor!

When you get started using XML, it's perfectly acceptable to use a simple ASCII-based, plain-text editor.

When you save a document for the first time, most text editors have predefined settings for the document's extension, which is the piece that comes after the last dot (.) in a filename. If you use generic XML, just use .xml as the extension. For a particular use of XML, such as Channel Definition Format (CDF), use an extension that's more appropriate for that application. For CDF, the .cdf extension is certainly a good choice!

You can create XML documents using one of the more sophisticated document-authoring programs such as Microsoft Word or Corel WordPerfect. Keep in mind, however, that the native File⇨Save format of such programs is a binary format. For example, the native — and default — file format for a Word file is the .doc format. That format is not suitable for XML — or for HTML, either. Make sure to save your document as a text file (.txt) if you want to use it as an XML document.

You must insert all markup yourself when using simple editors. In other words, if you have a paragraph such as

```
This is about XML editing.
```

You need to add the required markup by hand, for example:

```
<Para>This is about XML editing.</Para>
```

If you use and edit XML files only occasionally, marking up by hand will probably do. However, if you're thinking seriously about making XML your primary document format, you need more sophisticated software. (See Chapter 21 for some suggestions.)

XML editors: More power, more convenience

XML editors often look like a blend of traditional word processors and HTML editors. To some extent, you might not even be aware that you're working with XML *per se*.

XML editors have two distinct features that are essential for creating good XML documents:

✔ **Ease of markup:** XML editors can add markup to text as simply as you can turn text bold in today's word processors. All XML editors provide the capability to select text with a cursor and choose which markup you want to apply through a menu of selections.

✔ **Enforcing document rules:** For many applications, XML editors can determine which element types are allowed to appear in certain contexts. In this way, the editor helps you avoid making syntax or structure mistakes. For example, if you specify that a `<ChapterTitle>` is valid only at the head of a chapter, not within an ordinary paragraph, the editor can make sure that no `<ChapterTitle>` tag appears outside its proper place.

The Power of XML

XML is not limited to any fixed set of *tags,* or *element types* (which is the proper name for the whatchamathingies that show up between the opening < and closing > characters in XML markup). Using XML, you can define your own set of elements and even your own attributes to use within your document.

XML enables you to give more meaningful names to your markup. In HTML, the paragraph tag (`<p>`) is one of the most frequently used elements in Web documents. In XML, you can replace the paragraph tag with something more descriptive. For example, if you were writing a cookbook, you could use a `<CookingIntruction>` tag instead of the `<p>` tag.

More meaningful names in your documents

Suppose you have HTML text that looks like this:

```
<html>
<p>
This book is about the foundations of the Extensible
Markup Language and how to use it for your own
applications.
</p>
<p>
The authors are Ed Tittel and Frank Boumphrey
</p>
</html>
```

This is a normal HTML document; you know nothing about the meaning of the data contained in the document. In other words, you don't know whether that first sentence is a very long title, a description in a catalog, the first line of a book, the chorus of the new Britney Spears song, or something else.

Consider this alternate form of expression, in which cover copy (the information found on the cover of a book) for a book is provided and broken into specific, named elements:

```
<Cover>
<Abstract>
This book is about the foundations of the eXtensible
Markup Language and how to use it for your own
applications.
</Abstract>
<AuthorInfo>
<P>The authors are <Author>Ed Tittel</Author> and
<Author> Frank Boumphrey</Author>. </P>
</AuthorInfo>
</Cover>
```

Based on the markup tags, we can now identify that this is cover copy, and that it includes an abstract plus a section of author information. Furthermore, we can identify each of the book's authors individually. It shouldn't be hard to think of ways to increase the information associated with any particular element. For example, perhaps the <Author> tag could include not only the author's name but also a brief biography.

XML allows you to define and use your own elements and attributes. This is what XML is all about and also why XML is the *Extensible* Markup Language.

XML defines new languages

You can define your own markup languages using XML as well. If you aren't satisfied with HTML or need something completely different, you can create a markup language. XML provides a general syntax that you can use to describe exactly how a markup language looks and behaves.

To specify which *elements* (the markup tags) and *attributes* (values associated with specific tags) are allowed in your documents, you must define the rules for your markup. This statement of rules is called a *Document Type Definition* (DTD). A DTD can be a separate document (a good idea if you want to reuse your work repeatedly), or you can include it at the head of an XML document using additional markup.

But you don't even have to go through the step of adding introductory markup. You can just get started and use your own elements right away. However, if you want others to use your markup language, you must explicitly state which elements and attributes are allowed, where they are allowed, and which elements can appear within other elements. That's where the DTD, or equivalent markup, comes into play.

We cover all the details on how to do this kind of stuff later in the book. By now, you're probably asking, "Geez, do I have to go through this to get going with XML?" The answer is no. Experts in many applications and industries have already created specific markup languages that you can use as-is. Here are a few popular examples — some of which are described in detail later in this book:

- ✔ **The Extensible Stylesheet Language (XSL):** In addition to supporting Cascading Style Sheets (CSS), XML boasts its own style sheet language called XSL to provide pinpoint placement and appearance controls for documents. Read more about XSL in Part IV, in Chapters 11 through 14.

- ✔ **Linking languages:** XML currently supports three languages to help authors manage the appearance and behavior of hyperlinks in documents. These languages are the XML Linking Language (XLink), the XML Pointer Language (XPointer), and the XML Path Language (XPath). All are covered in Part V in Chapters 15 through 17.

- ✔ **Channel Definition Format (CDF):** CDF provides an open way to exchange information about channels on the Internet. If you're not sure what channels and CDF are, please read Chapter 18. If you've already used the channel features in programs such as Internet Explorer 4.0 or 5.0, read the chapter anyway for all the details and to find out how to use CDF for your own applications.

- ✔ **Mathematical Markup Language (MML):** Exchange of mathematical formulas has always been a big challenge for the Web. MML defines the vocabulary necessary to describe all the important notation you use for higher math. Even if you're not a math expert, don't miss Chapter 19 for more coverage of MML.

- ✔ **DocBook for XML:** This set of notation was developed for building books using SGML. It has been recast into a kinder, gentler XML-based form to make it easier to use. Check it out further in Chapter 20.

The universe of XML-based markup languages, also called XML applications, is constantly expanding. The odds are high that you'll find a markup language for your particular needs soon. If the language doesn't completely satisfy you, extend it — after all, XML is the *Extensible* Markup Language.

Web Pages before — and after — XML

XML changes the way we publish information on the Internet. XML is not a replacement for HTML. Rather, it enables the Internet industry to invent a new set of powerful tools.

XML: One document, many different outputs

Authors of XML-based Web documents do not make any assumptions about how the documents will be used on the client side. In other words, if you look at HTML pages, they are designed for one particular purpose, and that is to display information inside a browser. Browsers process HTML documents easily, but software sometimes has a difficult time post processing the information that such documents contain. This limitation does not apply to XML documents.

When we say *post processing,* we mean taking information delivered within a document and using that information in some other process or program. For example, suppose you receive a purchase order in the form of an XML document. An application that understands XML purchase orders can use that data to determine which items in what quantities have been ordered, and can even send instructions to another piece of software to generate a pick-list so the order can be picked, packed, and shipped from the warehouse. Now that's what we call post processing!

In many cases, XML documents are used with style sheets to provide high-quality output on-screen. You can use the same data, however, to send information to a speech-synthesis program that reads the text to a person who is blind or has low vision. Alternatively, that same data might also create output on a Braille reader. The same document with a layout program and a style sheet might be used also for high-quality printouts. (See Figure 1-2 for an illustration of this process.)

The beauty of this concept is that you never need to change the XML data to create output for different devices. You need only to use different pieces of software that can provide the output for a particular format or output device.

XML for data — HTML for display

In many cases, you'll see a combination of XML and HTML in everyday use. XML is all about preserving information. HTML is all about, or at least it is accomplished at, displaying information within a browser. Why not combine the best of these two worlds?

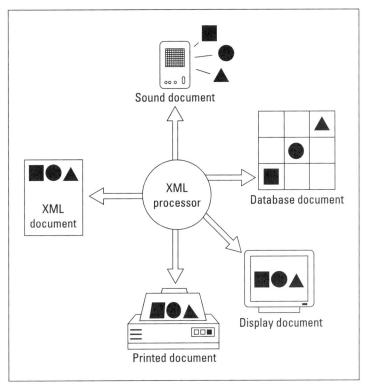

Figure 1-2:
XML for
different
outputs.

The basic idea is to have the original data based on XML, where all the rich markup and additional information about a document is available. Then you can use the same document for many different purposes and use the "intelligence" in the data to build powerful applications to display the data on-screen and translate it into HTML, a concept illustrated in Figure 1-3.

This conversion from XML to HTML can happen in one of two ways. XML stores and organizes the data, and HTML renders it inside your browser. The methods differ depending on when XML data is translated into HTML for display inside a browser.

The conversion experience can occur in the following ways:

- XML data is sent to the client (your browser), and the browser uses a style sheet — extra information that helps your browser to translate XML into HTML — to display HTML on the client.

- The XML data resides on the server, where it is converted to HTML before it is sent to a browser.

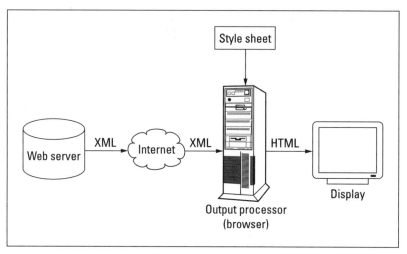

Figure 1-3:
XML to
HTML on
the client
side.

Better post-processing

HTML has been criticized because the data in an HTML document is display oriented — the data is hard to use for post-processing, such as constructing searchable local indexes. You can see the effect of this on your favorite search engine when you query for a particular subject. Very often, you get back either 0 hits or 100,000.

Because XML data preserves both context and semantics, it's much easier to build applications that apply some smarts to electronic documents. Suppose some XML documents contain an ⟨Author⟩ tag. This means you can search the Web for all documents in which Chelsea Valentine is the author, for example. (You'd probably choose another author — Chelsea happens to be one of our favorites.)

XML makes it much easier for search engines to access information inside documents because those engines can use XML tag contents and attributes to find specific entries or text. Therefore, instead of relying on the document titles and headings that robots usually gather from HTML documents to index their contents, you'll be able to access the entire content (and markup) inside XML documents instead. This not only covers the ground more closely but also makes it far more likely that you'll be able to use the results of your searches on the first try!

Chapter 2

The Beginnings of XML

*H*TML, XML, SGML, and XHTML — what's up with all the acronyms? As you delve into the world of Web creation, you'll hear — or at least read about — some of these acronyms. You may even know the extended name for each one. How do they all relate?

It's no mistake that they all end in *ML*. XML and HTML are derived from the same parent: Standard Generalized Markup Language (SGML). And Extensible HTML (XHTML) is the product of both the Hypertext Markup Language (HTML) and the Extensible Markup Language (XML).

But, wait, we get to that soon enough. For now, take a quick peek at the markup language family tree shown in Figure 2-1.

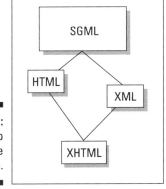

Figure 2-1:
The markup
language
family tree.

We won't go so far as to say that if you know HTML, XML is a snap to understand and use. However, knowing how a markup language works will help you understand and be able to use XML efficiently. If you're familiar with HTML, you need to shelve some of your ideas about it — such as doing whatever it takes with the markup to make your page look right — to work with XML successfully.

Many of you are approaching the topic of XML with at least a smattering of HTML knowledge, so we want to expose the similarities — and differences — between these two markup languages. Our goal in this chapter is to remove any misconceptions you might have that "XML is just another version of HTML." We compare HTML to XML, introduce you to the next wave of HTML — XHTML — and even convert an HTML document to a well-formed XML document.

The most important thing to take home from this chapter is that although XML and HTML are similar in lineage and construction, they are two very different markup languages. You might not have to convert all your HTML documents into valid XML; rather, you need to decide which markup language is best for your content and information handling needs.

Enough with the introductions! Please make sure your seat is all the way forward, and your tray table is in the upright and locked position. Here goes!

What HTML Does Best, and Where Its Limits Lie

Although you purchased this book to find out about XML, you wouldn't get your money's worth if we didn't take some time to talk about HTML. As a Web designer, you're forced to work in an imperfect world. For example, new language capabilities take center stage every few months, but new browser versions do not. Therefore, the user's browser doesn't always support the language. The two main browsers, Microsoft Internet Explorer and Netscape Navigator, still don't fully support Cascading Style Sheets (CSS); so don't expect the next versions to completely support XML either. If your target audience is the world-at-large, you might have to work with HTML for some time to come.

If you're one of the people who still must work with HTML (in other words, your audience is still the general public), here's a little background: HTML is a presentation language used to create documents for display on the Web.

HTML tags define how text is displayed in your Web browser. Add HTML markup to some text, add some links to graphics, throw in some hyperlinks for good measure, and you have an HTML document.

HTML makes our Web world look pretty. In some instances, "pretty" is all that is needed for a Web page, such as a personal site created for your family. You want an easy, cheap way to let others know what you've been doing and to post a few pictures of your latest addition.

The Web site in Figure 2-2 is a good example of straight HTML. The site has little need for flexibility and doesn't need a database. (If you need a database for your family's site, we wouldn't want to organize your next family reunion.)

If you want to sell the infamous widget from your Web site, however, you have to jump through some additional hoops. You'd want to create a database with product codes, styles, and colors, and you'd also want your customers to be able to select any combination of this data. In this case, HTML is not your best tool for representing the data in textual form.

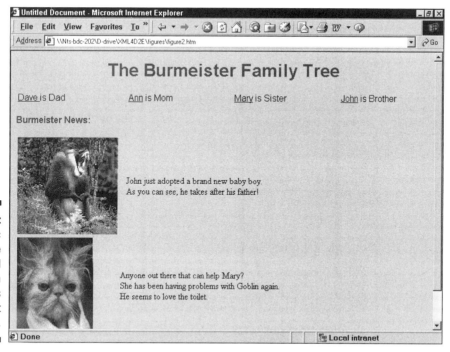

Figure 2-2:
A basic HTML page displayed with a browser's default settings.

The idea behind HTML was a modest one. It was meant to describe not the page content but rather how that content should be displayed in your browser. Since its introduction to the public, however, HTML has been called on to provide solutions to problems it was never meant to solve. Some of the things HTML wasn't meant to do include the following:

✔ Tightly control document display

✔ Be flexible enough to describe different, specific types of information

✔ Convey information in a variety of media and formats

✔ Define complex linking relationships between documents

✔ Publish a single set of information across a variety of media

Web designers (like us, for example) sometimes catch themselves thinking, "But my heading has to be in 45.5 Arial and centered in the second two-thirds of the page." Although this sentiment is a bit exaggerated, it's not far from what Web designers expect their HTML to do, leaving them wondering why HTML doesn't live up to their expectations.

Remember, HTML was created not as a page layout markup language but as a document-description markup language. Users would be able to describe a document's structure as well as the role each part of the document played, regardless of how it looked on a monitor.

Today's Web designers want to achieve the same formatting control over their Web documents that they have over printed documents. They want what they see on their screens with their browsers to be exactly what any visitor to their sites will see. Two overarching problems prevent Web designers from achieving this control using HTML:

✔ **HTML lacks fine controls.** First and foremost, HTML doesn't include the mechanisms for maintaining fine control. You can't specify the display size of a document or control the size of a browser window. These two variables are affected by the user's screen size and personal preferences. Although HTML 4.0 includes `<font>` tags to help you manipulate font style, size, and color, users can override your settings with their own.

✔ **Browsers' displays vary.** Along with the different versions of the two most common browsers — Internet Explorer and Netscape Navigator — Mosaic, HotJava, and other graphical browsers make it impossible to know exactly which browser and platform are being used to view your pages. And you can't realistically test every Web page on every available browser on every platform just to see what your users will see.

Recently, new tags and style sheets have been introduced to Web designers that will, we hope, provide them with the control they want. Although adding style sheets and tags to your arsenal gives you an enormous amount of flexibility in comparison to earlier versions of HTML, they do not solve every Web design problem. That's where XML comes in.

Style sheets have become an integral part of the XML discussion. For an in-depth look at the use of style sheets and XML, please visit Chapter 11.

XML and HTML Compared and Contrasted

Right off the bat, we want to tell you in no uncertain terms that XML won't — and can't — replace HTML. XML and HTML are not the same markup languages.

But XML and HTML both derive from the same parent, SGML, so they must be similar, right? The answer is yes and no.

HTML and XML both use tags and attributes, right? Yes, XML and HTML look similar. But whereas HTML tells us how text is displayed in a browser window, XML tells us what each word means.

In the preceding section, we outlined HTML's limitations. Perhaps you're now wondering why you should still use it. HTML has several advantages and, in the short term, you have no choice in the matter. Besides, HTML is good at the job for which it was created. It uses markup to provide users with a reasonably consistent Web-page presentation. As the expectations of businesses and the end-users increases, however, so does the need for a more flexible solution. XML rises to meet that challenge.

The benefits of using HTML

Why use HTML? Because it's quick, easy, and cheap.

Anyone can create an HTML document with a text editor and a little knowledge. Even if you don't know HTML, you can use an HTML editor — WYSIWYG style — and produce Web pages in minutes.

The most important reason not to write off HTML lies in where it's headed: XHTML 1.0. HTML is not out of the game yet. (See the "XHTML 1.0: Best of Both Worlds section" later in this chapter for more information on XHTML.)

The benefits of using XML

XML seems to be brimming with benefits. Here's a list of these benefits, in a nutshell:

- ✔ **Structured data:** Applications can extract the information they need.
- ✔ **Data exchange:** Allows you to exchange database contents, or other structured information over the Internet.
- ✔ **XML complements HTML:** XML data can be used in an HTML page.
- ✔ **Self-describing:** No prior knowledge of an application is needed.
- ✔ **Search engines:** Increase in search relevancy because of contextual information found in XML documents.
- ✔ **Updates:** No need to update the entire site page by page; the Document Object Model (DOM) built into XML documents permits individual elements to be accessed (and updated).
- ✔ **User-selected view of data:** Different users can have access to different information, or present the same information in a variety of ways.

As a user, the potential for intelligent pages that contain human-readable data is exciting. For example, HTML-based search tools use keywords and text strings. XML-based search tools can use them too, but they can also use metadata and data structure. This means your searches produce relevant results more quickly.

A Web designer reaps several benefits as well. For example, if you maintain a site that sells widgets and inflation kicks in, raising your price by $1.50 per widget, you could implement the change across the entire site. Forget the late nights of changing each page. You're working with intelligent data now.

The benefits of XML are endless. Trust us, there's a reason why large corporations now use XML-like languages to maintain their intranets. It also explains why XML is all that Web designers (like us) want to talk about.

Making the Switch: HTML to XML

Converting HTML documents to XML can deliver certain benefits. That's because XML documents organize information rather than merely display it. Because XML is still in its infancy, however, creating viewable documents in XML using current tools *can* be problematic. And although both Microsoft and Netscape are adding XML support to their browsers, how this support will be implemented remains to be seen. For now, using an XML editor or a special XML-capable browser (and such browsers work best on UNIX operating systems at present) is the best way to view your work in native XML format.

In this section, we show you how to turn HTML into a well-formed XML document to illustrate the relationship between XML and HTML. And, as you can imagine, with new developments and technology come new tools, so we also mention some nifty tools that will do the hard work for you.

In this section, we toss around some terms that you might not know; you don't need to understand them 100 percent for this exercise. Our goal is to demonstrate how XML builds on what you already know about HTML.

It isn't as difficult as you might think to create a well-formed XML document from an HTML document, especially if the original HTML document uses correct syntax. When converting HTML to XML, the most important characteristics are that

- All tags have distinct start and end components
- All tags are nested correctly
- All attribute values are quoted
- Empty elements are formatted correctly

The first three requirements are pretty straightforward (even though they aren't strictly necessary in HTML). XML doesn't allow you to use many HTML shortcuts and is quite unforgiving of syntax errors. That's why HTML documents must be altered to turn them into acceptable XHTML (which is a specialized form of XML). On the other hand, these requirements make XML and XHTML documents easy for computers to read and digest.

Now that you know the HTML characteristics that must change to create XML documents, let the switching begin. Our sample HTML page is a short page that lists a few of our favorite XML Web sites. It appears in Figure 2-3, and uses the following HTML code:

```
<html>
<head>
<title>XML Sites</title>
</head>
<body>
<h1>Web sites on XML</h1>
<p>Below you will find a list of some our favorite <em><font
        color=green>XML Web sites</em></font>
<ul>
<li>http://www.xml.com
<li>http://www.xml.org
<li>http://www.w3.org/XML/
<li>http://www.oasis-open.org/cover/sgml-xml.html
</ul>
<br>
<img src="file.gif" alt="image name">
</body>
</html>
```

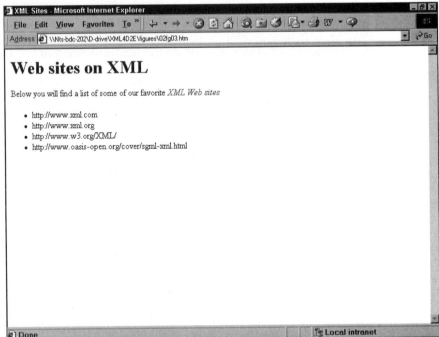

Figure 2-3:
A short
page listing
some of our
favorite
XML Web
sites.

Next, we turn this HTML page into a proper XML page by making sure that it meets each requirement.

All elements have a start tag and an end tag

The first requirement is that all elements have a start tag and an end tag. As you know, several HTML tags, such as `<p>` and `<li>`, act as text containers but don't require ending tags. Those tags work in non-pair containers because of a special SGML shortcut that allows the parser to assume an ending tag would have occurred right before another start tag of the same element. So, in effect:

```
<p>text text text
```

is the same as

```
<p>text text text</p>
```

Doing without an end tag doesn't fly in XML. So, in our sample document, we'll need to add a closing paragraph tag to this line of code:

```
<p>Below you will find a list of some our favorite <em><font
        color=green>XML Web sites</em></font>
```

We also must add ending list item tags (</li>) to all four selections in the unordered list. Our new code, with the appropriate additions, looks like this:

```
<html>
<head>
<title>XML Sites</title>
</head>
<body>
<h1>Web sites on XML</h1>
<p>Below you will find a list of some our favorite <em><font
        color=green>XML Web sites</em></font></p>
<ul>
<li>http://www.xml.com</li>
<li>http://www.xml.org</li>
<li>http://www.w3.org/XML/</li>
<li>http://www.oasis-open.org/cover/sgml-xml.html</li>
</ul>
<br>
<img src="file.gif" alt="image name">
</body>
</html>
```

Tags are nested correctly

The rules of both XML and HTML syntax say that tags must be nested in a certain order. The rule is always to close first what you opened last. So, even though this HTML code

```
<em><font color=green>XML Web sites</em></font>
```

looks fine in a browser, it's not correct technically. Instead, it should be as follows:

```
<em><font color=green>XML Web sites</font></em>
```

Two down, two to go.

All attribute values are quoted

HTML requires that only certain attribute values, such as text strings and URLs, be quoted. Other values, such as image height and font size, produce the desired results regardless of the quoted state. In XML, all attribute values must be quoted.

To bring our sample into compliance with this rule, we must change the following code, which works just fine in a HTML Web page:

```
<em><font color=green>XML Web sites</font></em>
```

to this correct XML syntax:

```
<em><font color="green">XML Web sites</font></em>
```

Both the single and the double quotation marks are legal in XHTML. However, you'll see the double quotation mark used most often.

We're almost finished!

Empty elements are formatted correctly

The XML way of formatting empty elements may seem a bit strange, but remember that all other elements must have both a start-tag and an end-tag to be correct in XML.

Empty elements are singleton tags (also called *empty tags*); they don't have text sandwiched between a pair of tags.

An `<img>` tag or a `<br>` tag that looks like this in our HTML example:

```
<br>
<img src="file.gif" alt="image name">
```

Looks like this in XML:

```
<br />
<img src="file.gif" alt="image name" />
```

How easy is that?

So, we've made all the necessary corrections and now our proper XML document looks like this:

```
<html>
<head>
<title>XML Sites</title>
</head>
<body>
<h1>Web sites on XML</h1>
<p>Below you will find a list of some our favorite <em><font
        color="green">XML Web sites</font></em></p>
<ul>
<li>http://www.xml.com</li>
<li>http://www.xml.org</li>
<li>http://www.w3.org/XML/</li>
<li>http://www.oasis-open.org/cover/sgml-xml.html</li>
</ul>
<br />
<img src="file.gif" alt="image name" />
</body>
</html>
```

Wow, wasn't that simple? And you thought XML was going to be hard! Sure, you must remember some new rules, and things in XML are a bit more formal and less forgiving than in HTML, but XML and HTML remain similar in form and function.

XHTML 1.0: Best of Both Worlds

Simply put, Extensible Hypertext Markup Language (XHTML) is the reformulation of HTML 4.0 as an application of XML 1.0. If you're familiar with HTML 4.0, XHTML 1.0 should be easy. Don't let the new acronym scare you; think of it as HTML 4.0 with a face-lift.

XHTML is intended to conform to XML and, if you follow some simple guidelines, it will operate in HTML 4.0-conforming user agents (for example, browsers). XHTML looks a lot like HTML but has a few notable exceptions:

- ✔ Tags must be written using lowercase only, for example

    Correct: `<b>This text is bold</b>`

    Incorrect: `<B>This text is bold</B>`

- ✔ Empty tags must include a space before the trailing / and > in all empty elements:

    Correct: `<img src="pajamacus.gif" alt="pajamacus" />`
    `<br />`

    Incorrect: `<img src="pajamacus.gif" alt="pajamacus"><br>`

✔ All nonempty elements must have closing tags.

> **Correct:** `<p>Closing tags mean no errors</p>`

> **Incorrect:** `<p>Closing tags mean no errors`

✔ All elements must be nested properly; elements may not overlap.

> **Correct:** `<b>this text is in <em>bold</em></b>`

> **Incorrect:** `<b>this text is in <em>bold</b></em>`

✔ Attribute values must always be in quotes.

> **Correct:** `<body color="#ffffff">`

> **Incorrect:** `<body color=#ffffff>`

Before, Web designers could be sloppy, for example:

```
<body>
<p>I am late for lunch and have to run
<p>My boss is yelling at me, I must finish that report!
</body>
```

Now, XHTML demands respect — and closing tags, for example:

```
<body>
<p>I am late for lunch, but I cannot forget my closing
        tag.</p>
<p>My boss is yelling, but those creators of XML will yell if
        I don't close my tags.</p>
</body>
```

Why do we like XHTML? The benefits of XHTML aren't clear until you understand what's so great about XML. With the strictness of XML comes an increase in predictability. With XML (and, possibly, XHTML), either your code will work without a hitch or you'll receive an error message. To a Web designer, this is wonderful news — no more late nights praying that a universal browser will be mandated!

The following is a list of some of the advantages of XHTML:

✔ XHTML documents can be viewed, edited, and validated with XML tools.

✔ Well-formed XHTML documents mean better-structured documents.

✔ XHTML documents may be delivered using different Internet media types, such as palm computers.

Remember to follow our guidelines presented at the beginning of this section and you will be authoring XHTML documents in no time at all.

Here's a simple example of XHTML 1.0 at work:

```
<?xml version="1.0" encoding="UTF-8"?>
<!DOCTYPE html PUBLIC "-//W3C//DTD XHTML 1.0 Strict//EN"
          "http://www.w3.org/TR/xhtml1/DTD/strict.dtd">
<html xmlns="http://www.w3.org/TR/xhtml1/strict"
          xml:lang="en" lang="en">
<head>
<title>Visit My Famous Widget Factory</title>
</head>
<body>
<p>Purchase your first widget, visit
<a href="http://www.widgetsAREus.org/">
www.widgetsAREus.org</a>.</p>
</body>
</html>
```

What if you create a site using HTML 4.0 and you want to update it to XHTML 1.0? Not a problem. A few tools are available to help you do this, or you can do it yourself by hand. Make sure your XHTML documents render on existing HTML user agents (also known as browsers).

Convert your HTML document to an XHTML document with ease using HTML Tidy, an open-source program available at `www.w3.org/People/Raggett/tidy/`.

Cool Tools for Building XML Documents

XML is a subset of SGML, so authoring many tools once used for SGML have been re-casted and are now ready to take on XML. Here's a list of some of our favorites:

- ✔ **Adept Editor,** from Arbor Text, is an expensive but fully equipped XML authoring tool. You can use this software to define data structures and demonstrate how they should look on the screen. Adept Editor is available for Windows at `www.arbortext.com`.

- ✔ **FrameMaker + SGML 5.5,** from Adobe Systems, provides control and flexibility while allowing users to select XML elements, attributes, and document structure from a list. In addition to publishing XML documents, you can create HTML, PDF, PostScript, and SGML documents. FrameMaker + SGML 5.5 is available for Windows and Macintosh at `www.adobe.com`.

- ✔ **XMetaL,** from SoftQuad Software, is an advanced XML authoring tool. Its familiar, word-processor-like environment makes XMetaL an easy-to-use solution that reduces training and implementation costs. XMetaL is available for Windows at `www.softquad.com`.

- ✔ **XML Pro,** from Vervet Logic, is a basic XML editor that enables you to create and edit documents using menus and screens. There's no support for document conversion, but if you're starting from scratch, XML Pro's wizards can put you on the right track. XML Pro is available for Windows at `www.vervet.com`.

- ✔ **XML Spy,** from Icon-Information Systems, lets you edit XML, XHTML, Extensible Stylesheet Language (XSL), and Document Type Definition (DTD) files. In addition, it provides three advanced views of your documents: an Enhanced Grid View for structured editing, a Source View with syntax coloring for low-level work, and an integrated Browser View that supports CSS and XSL style sheets. XML Spy is available for Windows at `www.xmlspy.com`.

Building XML Documents by Hand

Building XML documents by hand is easy. Before jumping in, however, get an overview of the process by taking a quick look at these steps:

1. **Make an XML declaration.** By including an XML declaration, you allow browsers and document readers to identify how the document should be processed.

2. **Create a root element.** The root element can describe the function of the document; it can't be repeated.

3. **Create XML code.** Invent your own elements (and attributes) as needed. Don't forget to make a well-formed document.

4. **Check your document.** If your document does not follow XML rules, and is therefore not well formed, it can't be read by the XML reader (in most instances, your browser).

With all you have discovered so far in the chapter, you're ready to step through your first XML document. Here you go!

Step 1: Making an XML declaration

The first step, creating an XML declaration, is easy. An XML declaration is optional (but highly recommended) and can have up to five parts. All together, these parts look like this:

```
<?xml version="1.0" standalone="no" encoding="UTF-8"?>
```

What does it all mean? Each part of this sample declaration works as follows:

- ✔ `<?xml` begins the XML declaration.

- ✔ `version="1.0"` describes the version of XML in use. Currently, XML 1.0 is the only version; therefore, `version` must equal 1.0.

- ✔ `standalone="no"` specifies whether external markup declarations exist. You may set this attribute equal to `yes` or `no`. Yes means that external declarations are not used; no means that an external declaration will be referenced.

- ✔ `encoding="UTF-8"` specifies the character encoding the author used. UTF 8 corresponds to what most of us know as 8-bit ASCII characters.

- ✔ `?>` closes the XML declaration.

Step 2: Creating a root element

The root element is the most important element in any XML document. In HTML, `<html>` is the root element. In XML, however, the root element can be anything. You create the root element and all XML elements and then use them in the same way that you use predefined HTML tags.

For our example, we use `<Book>` as our root element. Because the document is about a book, our root element name sets the stage for the sample document.

This is what we have so far:

```
<?xml version="1.0" standalone="no" encoding="UTF-8"?>
<Book>
</Book>
```

Step 3: Creating XML code

For now, we'll keep our XML code simple. For a more in-depth look at creating XML documents, see Chapter 4. Here, we just show you the bare bones of a well-formed XML document.

Remember, the characteristics of a well-formed XML document include the following:

- ✔ All tags have both distinct start and distinct end components. (Sometimes both components appear in a single tag, called an empty element.)
- ✔ All tags are nested correctly.

> ✔ All attribute values are quoted.
>
> ✔ Empty elements are formatted correctly.

That said, the body of our document looks like this:

```
<?xml version="1.0" standalone="no" encoding="UTF-8"?>
<Book>
<Title>XML For Dummies, 2nd Edition</Title><Br />
<Author>Edward Tittel</Author>
<Author>Frank Boumphrey</Author>
<Publisher>IDG Books Worldwide</Publisher>
<Date>2000</Date>
</Book>
```

There you have it, XML code complete!

Step 4: Checking your document

An XML document with an error is a dead document. Even omitting a single closing bracket renders a document unreadable. An easy way to check XML documents is to use a *parser,* which looks for errors.

Following are some Web sites where you can go to check XML documents for errors:

> ✔ Robin Cover's Check or Validate XML page at `www.oasis-open.org/cover/check-xml.html`
>
> ✔ IBM's DOMit Validation Servlet at `www.networking.ibm.com/xml/XmlValidatorForm.html`
>
> ✔ Microsoft's XML Validation page at `http://msdn.microsoft.com/downloads/samples/internet/xml/xml_validator/`
>
> ✔ XML.com RUWF? page at `www.xml.com/pub/tools/ruwf/check.html`

There you have it. Four steps to a well-formed XML document!

Chapter 3

Shake Hands with XML!

. . . .

In This Chapter

▶ Exploring a simple XML example

▶ Playing by XML's rules

▶ Adding context to XML documents using style sheets and DTDs

▶ Building an XML solution

▶ Looking at XML at work in the world

. . . .

So you're psyched about XML — you should be. After all, if you know HTML, you already have a grasp on some of the most basic fundamentals of markup, and XML is just markup.

XML is a powerful tool that allows you to identify the pieces and parts of all kinds of structure data — from catalog information to chemical equations — in a pretty simple way. And to top it all off, XML documents are text based. After you create your document, you can share it with all your friends and family (okay, and coworkers and business partners) regardless of the computer or operating system they use.

In a nutshell, XML is one of the coolest technologies to arrive on the scene since Tim Berners-Lee invented HTML. All you have to do now is find out how to use XML, and you can implement your own way-cool, cutting-edge solutions. In this chapter, you discover the bare basics of XML so you can begin building your own XML documents and solutions.

When you work with a truly simple XML document, you find out the rules you must follow when you build XML documents. You also get a glimpse of how style sheets and Document Type Definitions (DTDs) can provide complex contextual data for otherwise simple documents.

The chapter also includes a brief overview of the different components you should expect to find in every XML solution, so you're aware up-front of the collection of pieces and parts you must have to bring a complete XML solution online. Finally, to prove that XML really is as powerful as we claim — and to provide you with a bit of inspiration — the last few pages in the chapter showcase three real-world XML solutions.

A Truly Simple XML Document

You're probably thinking "Enough hype already. Show me the money." (Or the XML in this case.) Your wish is our command. One simple XML document coming up:

```
<?xml version="1.0" standalone="yes"?>
<Recipe cook="The XML Gourmet">
    <Title>Bean Burrito</Title>
    <Category name="tex-mex" />
    <Ingredients>
        <Item>1 can refried beans</Item>
        <Item>1 cup longhorn colby cheese, shredded</Item>
        <Item>1 small onion, finely chopped</Item>
        <Item>3 flour tortillas</Item>
    </Ingredients>

    <CookingInstructions>
        Empty can of refried beans into medium saucepan.
        Heat over medium-high heat until beans are smooth
        and bubbly.
        Warm tortillas in microwave for 30 seconds.
    </CookingInstructions>

    <ServingInstructions>
        Spread 1/3 of warm beans on each tortilla.
        Sprinkle with cheese and onions.
        Roll tortillas and serve.
    </ServingInstructions>
</Recipe>
```

So that's how you make a bean burrito. Oh yeah, it's also how you use XML to describe how to make a bean burrito. That wasn't so bad now, was it?

This sample XML document uses our own markup language, the Recipe Markup Language (RML), to describe the different components of a recipe, including its title and author and the ingredients and steps for preparing and serving the finished dish. Although the recipe is described only with markup tags, you can easily identify its different pieces and parts based on the markup alone. You can also tell what kind of information each tag is designed to describe — <Ingredients> identifies the recipe ingredients and <CookingInstructions> identifies cooking instructions. That's what XML is all about. A few HTML tags and some descriptive tags and poof, you have an XML document. It's almost as easy as making a bean burrito.

We're sure that you can think of different ways to describe this same recipe using more or different tags. Maybe you would identify the steps in the cooking and serving instructions with <Step>. . .</Step> tags inside the <CookingInstructions>. . .</CookingInstructions> and <ServingInstructions>. . .</ServingInstructions> tags. Or maybe you'd rather see the author of the recipe identified as author instead of cook. Keep in mind that we wanted to show you a truly simple document.

Given time, we could turn even this simple bean burrito recipe and its RML tags into a deeply complex document. The great thing about XML is that you can create your own markup. So if you have a burning desire to flesh out our RML, go for it. And as you work your way through other chapters in the book and discover the fine points of creating XML DTDs and documents, change our RML as you see fit. It's a great exercise and you'll end up with a tool for describing your favorite recipes.

The Least You Need to Know: Basic Rules for XML Markup

XML documents are exactly as simple or as complex as they need to be. There's no extra fluff along the way just for good measure. Obviously, a document that describes the different elements in a complex chemical formula is a bit more complicated than one that describes the different pieces and parts of an address book, a recipe, or a novel. Regardless of how complex or simple a given XML document might be, each and every such document must follow the same set of rules to function properly.

XML documents that play by all the official rules are known as *well formed*. A document that isn't well formed won't go far in the XML world (because it's not actually considered an XML document), so you want to make sure that every document you create plays by these very basic rules:

The following short rundown of rules only breaks the ice of what you need to know about well-formed XML documents. Remember that this chapter is about the least you need to know to write XML, not all you need to know. Because being well formed is such an important topic, it's covered in detail in Chapter 4. Any questions you might have as you read through this abstract version of the XML rulebook are answered there. For now, the short version of the rules is as follows:

- **First things first: the XML declaration.** The first thing you should include in every XML document is a simple declaration specifying that the document is XML compliant. Looking back at our burrito document, you see the XML declaration at the very top: <?xml version="1.0" standalone="yes"?>.

Good tools can help you stay well formed

You're probably wondering how you can possibly remember all the rules described in this chapter as you develop XML documents. Even veteran document designers forget a quotation mark or two here and there — not to mention the occasional absent closing tag or forgotten slash at the end of an empty tag.

The best way to make sure your documents are well formed is to build your XML document in an XML editor that checks the document as you write for easy-to-make mistakes that can lead to malformed documents. Before you begin to do much work in XML, we recommend that you go out and get yourself a good editor. You'll be a happier and less-stressed camper if you do — we promise!

Editors are available for a variety of platforms and range in price from free to fairly expensive. Although each editor's feature set is a bit different, nearly every XML editor checks documents to make sure they're well formed.

Chapter 21 focuses entirely on XML-related tools and includes a section on XML editors. Read more about the editors that are available for your platforms of choice, and then download a few and try them out. The best online resource we've found for XML software is `www.xmlsoftware.com`.

- ✔ **One tag contains all the others.** All tags and content within an XML document must live within a single top-level tag, appropriately called the *document element*. In our sample, `<Recipe>. . .</Recipe>` is the document element. Every document that uses RML (our recipe markup language) should begin with `<Recipe>` and end with `</Recipe>`, in the same way that every HTML document should begin with `<html>` and end with `</html>`.

- ✔ **Every element must have a start tag and end tag.** If you open a tag, make sure you close it. It's really that simple. If our burrito recipe were missing `</CookingInstructions>` somewhere in the document after the opening `<CookingInstructions>`, our document wouldn't be well formed. HTML browsers are forgiving about missing ending tags; XML tools are not.

- ✔ **Empty elements end in `/>`.** But what about tags that have only a start tag, such as the `<Category>` tag in our example and the `<img>` tag in XHTML? These tags are called *empty tags* because they don't hold content between open and close tags. To avoid confusion and prevent XML tools from searching endlessly for closing tags that don't exist in the first place, identify all empty tags with a slash (/) before the closing greater than sign (>), like this: `<Category name="tex-mex" />`.

✔ **Nest your elements like measuring cups.** Nesting elements means including one within the other, as we did with our `<Ingredients>`... `</Ingredients>` and `<Item>`... `</Item>` tags. The `<Item>`... `</Item>` tags sit within the `<Ingredients>`...`</Ingredients>` tags to identify the different items in a recipe's ingredient list. Notice how the `<Item>`... `</Item>` tags are completely enclosed within the `<Ingredients>`...`</Ingredients>` tags: `<Ingredients></Item>1 can refried beans</Item></Ingredients>`.

The easiest way to make sure you abide by this rule is to always close first the tag that you opened last.

✔ **Quote all attribute values!** XML tags use attributes just like HTML tags do. The key difference between the two is that you *must* enclose every attribute value in quotation marks (either single or double quotes — double quotes are used most often), as we do in our burrito recipe when we identify the recipe's author `<Recipe cook="The XML Gourmet">`. If you forget even one set of quotation marks, you can count on the code to break somewhere along the line.

✔ **Tags and entities always begin the same way.** Every XML tag must begin with a less than sign (`<`) and every XML entity must begin with an ampersand (&). (An *entity* is a virtual storage unit that can contain text, or binary files, such as graphics or sound clips, or represent a non-ASCII character, such as the copyright symbol. You reference an entity in an XML document using a string of characters that begins with an ampersand (&) and ends with a semicolon (;). Entities are covered in detail in Chapter 10.) It's really that simple. XML tools won't know what to do with tags and entities that don't play by this rule and will usually treat them as plain ol' content. Not a total disaster, but certainly not a boon for your document either.

✔ **Stick with a handful of entity references:** HTML offers an entire set of entity references that you can use to include non-ASCII characters. Examples include `&copy;` for the copyright symbol ((c)) and `&Aacute;` for an uppercase letter A with an acute accent (À). XML doesn't support this extended set of codes. XML's support for entity references is limited to `&amp;` for an ampersand (&), `&lt;` for a less than sign (<), `&gt;` for a greater than sign (>), `&apos;` for an apostrophe ('), and `&quot;` for a quotation mark (").

Never fear, XML does support non-ASCII characters — it just does so in a different way than HTML. Chapter 10 discusses XML's use of characters and entities in depth.

Style Sheets, Document Type Definitions, and Documentation

A quick note about XML and context: One of the most powerful features of XML is that it allows you to describe data in a consistent way even though the data's context may change. "But when would the data's context change?" you ask.

Think about our bean burrito recipe again for a second. If you store a recipe as part of your personal collection, it has one context. If you submit that same recipe to an online recipe repository, its context has changed.

That said, how does XML deal with changing contexts? More importantly, why should you care?

Free at last, free at last: Data independent of context

XML documents aren't tied to any particular context. They are text documents that can be stored anywhere and processed on any platform. They don't depend on a particular application for display. This last is in contrast to many other types of documents, such as word-processor documents, which are not terribly readable unless you have access to a copy of the program that created them (or some reasonable facsimile thereof, such as WordPad for Microsoft Word).

Because XML documents aren't tied to one system or application, you can use a variety of tools with one document and its data. This means our bean burrito recipe can be displayed on a miniature recipe computer sitting by your kitchen sink or on a Web page at the online recipe repository — same data, same markup, different context.

This lack of context also means that a standalone XML document can't do much. The tags that describe the document's content don't include information about how the document should look when it's displayed or printed. In addition, the document uses only the tags that describe its content. If other tags are in the document's DTD, you won't know what they are. This lack of context information makes the document very flexible, but it also means that you often have to provide a context for the document using style sheets and DTDs to supply the necessary information about looks and behavior. DTDs are covered in the "DTDs and context" section later. If you need even more detail on DTDs, go to Chapter 5.

With style comes context

We have one bean burrito recipe and two potential contexts: a countertop recipe computer and an online recipe repository. Both are XML-aware and both will display your recipe. However, the context for display is different in each case. The recipe computer has a small six-by-four-inch screen and displays recipes in a simple way with no graphics or other splashy effects. The Web-based recipe repository is designed for users with computer monitors that can display resolutions of 800 by 600 pixels or larger. Thus, the site displays recipes using an advanced layout, colors, and more that the recipe computer can't handle. Figure 3-1 shows how the burrito recipe might look as displayed on a countertop computer. Figure 3-2 shows how it might look if you viewed it online at the repository's Web site.

Figure 3-1:
A counter-top recipe computer displays a recipe simply and compactly.

So the question becomes, "How can one document be displayed differently, without the markup changing?" Remember that XML only describes data. It doesn't include information about how that data should be treated in any way, including its display. This is a good thing because it makes a single document incredibly flexible and supports many possible forms of display.

Style sheets control how XML documents are displayed by specifying how certain elements in a document should look. The style sheet for the countertop recipe computer specifies that the entire recipe should be displayed in a monospace font. The style sheet for the recipe repository Web site adds a title banner and a navigation bar and displays the recipe in a standard serif font — same document, two different displays.

Figure 3-2:
An online
recipe
repository
adds flash
and
substance
to the
recipe's
display.

Because style sheets are the driving mechanisms behind the display of XML documents, they are a major topic in and of themselves. All of Part IV is dedicated to this important topic. Turn to it for all you need to know about stylin' your XML.

DTDs and context

There's more to a document's context than its appearance when displayed on a monitor or printed on paper. A document's *context* is provided by its content — and not the way it looks on a screen. Each bit of content in a document plays a role — as a header, a paragraph, and so on — and the role a bit of content plays is far more important than the way it looks on a screen or piece of paper.

The tags that describe a document tell us about the role of each piece of a document's content. To do this, the tags must work together. In our recipe markup, the `<Item>` tag relies on the `<Ingredients>` tag to completely identify different ingredients for the recipe. Without the `<Ingredients>` tag, you don't know what the item is — it could be a grocery list item for all you know. The `<Ingredients>` and `<Item>` tags together identify each recipe ingredient as an individual ingredient item. Together, all the tags describe a complete recipe.

A *DTD, or Document Type Definition,* identifies which tags you can use to describe data in an XML document. You don't necessarily need a DTD, however, to create XML. Instead, you can just make up tags as you go along and as you need them to describe different kinds of data. When you add a DTD to a document, however, you provide it with the context defined by the tags that the DTD supports. Two different DTDs might have two different sets of tags for identifying the content of a document and the roles that each individual chunk of information plays in the document. If you didn't like our Recipe Markup Language (RML), for example, you could write your own (and make it as complex or as simple as you like). You could then use your own set of tags to describe the same bean burrito recipe we described with RML. Because the sets of tags would be different, however, the recipe would have two different contexts.

Often, DTDs have style sheets already written for them or special processing tools designed to work with data described in that specific DTD. When you link a DTD to a document, it works with those style sheets and special processors. In addition, many industry groups — from high finance to chemists — are getting together and building their own DTDs to describe data common to their industries.

Using a DTD established by a common group for describing common data provides yet another context for a document. Of course, when you use a DTD, it means you have to abide by the rules of the DTD, but that's a topic for another chapter.

DTDs are a crucial part of XML development and are an in-depth topic that you must understand to some extent if you want to build customized XML solutions. Chapter 5 discusses DTDs in detail, and Part VI is devoted to the description of some of the many XML DTDs already under development.

Ready to Roll Your Own XML?

An XML solution involves more than simply building an XML document — if only it was that easy. A complete XML solution includes many pieces. Before you dive into putting together a customized XML solution, you must know what those pieces are. You also have to decide whether you want to build those pieces yourself or take advantage of the work of others. Luckily, a variety of developers and organizations jumped on the XML bandwagon early and are now providing many tools for others interested in using XML.

When you're planning your own XML implementation, you should think about the following:

- ✔ **To DTD or not to DTD?** Will you need a DTD to follow as you describe your content with XML tags? We recommend that you think seriously about the benefits of a DTD. When you build a DTD, you're forced to think carefully about your data and how it's structured. It's been our experience that documents described with DTDs are better structured and more robust than those without DTDs. In addition, you might be able to take advantage of DTDs available from other members of your particular industry. Before you delve into DTD development or decide to skip the venture entirely, visit www.schema.net to see what others are doing.

- ✔ **Build a document and they will come.** If you're going to use XML, you have to build XML documents; there's no avoiding it. Because XML documents have to play by a specific set of rules, you need to devote some serious resources to document development. If you have quite a bit of existing content that you need to "XMLize," make sure you give yourself plenty of manpower and time to do so. At the risk of sounding like a broken record, we once again stress that a good XML editor will save you time, energy, and grief.

- ✔ **Don't forget a touch of style.** If your XML solution involves displaying or printing documents, you need to build style sheets. Think about the many different ways you might want to display your content — that's the number of style sheets you need to build.

  Remember that style is more than just how things are formatted. Take advantage of the fact that XML separates content from display and have someone with a good sense of style create your style sheets for you. And yes, style sheet tools are available to make your style life easier, too.

- ✔ **Processors make XML documents palatable.** We've talked quite a bit about creating XML documents and even creating style sheets that drive their display. What we haven't touched on is how you get from an XML document to an XML display or other use of the content you describe with XML tags.

  XML documents must be processed by an XML-aware application. In our recipe example, the countertop recipe computer and the Web browser are the processing applications that read XML files and generate output. They do other things as well, but they do read XML. You need some sort of a tool to process your XML documents. Although you can create such tools from scratch, a plethora of them are available already.

The fine details of processing XML and using the results to build an application are a bit beyond the scope of this book. However, Chapter 21 discusses some of the tools used for processing, and Chapter 22 points you to a variety of Web sites that discuss this technical issue in depth.

XML by Excellent Example

Large numbers of individuals, organizations, and businesses plan and implement XML solutions every day. You know this, or you wouldn't be reading this book. To show that XML applies across a variety of industries and is useful in ways too numerous to count, this section includes a short review of how XML is being used in three very different ways.

Exchanging business data with XML/EDI

Electronic Data Interchange (EDI) is a standard for the electronic exchange of basic business information. Businesses that use EDI systems can share a variety of information, including invoices and project data. EDI has been around for a while but the data format is proprietary and a business must run an EDI-compatible system to use EDI. The goal of XML/EDI is to employ basic EDI practices but describe the data using XML instead of a proprietary system. This solution takes advantage of the flexibility of XML but works within an established data exchange system.

The hope of those involved in XML/EDI development is that it will become the cornerstone for business communications and make setting up electronic commerce sites faster and easier. If the business community agrees to use XML/EDI as an operating standard, everyone's data will be in the same format, making it easier to share information regardless of the computer system that each individual business uses. You can read more about XML/EDI at www.xmledi-group.org.

Using OFX to describe financial data

Microsoft's Money and Intuit's Quicken applications are the two most popular personal financial software packages that people use to balance their checkbooks and track their expenses. A majority of banks, large and small, offer online, Web-based access to account information. Some even provide that information in Money and Quicken formats. Even so, this means your checking account information has to be available in as many as four formats: in the bank's format, in a Web-based format for online access, and in Money and Quicken formats.

Wouldn't it be easier if financial data was described in one standard way that the banks, the Web, and your personal financial software could all understand? That's the goal of the Open Financial Exchange (OFX) effort. OFX uses XML to describe bank data and transfers that data electronically via the

Internet. Although Microsoft and Intuit are direct competitors in the software world, they've come to realize that standardizing on one data type is a good thing. They can still compete for your hard-earned dollars based on the different functionality they include in their software as well as how easy it is to use. The data format should be irrelevant.

If Microsoft, Intuit, and the banking organizations can all agree on a single format to describe banking data, information exchange will be as easy as pie. Although they're still working the kinks out of the specifics of OFX, the one thing they all agree on is that XML is the right vehicle for describing such data. For more about OFX, check out www.ofx.net.

Tracking ancestry with GedML

Thanks in large part to the efforts of the Mormon Church, genealogical data is abundant and widely available. One of the hardest parts of tracking your ancestors is reconciling all the information you uncover. You might find a birth record here and a hospital record there, and of course you hear all sorts of stories. After you gather this information, you must put it together and see what it adds up to.

The Genealogical Markup Language (GedML) is a set of XML tags to describe genealogical data. GedML is based on GEDCOM, a common format for describing this kind of information. It simply uses XML to describe the data involved. If you're thinking that this is similar to what the XML/EDI folks are doing — not reinventing the wheel but simply using XML with existing standards — you're right.

One of the best ways to find out about implementing a solution is to see what others are already doing with it. In Part VI, we take a detailed look at a variety of XML implementations already at work in the world.

XML for Everyone

As you can see, XML isn't just for computer geeks. Instead, it's utilized by everyone from genealogical hobbyists to the banking industry. Even the authors of this book — all of whom enjoy cooking — have found a household use for XML. XML's versatility lies in its ecumenical capability to describe any kind of data. No matter who you are or what you're doing, if you have a need to work with data, you have a need for XML.

Part II

Structuring XML Documents

The 5th Wave   By Rich Tennant

"Great goulash, Stan. That reminds me, are you still scripting your own Web page?"

In this part. . .

It's a good idea to get a thorough grounding in the pieces and parts that make up any XML document. Starting in Chapter 4, you study a little XML document anatomy and observe the differences between a document prolog and a document body. You also encounter two important terms that apply to XML documents: *well-formed* (which means the document demonstrates good intrinsic structure) and *valid* (which means it not only demonstrates good intrinsic structure but has been checked to ensure that it follows a specific set of markup rules).

In Chapters 5 and 6, you begin to plumb the mysteries of the markup description known as a Document Type Definition (DTD), which governs most XML documents. Chapter 5 takes you through the concepts and related terminology that control what DTDs do and how they behave. Chapter 6 describes what's involved in building your own DTDs (and hence, your own customized XML markup).

Chapter 4

Understanding XML
Document Structure

*I*n this chapter, we explore the meaning of the terms *valid* and *well formed* in relation to XML documents. Then we demonstrate good XML coding techniques.

After you master the concept of good coding, you find out how complete XML delivers good structure overall. This leads to a discussion of what *well formed* really means in an XML document. After you get all that under your hat, you find out how to tell whether you've coded your XML correctly.

Mastering the Basics: Pieces and Parts

Writing XML code is easy. All you need is a text editor — you can even make up your own tag names! Before you begin creating XML documents, however, we need to talk about a few things.

You must understand a couple of buzzwords in order to create correctly for-matted XML documents: *valid* and *well formed*. These two terms are often bantered about whenever techie types discuss XML. In this section, you uncover what these two terms mean — without the usual jargon.

A well-formed road is a good road

All XML documents must be well formed — end of story! A well-formed XML document follows a few specific rules to make the document easy for a computer program to read. See the section entitled "Making XML Well-Formed" later in this chapter for the complete scoop on creating well-formed XML.

Seeking validation

Although all XML documents must be well formed — or else they aren't XML — not all XML documents have to be *valid.* This doesn't mean you don't want valid XML documents. Validity just adds another layer of structure that can be helpful when you want to use or reuse a document. After all, a structured document is better than one that can contain any old set of tags in any old order.

A valid XML document adheres to a Document Type Definition (DTD). To answer the next inevitable question, a DTD defines a set of rules that specify which tags can legally appear in your document. A DTD also spells out how those tags can appear: It indicates their order and which tags can appear within other tags. Simply put, a DTD tells you what your tags can and cannot do; therefore, a DTD defines the rules that XML markup in a document must follow.

DTDs are not necessary, or required, for every instance of XML. However, they do give your XML documents an extra layer of organizational structure that can make your life easier. DTDs also help developers share expectations about document structures. If you're interested in reading more about DTDs, please see Chapter 5.

Now that you know what to look out for, open your text editor so we can get started.

Preambles and Definitions Start the Game

A well-formed XML document always begins with a declaration that announces that the document is written using XML 1.0, so speak up and declare yourself!

Declare yourself!

A declaration for an XML document is simple. It occurs in the first line of your XML document. Currently, a declaration must point to XML version 1.0 — after all, it's the only version out there. An XML declaration looks like this:

```
<?xml version="1.0"?>
```

To be honest, you don't have to include an XML declaration in every XML document. If you don't point to a particular version, XML 1.0 is the default. However, we suggest that you get in the declaration habit for all XML documents because when version 2.0 comes out, XML declarations might be required.

You can write fancier declarations for XML documents if you want. For more XML declaration details, see Chapter 2.

Document it

If you decide to use a DTD to add organization and structure to an XML document, you must declare that DTD. (Remember that a DTD defines the rules of the game for your XML document. To find out more about creating and using DTDs, consult Chapter 5.) To declare a DTD in an XML document, you need just one simple line:

```
<!DOCTYPE Document-Name SYSTEM "Document-Name.dtd">
```

There you have it — one line of code that says it all for the related DTD!

Good Bodies Make for Good Reading

Have you ever picked up an instruction manual and wished you hadn't? You know the ones we mean — chock full of grammatical errors, poor syntax, and just plain lousy sentence structure. After hours of struggling to finish assembling a do-it-yourself bookcase, you wonder why the author took the time to write a manual at all. You might be tempted — and rightfully so — to make the same value judgment about XML code. If the code lacks structure from a human-readable standpoint, perhaps the document containing that code is of poor quality.

This section explains how to write good — that is, well-formed — XML code to keep others from saying bad things about your work later!

The root of the matter

In HTML, you begin every HTML document with `<html>`. The `<html>`. . . `</html>` tag pair is the *root element* for an HTML document. With XML, you create elements just like you use predefined HTML tags. The only difference with XML is that you get to choose the name for your root element. For example:

```
<?xml version="1.0"?>
<!DOCTYPE Validators-Xml SYSTEM "Validators-Xml.dtd">
<Validators-Xml>
<Validator>
. . .
</Validator>
</Validators-Xml>
```

In this example, `<Validators>` is the root element. It's important to remember that a root element is the outermost element that contains all other elements in an XML document.

Although it might seem that tags and elements are interchangeable, they're not. One example of a tag is `<p>`; an example of an element is `<p>text</p>`. An *element* includes an opening and closing tag of a tag pair and everything in-between. A tag is just a tag, all by itself.

It's elementary, my dear

Elements make up the bulk of any XML document, so you need to get them right. Although XML's cousin, HTML, is forgiving in this respect, XML does not extend that sentiment.

XML elements must follow a few basic rules that you can't break, even if you try:

- ✔ All tags include distinct start and end components (sometimes both components appear in a single tag, called an empty element).
- ✔ All tags must be nested correctly.
- ✔ All attribute values must be quoted. (Either single or double quotes is acceptable; we use double quotes.)
- ✔ Empty elements must be formatted correctly.

Here's what proper XML code should look like (Note this is only part of an XML document):

```
<Music-List>
<Song>
<Title>Oh, Maria</Title>
<Band>Nothing But Gil</Band>
<Artist>
<Name age="22">Sam Williams</Name>
<Name age="23">Karl Lundin</Name>
</Artist>
</Song>
<Song>
<Title>A Little Duet for Zoot and Chet</Title>
<Band>Chet Baker</Band>
<Artist>
<Name age="deceased">Chet Baker</Name>
</Artist>
</Song>
</Music-List>
```

Note how each element is nested properly. For example, the first `<Name>` element is closed before we open a second name element, and both these elements close before we close the `<Artist>` element. One important rule to remember is to close first what you opened last!

Attributes add information

Attributes provide more information about individual XML elements. If you've worked with HTML, you're already familiar with attributes. For example, `color` is an attribute of the `<font>` tag:

```
<font color="red">
```

The difference with XML attributes is that they never define formatting characteristics. Instead, attributes in XML documents provide additional data about an element. For example, `age` is an attribute of the `<Name>` tag:

```
<Name age="32">Tom</Name>
```

Attributes and the information they contain are defined in your DTD. In Chapter 5, we jump right in and explain how to create and use a DTD. For now, the most important thing you need to know about attributes is that they must always be enclosed in quotes.

The Virtues of Completeness

Figure 4-1 shows you, in flowchart fashion, how complete XML relates to structure and content. The presentation is the goal that drives the coding process. Attaining this goal requires that you keep the presentation in mind throughout your coding project.

In XML, many factors contribute to a successful project. Although you don't need a DTD or even a style sheet to create Web pages using XML, you'll see the benefits of adding these weapons to your arsenal if you stick with XML long enough.

Style sheets for XML may use either Cascading Style Sheets (CSS) or the Extensible Stylesheet Language (XSL). Both these forms of markup define formatting rules that allow your pages to take on different styles. Whereas CSS and XSL govern format, DTDs define additional structure. Combining a style sheet and a DTD with XML content creates a presentation even your boss can admire. Okay, so that last sentence was a little hard to swallow. Never fear — Chapter 5 covers DTDs, and Chapters 11 and 12 cover style sheets.

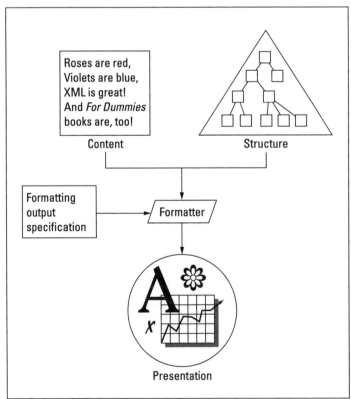

Roses are red,
Violets are blue,
XML is great!
And *For Dummies*
books are, too!

Content

Structure

Formatting
output
specification

Formatter

Presentation

Figure 4-1:
Piecing
together
XML.

Making XML Well-Formed

When an XML author creates a well-formed document, the results should be clean and logical to the eye. Every language (programming and non-programming alike) has a set of rules. We've touched on XML rules in previous sections, but we'd like to take a moment to make sure we're all on the same page. Here goes!

XML's rules are simple, so you don't need to be a rocket scientist to follow them. But why do they exist? The legacy of HTML forced important changes in the way that XML was designed. One of HTML's most galling shortcomings is its lack of coherence. At first blush, it might seem that HTML is subject to few rules. Worse yet, browsers interpret those rules loosely, if they pay any attention to them at all. Although rules can sometimes get in the way, the idea of adding rules to the Web makes your Web experience better in the long run — trust us! That's why XML defines and enforces its rules across the board, without exceptions.

Now that you know why you must create a well-formed document, here are some of the rules (often called *constraints* by geeky guys) for creating one:

- All elements must have an explicit closing component (for example, `<p>text</p>`).

- All tags must nest properly (for instance, `<em><b>text</b></em>` is correct and `<em><b>text</em></b>` is incorrect).

- Empty tags, those that stand alone, use special XML syntax that opens and closes the tag in a single expression (for example, `<br />` or `<Space />`).

- All attributes values appear between quotation marks (for example, `<a href="http://www.w3.org">`).

- All entities (reusable chunks of data, much like macros) in a document must be declared explicitly in the DOCTYPE declaration.

- All tags are case sensitive (for example, `<Name>` is not the same as `<name>`).

The syntax for empty tags in XML and XHTML differs. Whereas XHTML requires a space after the tag and before the forward slash (such as `<br />`), XML does not require that space. See Chapter 2 for more information on XHTML.

If you take it from here and create your own well-formed document, you might come up with something like this:

```
<?xml version="1.0"?>
<Validators-Xml>
<Validator>
<Product-Name>Richard Tobin's Validating XML
         Checker</Product-Name>
<Url>http://www.cogsci.ed.ac.uk/~richard/xml-check.html</Url>
</Validator>
<Validator>
<Product-Name>Scholarly Technology Group's XML
         Validator</Product-Name>
<Url>http://www.stg.brown.edu/service/xmlvalid/</Url>
</Validator>
<Validator>
<Product-Name>DOMit XML Validation Servlet</Product-Name>
<Url>http://www.networking.ibm.com/xml/XmlValidatorForm.html
         </Url>
</Validator>
</Validators-Xml>
```

You don't always have to use a DTD. Our example doesn't point to one. This means our document is well formed but not valid. To be valid, the document would have to point to a DTD and follow the rules outlined in that DTD.

Checking Your Work

Did you forget to close any tags? Did you forget to put quotes around your attributes? Remember, one mistake can render an XML document unreadable. So the rule is: Check until you can check no longer!

Lots of tools — many free — can check your work for you. To find a few of our favorites, visit Chapter 2.

Chapter 5

Understanding and Using DTDs

*A*n XML Document Type Definition (DTD) defines the rules of the game for XML documents. DTDs are used to add structure and logic and to make it easier for everyone to understand what all the elements in an XML document mean. Although DTDs are not absolutely necessary when creating XML, it's important that you understand what they are and how they work.

Using a DTD properly means that your document will be valid. In Chapter 2, we outline what it takes for an XML document to be well formed. In this chapter, we tell you what it takes to create an XML document that's valid.

You must throw away all preconceived notions about HTML and tighten the reins on your coding habits. Unlike HTML, XML is strict and requires that you follow the guidelines of the World Wide Web Consortium (W3C). This is not a tall order; as a matter of fact, it's quite easy. But keep in mind that if you break any rules, your documents will fail.

What's a DTD?

A *Document Type Definition* (DTD) is a set of rules that defines the elements — and their attributes — in an XML document. Some people like to call it the grammar of the XML document because it tells applications — and individuals — just what each element means and how to use it. We're all accustomed to rules that govern the way we speak. Well, now we have a bunch of rules telling us how to write — code that is.

DTDs consist of declarations for elements and their attributes. DTDs are nothing new. In fact, in techno years, they're pretty darn old. DTDs were created as part of the Standard Generalized Markup Language (SGML) — XML's parent. HTML is described in an SGML DTD for producing that famous document type, the Web page.

DTDs aren't required because, unlike SGML, XML follows strict rules of construction. This enables XML processors to read a well-formed document and infer the rules. They do this by building a tree of all elements and their children and then drawing conclusions from the nesting relationships that may be observed therein.

A DTD has many parts and many technical terms with which you should become familiar. After you can define terms such as *attribute list declaration* and *name token,* you'll be well on your way to knowing your DTD lingo, and better yet, creating a DTD! But before you jump in, Table 5-1 lists some of the important components that you find out about in this chapter.

Table 5-1	DTD Lingo	
Term	*Example*	*What It Does*
XML declaration	`<?xml version="1.0" encoding="UTF-8" standalone="yes"?>`	Tells the processor which version of XML to use
Document type declaration	`<!DOCTYPE Root-Element SYSTEM "Root-Element.dtd">`	Tells the processor where the DTD is located
Element type declaration	`<!ELEMENT Name (#PCDATA)>`	Defines the element type
Attribute list declaration	`<!ATTLIST Element-Name Name Data-Type Default>`	Defines the name, data type, and default value (if any) of each attribute associated with an element

Term	Example	What It Does
Entity declaration	`<!ENTITY Entity-Name "text">`	Defines a set of information that can be called by using its entity name
Notation declaration	`<!NOTATION Name System "externalID">`	Associates a notation name with information that can help find an interpreter of the notation

Reading a Simple DTD

Even if you don't plan to create your own DTDs from scratch, it's helpful to know how to read them. In theory — and we hope in practice — XML (and DTDs) should be easy to read and understand. You should be able to look at a DTD, list all elements and their attributes, and understand how and when to use those elements and their attributes.

Create a document tree to help you better understand the hierarchy among document elements. A document tree begins with one root element. All other elements are children of (or nest within) that root element. See Chapter 16 for more information on document trees.

In the following sections, we dissect a DTD. We want you to understand all the pieces and parts of a DTD before you try to create one yourself. (If you already recognize all the pieces of a DTD, read Chapter 6 to build a DTD.)

XML prolog

The *XML prolog* is the first thing a processor — or human — sees in an XML document. You place it at the top of your XML document, and it describes the document's content and structure. An XML prolog may include the following items:

- ✔ XML declaration
- ✔ Document type declaration
- ✔ Comments
- ✔ Processing instructions
- ✔ White space

Notice that we use the phrase *may include*. That's because an XML prolog doesn't have to include any of that information. If you want to use a DTD, however, you must include in your prolog a few items in addition to an XML declaration. Here's an example:

```
<?xml version="1.0" encoding="UTF-8" standalone="yes"?>
<!DOCTYPE Book-Review SYSTEM "Book-Review.dtd">
<!--  End of Prolog  -->
<!--  Beginning of Document Body  -->
<Book-Review>
. . .
</Book-Review>
<!--  End of Document Body  -->
```

Take a second to look over what we included in the prolog:

- ✔ First, we include the XML declaration itself.
- ✔ The second line is a document type declaration.
- ✔ The last lines are comments signifying the end of the prolog and the beginning of the document.

Don't worry! We don't expect you to understand any of this yet. You're just getting started.

XML declaration

Generally speaking, a *declaration* is markup that tells an XML processor what to do. Declarations don't add structure or define document elements. Instead, they provide instructions for a processor, such as what type of document to process, what standards to use, and even where the DTD can be found. Specifically, the *XML declaration* tells the processor which version of XML to use. The XML declaration is found in the XML document prolog.

An XML declaration is easy to write. A simple XML declaration reads

```
<?xml version="1.0"?>
```

This XML declaration tells the processor to use version 1.0 of the XML specification. Right now, version 1.0 is the only XML version on the market, so there's no flexibility here. This means that, for now, a simple XML declaration looks exactly like our example, no ifs, ands, or buts!

However — and there's always a *however* — you can write a more complex XML declaration, such as

```
<?xml version="1.0" encoding="UTF-8" standalone="yes"?>
```

The second part of the statement, `encoding="UTF-8"`, is called an *encoding declaration*. This statement describes the character coding used. The next set of code, `standalone="yes"`, implies that the document does not rely on markup declarations defined in an external document, such as an external DTD. If `standalone` is set to equal `"no"`, it leaves the issue unresolved — translation, it may or may not reference one or more external DTDs.

A `standalone` declaration is rarely used; just by reading our few sentences you might understand why. It's obscure and doesn't provide much useful information. Use a standalone declaration only when necessary, such as when creating or experimenting with new markup. Don't just throw it in for the heck of it!

Document type declaration

The *document type declaration* is markup that tells the processor where it can find the DTD. In other words, it's used to link an XML document to its corresponding DTD.

As you read this chapter, do not confuse document type declarations with Document Type Definitions (DTDs). The document type declaration is the locator for the DTD.

First, take a look at the basic markup of a document type declaration:

```
<!DOCTYPE Book-Review SYSTEM "Book-Review.dtd">
```

`<!DOCTYPE` is the tag that starts a document type declaration. `Book-Review` is the name of the DTD used. This name must correspond with the name of the root element for that document. `SYSTEM "Book-Review.dtd"` instructs the processor to fetch an external document, in this case, a DTD called `Book-Review`.

We know it might seem like you're duplicating information by using `Book-Review` twice, but keep in mind that the first instance of `Book-Review` in the code is the root element for the document. The second instance — `Book-Review.dtd` — is the DTD file name.

In the preceding example, `Book-Review.dtd` is a relative Uniform Resource Identifier (URI). URIs are basically filenames — or locations. This particular one is used to point to an external DTD. This means the XML document and the DTD reside in the same directory but not in the same document. We delve into how to reference external DTDs in the "Calling for outside support: Referencing external DTDs" section later in the chapter. Hint: You might notice the resemblance to the term *URL*. Well, a URL is a type of URI.

Now take a peek at a DTD included in the prolog of an XML document:

```
<!DOCTYPE Book-Review [
<!ELEMENT Book-Review (Book*)>
<!ELEMENT Book (Subject, Title, Author)>
<!ELEMENT Subject (#PCDATA)>
<!ELEMENT Title (#PCDATA)>
<!ELEMENT Author (#PCDATA)>
<!ENTITY Publisher "The Book Club">
]>
```

This is an example of an internal document type definition. In our first example, we referenced an external DTD; here, we include the DTD information within the document type declaration.

We do not expect you to recognize most of those tags because we haven't defined them yet. We talk about each declaration later in this section. But for now, take a look at the example and see whether you can find any structure.

What you should notice is that the third line, `<!ELEMENT Book (Subject, Title, Author)>`, contains the names for the following element declarations in the same order in which they appear. So, without even being told, you already know how these elements relate to each other (see Figure 5-1).

Figure 5-1:
Book and its
children
elements.

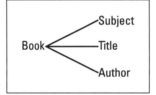

Comments

Comments — use them and read them! Sometimes the author (quite possibly yourself) wants to include text that explains the document a little bit better but doesn't want that text displayed or even processed. In that case, you use comments, which have been carried over from HTML.

Comments are like an owner's manual; they can help you navigate your way through a document when something breaks down or even when you need to change something. Use them with care!

As long as you follow the correct format, the comment will remain hidden. The correct format is

```
<!--  Include your comment here  -->
```

Look familiar? It should.

You have two rules to live by when using comments. Never nest a comment in another tag and never include - (hyphen) or - - (double hyphen) in the text of your comment. Those characters might confuse processors into thinking that you're closing the comment.

Processing instructions

Comments allow an author to leave instructions — or comments — to someone reading the code, without interfering with the structure of the document. *Processing instructions* are similar to comments but they provide a way to send instructions to computer programs or applications — not humans.

Another common processing instruction you're likely to find includes style sheets in a document. For example:

```
<?xml:stylesheet type="text/xsl"?>
```

All processing instructions follow the same format as shown in Figure 5-2.

Figure 5-2:
Dissection of a processing instruction.

```
Name of application
        |
   <?xml:stylesheet type="text/xsl"?>
                               \
                        Instruction information
```

All processing instructions must begin with <? and end with ?>.

What about that white space?

White space consists of invisible characters such as spaces, tabs, carriage returns, or line feeds. The XML specification allows you to add white space outside markup; it's ignored when the document is processed.

Think of it this way: If we wrote a book without paragraph breaks, readers would give up reading it after a few pages. Paragraph breaks and a line of white space between each paragraph are easier on the eyes. The same logic applies to XML documents. When you're writing code, you might want to add a line of white space between sections. This way, when someone such as your boss visits your code, he or she will be able to read it (if not understand it) without a hitch.

Some tags treat white space in a special way. It's safe to include white space outside XML tags, but do your homework before you add extra white space within tags. If you find yourself intrigued by the use of white space, you might want to read more about the `xml:space` attribute, which lets applications know when white space matters and when it doesn't. To read more on the `xml:space` attribute, check out Chapter 7.

Element Declarations

Because the heart of an XML document is made up of its elements, you must define them in your DTD. To do so, you use *element type declarations*. Element type declarations are important. They not only name your elements but also define any *children* an element might have.

We know, it sounds strange to bring family into it, but if you think about it, it makes sense! We start with the root element of a document:

```
<Book-Review>
. . .
</Book-Review>
```

Within that root element are other elements, all relating back to the root. Therefore, the root element is the topmost element in the hierarchy of elements. This is part of what makes XML so great. It's logical and easy to read and understand. If you nest an element within another element, the elements must be related — hence the family analogy.

Now, back to those children. Elements can be defined to contain four types of content, which are listed in Table 5-2.

Table 5-2	Types of Content Found in Elements	
Content Type	*Example*	*What It Means*
ANY	`<!ELEMENT Name ANY>`	Allows any type of element content, either data or element markup information

Content Type	Example	What It Means
EMPTY	`<!ELEMENT Name EMPTY>`	Specifies that an element must not contain content
Mixed content	`<!ELEMENT Name (#PCDATA | ChildName)>`	Allows an element to contain character data or a combination of subelements and character data
Element content	`<!ELEMENT Name (Child1, Child2)>`	Specifies that an element can contain only subelements, or children

If you're wondering what the commas (,) and the pipe bars (|) in the table's examples mean, be patient. We discuss them in the following section.

Any or empty can do the trick

There will be times when you'll want an element type to remain empty — does not contain content between those lovely little opening and closing tags. A common example would be the use of an image that would be located somewhere else. In this case, you would want to reference the image but you would not need to include anything between the opening and closing tags of an image element. To work with empty elements, you first must declare them like so:

```
<!ELEMENT Name EMPTY>
```

When using empty elements in your XML document, you don't have to use opening and closing tags. That would not make much sense, would it? Those XML geniuses knew we didn't want to add useless code, so they came up with a way to save us time. Instead of including an opening and a closing tag, all you have to do is remember to close the opening tag, like so: `<empty-tag/>`. Thanks, guys and gals!

Some day, you might want to use another type of content specification, `ANY`. If you declare the element to contain `ANY` content, you allow an element type to hold any element or character data. This renders no structure to speak of, however, so it's rarely used.

Mixed content mixes it up

Mixed content allows your elements to contain character data or character data with child elements. In other words, it allows your elements to contain a mixture of information. Even if an element contains only character data, it's still said to contain mixed content. Try this one on for size:

```
<!ELEMENT Name (#PCDATA | Child1 | Child2)*>
```

The `<!ELEMENT` begins the declaration, and `Name` is the element name. We know you got that part, but what about the rest? Now we get to the meat of defining elements.

First, keep in mind that mixed content is one of the four types of element content specification. Quick, think of the other three (element content, `ANY`, and `EMPTY`).

`#PCDATA` means that an element contains *parsed character data,* or in fewer words, text. Whenever your element contains parsed character data, you include `#PCDATA`. If you just want your element to contain character data, use (`#PCDATA`) by itself.

Next, you find an element name, `Child1`. This indicates that the element named `Child1` may nest within the parent element (`Name` in our example). `Child2` says pretty much the same thing, except it calls on a different element, `Child2`.

Note the * in the preceding code. The asterisk is required in element type declarations that contain both text and elements. The "why" will become clearer in the following section. For an even more detailed explanation, visit Chapter 9.

But what does | signify? In the preceding line of code, | means that the `Name` element may contain parsed character data, or `Child1`, or `Child2`. With mixed content, you can't control the order of the elements or even how many times they appear. The purpose of mixed content is to allow the author to specify an element that may contain both text and other elements.

You don't have to create or define symbols, such as |, in your DTD. They are already defined for you. Wait, we have one more helpful hint. White space is not significant within the parentheses. For example, (`#PCDATA`) is the same as (`#PCDATA`).

XML authors don't have much flexibility when working with mixed content. There are only two different ways to work with mixed content:

✔ Use only parsed character data

✔ Allow an element to contain both text and other elements (don't forget the asterisk!)

Next stop, element content model.

Element content keeps your children in line

The *element content model* is a little more involved than mixed content. Element content describes the child elements that an element can contain. This type of specification says that an element may contain only child elements. For example:

```
<!ELEMENT Book-Review (Subject*)>
```

As with all element declarations, `<!ELEMENT` begins the tag. Then the element receives its name, `Book-Review` in this example. Next comes the content specification, which states that `Book-Review` may have a child, `Subject`. Note the `*`; it's an occurrence indicator.

The element content model uses occurrence indicators to control the order and number of times that elements can occur. In fact, the element content model almost always uses one. Take a look at Table 5-3 and think about what the `*` means. Got it? It means that the `Subject` element is optional or repeatable. Translation: `Subject` may nest within `Book-Review` zero or more times.

Table 5-3	Occurrence Indicators	
Symbol	*Example*	*What It Means*
,	`<!ELEMENT Book-Review (Subject, Title)>`	All listed child elements must be used in the order shown
|	`<!ELEMENT Book-Review (#PCDATA | Title)>`	Either one or the other element may be used
	`<!ELEMENT Book-Review (Subject)>`	This nonsymbol indicates a required occurrence
+	`<!ELEMENT Book-Review (Subject+)>`	This child element must be used at least once or many times
*	`<!ELEMENT Book-Review (Subject*)>`	This child element may be used as many times as needed or not at all
?	`<!ELEMENT Book-Review (Subject?)>`	This child element may be used once or not at all

Now, you apply what you just read to our example. You may use the , occurrence indicator to imply sequence. For example:

```
<!ELEMENT Book-Review (Subject, Title)>
```

In this example, Subject must precede the Title element when nesting within its parent, Book-Review. To find out more about creating element type declarations, read Chapter 6, where we use them to build a DTD.

Attribute List Declarations

In the "Element Declarations" section, you discover how to declare an element. Well, in this section, you need to define the element's better half — its attribute. In techie terms, you need to include *attribute list declarations* in your DTD. This declaration lists all the attributes that may be used within a given element and also defines each attribute's type and default value.

The declaration begins with the string <!ATTLIST, followed by white space. Remember, XML is case sensitive, so don't forget to use capital letters.

Where were we? So far, we have <!ATTLIST with a space. Next up are the element name, the attribute's name, its type, and its default. That's a lot of information, so it's a good idea to dissect an example (see Figure 5-3).

Figure 5-3:
The dissection of an attribute declaration.

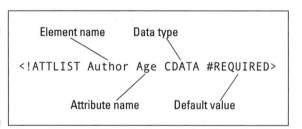

Wait! What does all that mean? Here's a quick glance at each term that appears in Figure 5-3:

- **Element name** is the name of the element that the attribute will describe.

- **Attribute name** is the name given to the attribute.

- **Data type** is one of the following ten kinds of data type attributes:

  - CDATA**, or character data,** enables the author to include any string of characters that does not include the ampersand (&), less than and greater than signs (< or >), or quotation marks ("). These four characters may be represented using special escape sequences (&, <, >, or ", respectively).

  - Enumerated is a list of possible values for the attribute, separated with vertical bars (|). The XML author has a choice!

- ID creates a unique ID for an attribute that identifies an element. This type is most often used by programs that process a document.

- IDREF allows the value of an attribute to be an element somewhere else in the document.

- IDREFS is just like IDREF but the value may be made up of multiple IDREFs.

- ENTITY allows you to use external binary data or unparsed entities.

- ENTITIES allows you to link multiple entities.

- NMTOKEN restricts the value of the attribute to any valid XML name.

- NMTOKENS allows the value of the attribute to be composed of multiple XML names.

- NOTATION allows you to use a value that is already specified with a notation declaration in the DTD.

✔ **Default value** consists of one of the following four options:

- #REQUIRED means you must always include the attribute when the element is used. <!ATTLIST element-name attribute-name CDATA #REQUIRED>

- #IMPLIED means the attribute is optional. The attribute may be used in an element type but no default value is provided for it if it isn't used. <!ATTLIST element-name attribute-name CDATA #IMPLIED>

- #FIXED means the attribute is optional. If used, the attribute must always take on the default value assigned in the DTD. <!ATTLIST element-name attribute-name #FIXED "value">

- value simply defines a specific value as the default value — end of story. Whereas the first three options use keywords to require a specific use of attributes, this last option provides the value to be used if none is set. If the element does not contain the attribute, the processor assumes that the element has an attribute with the default value. <!ATTLIST element-name attribute-name (option1 | option2 | option3) "default-value">

Entity Declarations

Entity declarations are a little trickier than the other declarations, but they sure save you time! An *entity declaration* defines an alias to another block of text. This means you can attach a name to a specific block of text and then call up this block using just one name.

Think about how quickly you could include your company's address in different documents if they all used the same DTD. Or what about if the company moved? You wouldn't have to change the address in each document — your information would be centralized.

This section provides you with a basic understanding of entities. We discuss them in detail in Chapter 6.

Before you can use an entity, you must declare it in your DTD. You can do this in either an internal or external DTD. The code looks like this:

```
<!ENTITY Name "text">
```

Name is the name of the entity and is used to call up the text in your document. Nice, huh? This allows you to take those long footers — that you normally have to type again and again and again — and reference them with one word. No more extraneous typing — almost.

Two types of entities exist: internal and external. Here's how it goes:

- ✔ **Internal (or general) entities** occur within the document and do not reference outside content, for example, `<!ENTITY Copyright "Copyright 2000, IDG Books Worldwide, Inc.">`.

- ✔ **External entities** refer to content that may be found outside the document using a system or public identifier. Both parameter and general entities may be used as external entities, for example, `<!ENTITY entity-name SYSTEM "file.gif">`.

A parameter entity is both defined and used within the DTD. For more on parameter entities, see Chapter 9.

Notation Declarations

Notation declarations allow XML documents to refer to external information. They announce to the XML processor that information from an outside source is needed and processed. Nine times out of ten, this external information is non-XML information. Take a look at the syntax:

```
<!NOTATION Name SYSTEM "file.exe">
```

You probably have it down by now. What comes first? And second? As with other declarations, you have the declaration name followed by the name given. In our example, we use the SYSTEM keyword, but you may also use PUBLIC identifiers. The file found in the quotation marks, file.exe, is an external ID.

SYSTEM is an XML keyword indicating that an entity appears in a URL or URI. PUBLIC indicates that a standard name for an entity is referenced. You find out more about notation declarations in Chapter 9.

Deciding Whether to Have a DTD

In the "What's a DTD?" section at the beginning of this chapter, we mention that it's not necessary to use a DTD. So the first step in including DTDs in your document is to decide whether you even want to jump off that bridge, right?

Why would you want to use a DTD? Well, here are several reasons:

✔ To create large sets of documents for your company. DTDs allow you create rules that all documents must follow.

✔ To make it completely clear what markup may be used in certain documents and how that markup should be sequenced. DTDs make document rules totally explicit.

✔ To provide a common frame of reference for documents that many users can share. Big name XML applications such as MathML, Channel Definition Format (CDF), and other applications covered in Part V all have their own associated DTDs.

Therefore, when it comes to working with DTDs, standardization is what they're about!

Why would you want to scrap this chapter and concentrate on creating a XML document? Reasons to not use a DTD:

✔ You're working with a few small documents. Remember why you would create a DTD: to make your life easier. If you find that your DTD is bigger than your document, you might be wasting your time.

✔ You're using a processor that is nonvalidating. If the processor checks only for a well-formed document, there's no need for an external DTD.

Now that we've outlined some good reasons not to use DTDs, we need to warn you that you should at least consider including a DTD in any XML document. Not only do we recommend that you create a DTD, we recommend that you create an external DTD. Why? Simply put, it's recyclable. Less time spent working means more time spent playing!

Ways to Include DTDs or Definitions

In this section, we outline the differences between an internal and an external DTD. Formally known as *internal* and *external subsets*, respectively, these two approaches follow the same markup structure but have some key differences, such as where they live!

More times than not, you'll find that it's best to utilize a combination of the two. But before we go there, here are some differences.

The inside view: Internal DTD subsets

The most important drawback to using internal DTDs is that they may be used only by the document that contains them. When you create an internal DTD, you're essentially keeping all the information in one document. However, internal DTDs have a few benefits, as follows:

- A single file processes faster than multiple files.
- Validity and well-formedness are kept in the same place. Any processor can process your document without looking elsewhere.
- And finally, internal DTDs can be used on your local system without logging on — you can even take that one file on the plane and run it on your laptop!

Calling for outside support: Referencing external DTDs

We just told you that internal DTDs are quicker, easier, and mobile. But that's not to say we recommend them!

No, we're not trying to confuse you (although it seems that way). However, external DTDs have many advantages that just might sway you to our side:

- They're recyclable. You can use one file for multiple documents.
- Your external DTD can simply be a public one already created by someone else.
- Editing an external DTD can be a breeze when you need to change one item found in multiple documents. (Remember entities?)
- With external DTDs, management doesn't mean late hours at work.

Two is sometimes better than one

Sometimes you'll need a large, complex external DTD; other times you'll not only need the monster DTD, but you'll also want to define some information internally. We find that more times than not, authors combine internal and external DTDs to get the most from their XML document structure.

You already know how to read internal and external DTDs. Combining DTDs is not much different. Two rules to live by when mixing these two types of DTDs are

✔ The XML processor always reads the internal subset first. Therefore, the internal DTD takes precedence.

✔ Entities declared in the internal subset can be referenced in the external subset.

For a complete example of building DTDs, see Chapter 6.

How Documents Digest DTDs

This chapter covers how to read DTDs, declarations, and lists, and even how to name children — no, not your children, but an element's children! Here, we take a few moments to explain what an XML document does with a DTD.

After you've created your XML document, defined all its elements in a DTD, and added a style sheet for formatting, you're ready to parse!

A *validating parser* compares your XML document to a declared DTD. If the parser finds that the document is valid (adheres to the DTD's rules), it passes the document along to an application, such as a browser. But — and this is a big *but* — if the parser finds a mistake, it yells, "Error!"

All you veteran HTMLers might need a moment to digest this because the good ol' days of leniency are over. Remember when you presented your Web page to the world, and low and behold you forgot to close your <p> tag. In those days, well-formedness for HTML was a pretty much nonexistent concept. The browsers said, "No problem," and interpreted it for you. Well, wave good-bye, because if you forget those wonderful — and well-formed — XML rules, you run the risk of marooning your user on a deserted island.

Enough with the analogies! What we're trying to tell you is that you must be careful and check your DTD and your XML document before allowing users to access them. Luckily, many validating parsers are available for checking your documents. To read about some of our favorites, go to Chapter 2.

REMEMBER

Time to review a few DTD rules. You must always

- ✔ Announce and define your elements
- ✔ Announce and define their attributes
- ✔ Announce and define any entities and notations

Chapter 6

Building DTDs

Creating a Document Type Definition (DTD) is one of the most important tasks you'll encounter when working with XML. DTDs define the different pieces of data you want to present — as well as the relationships between them.

In this chapter, you build a simple DTD, step by step. In Chapters 7, 8, and 9, you can read more details about the topics that are only skimmed over in this chapter.

Quick Recap

Before you begin marking up your own code, it's extremely helpful to know what you are working with. We cover DTD basics thoroughly in Chapter 5. Here, we take a few moments to run down a few essential components of a simple DTD:

✔ **Element type declarations:** Element type declarations provide a framework of names and content models that are then expressed as elements — sort of like tags — in XML documents. An element is what becomes a tag in the XML markup. Therefore, element type declarations in DTDs define the intent and the syntax of any tags you want to use in the body of your documents.

✔ **Attribute list declarations:** Attributes annotate elements with additional property information, add extra ways to control their meanings or values, provide a mechanism to associate files, Uniform Resource Identifiers (URIs), or other external data to tags, and so forth. Therefore, attributes provide a way to tweak or control the behavior of XML tags and the text that they bracket (if they're not empty tags, that is).

✔ **Entity declarations:** A shortcut that allows you to call on outside files or blocks of text with the use of symbols. If you get sick of typing your company name in every document, for example, using an entity declaration can solve the problem. (See the "Step Five: Creating Shortcuts with Entities" section for more information.)

✔ **Comments:** What an XML or SGML parser will cheerfully ignore may be the source of enlightenment to human readers forever afterward — including you, when enough time goes by. Always document your code to ensure readability later, especially when you use shortcuts or tricks.

✔ **White space:** Within tags, white space may be significant. For example, with entity declarations, you must remember the space after `<!ENTITY` or the declaration is invalid. White space that occurs in the XML document — outside the tags — is not significant. If it was, your text would be illegible and annoyingtoreadlikethis. See what we mean? If white space was always significant — had meaning attached to it — you could not use it to separate paragraphs or words used outside our favorite greater than and less than signs (< >).

Step 1: Understanding Your Data

Before diving into building DTDs head first, you need to identify — and understand — your data. Take a second to ask yourself where your data comes from. It might be sitting pretty in your head, tucked away in the company database, or even on scraps of paper scattered all over your office floor. Wherever it resides, take some time to map it.

XML documents are about organizing data. For example, if you take a sample of some of your favorite titles and want to organize that material as a detailed resource for others, you might elect to present the information using XML. This might look easy if you're charting just a few of your favorite books, but what if you work for the Library of Congress and you want to chart hundreds of thousands of titles? The easiest way to work with large doses of data is to structure it in a way that makes it easy enough for almost anyone to manage and understand.

Because XML's primary function is to define data, you need to get a grasp on what you're working with and how you want that information structured. After you understand your data, you can begin to look at how to present it using XML code. Whittling away at the data is the first step toward understanding what you plan to represent. Now is the time to think about the types of data you will use. For example, do you deal with numbers to price and sell your newest products, or do you need to set up a resource site to catalog numerous articles? After you know what type of data you want to use, you should begin to chop it up into small, manageable pieces. This allows you to get to know your data before you get into bed with it.

Step 2: Capturing Data Elements in Code

Every language, whether spoken or technical, follows some set of rules. One of the benefits of using XML is that you get the chance to create some of those rules for yourself — or at least for your documents. Although the World Wide Web Consortium (W3C) sets the rules that govern how to define a well-formed document, you still get some say about its validity.

Although all XML documents do not have to be valid, there's value in adding validity to your XML pursuits. In brief, a document is *valid* when it conforms to whatever rules are defined in the DTD that governs the document (which you may also have created yourself). In this chapter, we assume that you understand what a valid XML document is and that you're ready to begin creating some rules of your own. For a detailed explanation of validity, flip to Chapter 4.

For example, if you work for the Library of Congress, you need to be able to chart hundreds of thousands of books. Right off the bat, you should be able to identify specific items of data that must be present in any book listing, such as the title, author, and publisher. You can identify these items as element types, for example:

```
<Title>
<Author>
<Publisher>
```

It's important to understand that elements do not *mean* anything; they're simply a way to create and label a structure for your data. Meaning is something that gets addressed in documentation. The content that provides the meat of the matter falls between the start and end tags of some element type. Keep in mind that all this — content and element types — appears in the XML document, not in the DTD. For now, you want to identify what code you will use in your document so you can better understand what rules you need to define in your DTD.

If you frequently run in XML circles, you will hear both *element* and *element type* a lot. *Element types* are specific — or named — elements, such as ⟨Book⟩ and ⟨Title⟩. The word *element* is used as a more general reference. In the following example, we have three element types and four elements (because the ⟨Author⟩ element appears twice):

```
<Book>
<Title>XML For Dummies, 2nd Edition</Title>
<Author>Ed Tittel</Author>
<Author>Frank Boumphrey</Author>
</Book>
```

Elements are the root of all structure

Elements define the skeleton for any XML document. In a document, an element looks like any old HTML tag, such as ⟨title⟩. But after you define an element in a DTD, the element takes on a life of its own.

First, we map out the elements we want to use in our DTD; in the next section, we start to declare them. We stick with a Library of Congress example throughout this chapter to make it easier to follow. Table 6-1 maps out the pieces of data we use for that purpose.

Table 6-1	Data in the Library of Congress Example	
Data	**Element Type**	**Relationship**
Catalog	⟨Catalog⟩	Root element
Book	⟨Book⟩	Child of Catalog
Book Title	⟨Title⟩	Child of Book
Author	⟨Author⟩	Child of Book
Publisher	⟨Publisher⟩	Child of Book
Date Published	⟨Pub_Date⟩	Child of Book

Before you define your element types, you must identify relationships and any resulting hierarchy among elements. You need to think about several things here: sequence, hierarchy, and occurrence. The best way to understand what we mean is to work through an example. Here goes:

```
<Catalog>
   <Book>
     <Title> . . . </Title>
     <Author> . . . </Author>
     <Publisher> . . . </Publisher>
     <Pub_Date> . . . </Pub_Date>
   </Book>
   <Book>
   ...
   </Book>
</Catalog>
```

Because we want to demonstrate only the relationships between element types, we included no content. You need to know about several key relationships among these elements (they are shown to some degree by the indenting of the code):

✔ <Catalog> is the root element and is the parent of <Book>

✔ <Book> is the parent of <Title>, <Author>, <Publisher>, and <Pub_Date>

In the preceding bulleted list, one could also say that <Pub_Date> is the *child* of <Book> or <Book> is the *child* of <Catalog> — get the picture?

Remember the three keywords we identified when working with elements? They are *sequence, hierarchy,* and *occurrence*. All three terms occur within element declarations. Here's how they break down:

✔ **Sequence.** When using a DTD, you can define the order in which element types may appear.

✔ **Hierarchy.** DTD element declarations can define parent-child relationships between or among elements.

✔ **Occurrence.** Element declarations may use occurrence indicators (such as ?, *, and +) to specify the number of times an element type may be used or must occur. (See the "Remember how to mix it up" section later in this chapter for more details.)

Attributes shed some light

Now that you understand a little about elements, you need to turn your attention to the attributes that modify or manage the content that elements may contain. Not only can attributes help clarify what content elements may contain, but they can also help define what an element does. As with elements, attributes have a few rules of their own.

Later in the chapter, we define the two ways that attributes provide information: by defining a data type and by defining a default value.

Essentially, attributes provide the capability to

✓ Associate external data resources

✓ Manage how element content should be handled

✓ Identify element data types, associations, and so forth

In a DTD, when you define attributes for elements, you can also define the types of data those attributes take (and whether such attributes must be present), handle default values, and control the number of value instances that may occur.

The way attributes are handled in a DTD is particularly important because the DTD must cover all conceivable usage scenarios. Before you decide that you must use an attribute in a DTD, here are some of the questions you should ask:

✓ Are you defining a particular aspect of an element, such as size, height, or color?

✓ Are you defining formatting information?

✓ Are you pointing to an object such as a graphic or a cross-reference?

✓ Are you locating links or other external files or objects?

If the answer to the first two questions is yes, you might want to consider handling that kind of information in a style sheet instead. But if you're associating an element with external data, as in the final two questions, that's a great reason to add an attribute to an element — but of course not the only reason!

Step 3: Developing and Defining Your Elements

So, you're on top of the elements you'll use in your document. Now, you need to create the element declarations you'll include in your DTD. As explained in Chapter 5, you declare elements as follows:

```
<!ELEMENT name (content specification)>
```

With our Library of Congress example, you can define your elements as follows:

```
<!ELEMENT Catalog (Book)+>
<!ELEMENT Book (Title,Author*,Publisher*,Pub_Date*)>
<!ELEMENT Title (#PCDATA)*>
<!ELEMENT Author (#PCDATA)*>
<!ELEMENT Publisher (#PCDATA)*>
<!ELEMENT Pub_Date (#PCDATA)*>
```

This chapter is primarily concerned with the content specifications that occur between the parentheses that follow the element names as well as associated attribute declarations. Several types of information can be contained between these common characters!

We define the various types of content specification in Chapter 5 (ANY, EMPTY, mixed content, and element content). For the moment, we're concerned with only the last two types of content specifications: mixed content and element content.

Elements content can mix it up, too

We define mixed and element content in Chapter 5, but we want to recap that information before you begin writing code. In mixed content, you are allowed to use only two symbols (occurrence indicators): | and *. Following are the symbols you can use in element content:

	Either one or the other may be used
*	The child element may be used as many times as needed or not at all
,	All listed child elements must be used in the order shown
	The occurrence is required (yes, it's a nonsymbol)
+	The child element must be used at least once or may be used many times
?	The child element may be used once or not at all

Now we break down the Library of Congress example:

```
<!ELEMENT Catalog (Book)+>
```

<Book> must appear within <Catalog> one or more times.

```
<!ELEMENT Book (Title,Author*,Publisher*,Pub_Date*)>
```

<Title> may appear within <Book> only once, whereas <Author>, <Publisher>, and <Pub_Date> may appear within <Book> once or not at all. Here's an example of element content:

```
<!ELEMENT Title (#PCDATA)* >
<!ELEMENT Author (#PCDATA)* >
<!ELEMENT Publisher (#PCDATA)* >
<!ELEMENT Pub_Date (#PCDATA)* >
```

<Title> contains only parsed character data, or text, but may include one or more blocks of text. The same is true of <Author>, <Publisher>, and <Pub_Date>. These are all examples of mixed content. Getting the drift? If so, here's a closer look at element content.

Element content describes parent-child relationships between elements. Element content also uses occurrence indicators to define usage. In our example, one declaration sticks out:

```
<!ELEMENT Book (Title,Author*,Publisher*,Pub_Date*)>
```

This declaration requires the elements to follow the specified order — <Title>, <Author>, <Publisher>, <Pub_Date> — and allows all elements except <Title> to be used more than once. (Because we use *, some elements don't have to be used at all.)

Step 4: What about Attributes?

Declaring attributes is similar to working with elements in that you have to include a bunch of information within those pesky little greater than and less than signs — and don't forget the exclamation mark (!). Take a look:

```
<!ATTLIST elementname attributename (data type) defaultvalue>
```

But wait a second! Let's slow down. The first decision you must make is what type of data to use in an attribute. Attributes can use several types of data (see Chapter 5 for the details). Here's a short list of data types that you can use in attributes:

- CDATA, or character data
- Enumerated
- ID
- IDREF and IDREFS
- ENTITY and ENTITIES
- NMTOKEN and NMTOKENS
- NOTATION

You also have three options for any default values:

- ✔ #REQUIRED
- ✔ #IMPLIED
- ✔ #FIXED

In the code that follows, we define some attributes for our example:

```
<!ATTLIST Title ISBN CDATA #REQUIRED>
<!ATTLIST Author Status CDATA #IMPLIED>
```

In this example, the element type <Title> may be further defined by adding an ISBN number. The declaration states that the XML document must list an ISBN number for every occurrence of the <Title> element type. The second declaration follows similar logic. <Author> does not always have to include Status as an attribute.

Step 5: Creating Shortcuts with Entities

Have you ever been working and accidentally misspelled your own name? Imagine working for the Library of Congress and having to type the same string of letters (*Library of Congress*) hundreds of times every week. Wouldn't it be nice if you could take a shortcut and use the &loc; string instead? Entities offer a convenient solution to such problems.

The XML specification allows two basic types of entities: general and parameter. *Parameter entities* are created and used within the DTD; *general entities* are created in the DTD but used in the XML document. In this section, we cover the basics of general entities. For a detailed look at parameter entities, visit Chapter 9.

Internalize it

Instead of typing the same text over and over, you can define an internal entity to contain the text. Then you need to use only the entity where you want to see the text. Basically, they are abbreviations defined within a declaration. Because the parser expands any entity it finds, you can be assured that you'll get the same text in every location — spelled the same way!

To call on entities, you must insert an entity reference in your document. If you've worked with HTML, you've already used entities. The most common entity references in HTML are < and &. Even the quotation mark is an entity reference and is referenced using the " character entity.

XML is not that different. You must still use the ampersand (&), followed by the entity's name, followed by a semicolon (;). That's because the underlying syntax comes from SGML, which is the parent language to both HTML and XML.

In XML, for the most part, you'll create your own entities. However, five internal entities are already defined for your use:

- < is the less than sign, <
- > is the greater than sign, >
- & is the ampersand, &
- ' is the single quote or apostrophe, '
- " is the double quotation mark, "

All XML processors support these predefined references, even if you don't declare them. Even so, some XML experts recommend that you include the necessary declarations for this markup in any DTD you create, just in case you run across a dumb XML processor!

To declare an internal entity, you must use the follow syntax:

```
<!ENTITY entityname "replacement text">
```

Following is our Library of Congress example:

```
<!ENTITY loc "Library of Congress">
```

Now, every time you want the words *Library of Congress* to appear in your document, &loc; is all you have to type.

External entities save time

External entities offer a mechanism to divide your document into logical pieces. Rather than creating a monolithic document, such as an online book, you can store each chapter in a separate file and use external entities to insert that file.

The benefit of using external entities is that they're reusable. But be aware that you need to carefully manage all the pieces. Chapter 9 covers the concerns when using external entities.

To declare an external entity, you use the following syntax:

```
<!ENTITY entityname SYSTEM "system-identifier">
```

The `system-identifier` is defined as a URI. The most common URI is a file name. You may also use the following syntax to refer to a public identifier not stored on your system:

```
<!ENTITY entityname PUBLIC "system-identifier">
```

Step 6: Calling Your DTD

When working with a simple DTD, you can use it in two ways: internally (in the existing XML document) or as an external file. If you opt to include your DTD in your XML document, you work with what's called an *internal subset.* When you reference an external DTD, you work with an *external subset.* The guts of the DTD stay the same, but it resides in different places in each case.

We delve into the differences between internal and external DTDs in Chapter 5. For now, we're more concerned with how to invoke them in code.

Internal subset

Internal subsets are located in the prolog of the XML document, within the document type declaration. Remember, your first line of code in the document is an XML processing instruction. The second line should be a document type declaration.

When declaring your DTD internally, the declaration falls within the document type declaration, like so:

```
<?xml version="1.0" standalone="yes"?>
<!DOCTYPE Catalog[
<!ENTITY loc "Library of Congress">
<!ELEMENT Catalog (Book+)>
<!ELEMENT Book (Title,Author*,Publisher*,Pub_Date*)>
<!ELEMENT Title (#PCDATA)*>
<!ATTLIST Title ISBN CDATA #REQUIRED>
<!ELEMENT Author (#PCDATA)*>
<!ATTLIST Author Status CDATA #IMPLIED>
<!ELEMENT Publisher (#PCDATA)*>
<!ELEMENT Pub_Date (#PCDATA)*>
]>
<!--   Begin Document Body   -->
<Catalog>
  . . .
</Catalog>
```

Notice that the DTD code comes after the declaration and root element `<!DOCTYPE Catalog [ DTD code ]>`.

External subset

Creating an external DTD file has many advantages. The main advantage is that an external DTD file is reusable.

We create an external DTD in a moment, but for now, you need to find out how to reference it within your XML document. Take a look:

```
<?xml version="1.0" standalone="no"?>
<!DOCTYPE Catalog SYSTEM "bookcatalog.dtd">
<Catalog>
. . .
</Catalog>
```

For the previous sample XML document to be valid, it must adhere to `bookcatalog.dtd`. Note that the root element must be listed in the document type declaration.

Tricks of the Trade

We've covered all the bases — almost. We still have the following unfinished business to attend to:

- ✔ `<!-- Comments document your work -->`. Always use comments to add notes and navigational information.

- ✔ `<!ENTITY` **first.** Declare your entities before element and attribute declarations. This enables you to define entities you can use in the declarations that follow.

- ✔ `<!ENTITY` **practice.** Practice using entities; they can save you tons of time in the long run!

- ✔ **Tools do DTDs, too.** Visit Chapter 21 to find XML editors that can generate a DTD from an XML document on demand.

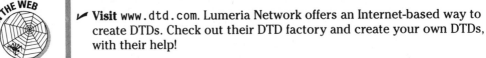

- ✔ **Visit** `www.dtd.com`. Lumeria Network offers an Internet-based way to create DTDs. Check out their DTD factory and create your own DTDs, with their help!

- ✔ **Remember your CAPS.** XML is case sensitive, so don't forget to capitalize all reserved DTD terms, such as `<!ENTITY`.

Creating a Simple External DTD

Now that you can write all the parts and pieces, it's time to put them together. We discuss the heart of a DTD and identify each piece as we go along. At the end of this adventure, you'll find a simple, yet thorough, DTD.

Insert comments to identify the beginning of the DTD:

```
<!-- Begin bookcatalog.dtd last updated January 1, 2000 --
          >
```

Declare entities first so they can be referenced within element and attribute declarations as well as in the XML document. Remember, the &loc; entity is an internal one.

```
<!ENTITY loc "Library of Congress">
```

State your element declarations. You'll be able to use these elements in your XML documents.

```
<!ELEMENT Catalog (Book+)>
<!ELEMENT Book (Title,Author*,Publisher*,Pub_Date*)>
<!ELEMENT Title (#PCDATA)>
```

Now it's time to declare all your attributes. As shown, an attribute declaration usually follows the corresponding element declaration:

```
<!ATTLIST Title Name CDATA #REQUIRED>
```

Again, we list an element that may contain parsed character data:

```
<!ELEMENT Author (#PCDATA)>
```

The <Author> element type also has an attribute, Status. In this case, the document is not required to include the attribute:

```
<!ATTLIST Author Status CDATA #IMPLIED>
```

The last of the element declarations are listed:

```
<!ELEMENT Publisher (#PCDATA)>
<!ELEMENT Pub_Date (#PCDATA)>
```

Throw in a closing comment for good measure.

```
<!-- End of bookcatalog.dtd -->
```

Don't forget to save your document with a .dtd file extension. As with naming elements, you may name your DTD anything you want. Remember that XML is case sensitive and don't forget to reference your DTD in your XML document. That's all she wrote.

But wait! Let's pull it all together for one final look:

```
<!--   Begin bookcatalog.dtd last updated
       January 1, 2000  -->
<!ENTITY loc "Library of Congress">
<!ELEMENT Catalog (Book+)>
<!ELEMENT Book (Title,Author*,Publisher*,Pub_Date*)>
<!ELEMENT Title (#PCDATA)*>
<!ATTLIST Title ISBN CDATA #REQUIRED>
<!ELEMENT Author (#PCDATA)*>
<!ATTLIST Author Status CDATA #IMPLIED>
<!ELEMENT Publisher (#PCDATA)*>
<!ELEMENT Pub_Date (#PCDATA)*>
<!--   End of bookcatalog.dtd  -->
```

Now take a look at the XML document with the DTD defined internally in the prolog:

```
<!--   Begin bookcatalog.dtd  -->
<?xml version="1.0" standalone="yes"?>
<!DOCTYPE Catalog[
<!--
     Description : Catalog of our favorite books
     Author : LANWrights
     Update : January 1, 2000
-->
<!ENTITY loc "Library of Congress">
<!ELEMENT Catalog (Book+)>
<!ELEMENT Book (Title,Author*,Publisher*,Pub_Date*)>
<!ELEMENT Title (#PCDATA)*>
<!ATTLIST Title ISBN CDATA #REQUIRED>
<!ELEMENT Author (#PCDATA)*>
<!ATTLIST Author Status CDATA #IMPLIED>
<!ELEMENT Publisher (#PCDATA)*>
<!ELEMENT Pub_Date (#PCDATA)*>
]>
<!--   Begin Document Body  -->
<Catalog>
<Book>
<Title ISBN="0316769533">Catcher in the Rye</Title>
<Author Status="deceased">J.D. Salinger</Author>
<Publisher>Little Brown and Company</Publisher>
<Pub_Date>1951</Pub_Date>
</Book>
<Book>
<Title ISBN="0316769541">Franny and Zooey</Title>
<Author Status="alive">J.D. Salinger</Author>
<Publisher>Little Brown and Company</Publisher>
<Pub_Date>1961</Pub_Date>
</Book>
</Catalog>
```

Part III

Building XML Documents

The 5th Wave   By Rich Tennant

"You'd better come out here — I've got someone who wants to run a banner ad on our Web site."

In this part. . .

*H*ere, we take the contents of Part II, which describe XML document structures in general and in particular, and explain how to put the particulars to work. In Chapter 7, you find out about element attributes and what they can do to further describe and control XML document content. In Chapter 8, you look at the ins and outs involved in using a DTD to create XML markup for organizing your content. Chapter 9 explains how to take multiple DTDs and combine them to good effect as well as how to customize a standard DTD to reflect your own special needs or requirements.

Chapter 10 explains how to use alternate alphabets, special symbols, and all kinds of character sets in your XML documents. This is especially interesting to those who seek to represent text in languages other than English in their XML documents. It also explains the mechanisms that make specialized character displays possible for XML applications such as the Chemical Markup Language (CML) and the Mathematical Markup Language (MathML), both of which require lots of specialized notation to display their content correctly.

Chapter 7

Attributes Add Flexibility to XML

* *

* *

*I*n Chapters 5 and 6, you find a lot of discussion about inserting attributes for XML elements into DTDs. In this chapter, we dig down deeply into this important subject. You uncover not only the syntax and structures involved in declaring and using attributes but also how to recognize when attributes are required or helpful. In addition, you find out how to create and use attributes properly in your XML documents.

The Truth about Attributes

In XML, either the start tag of a tag pair or an empty tag may contain one or more attributes. Such attributes are optional, in that there's no requirement that such tags must contain an attribute. In practice, some do and some don't.

In XML markup, attributes often appear in the form of name-value pairs, where the name is separated from the value by an equal sign, and the value is always contained within a pair of quotes, as in:

```
<graphic image="figure1.gif" alt="Book cover"/>
```

This format might look familiar to you — it's the same format used in HTML. The main difference is that the quotation marks are required in XML. Both the single and the double quotation marks can be used; however, you'll see double quotation marks used most often.

Now we break the previous element down, according to the book catalog DTD we use in Chapter 6:

- ✔ `<graphic` is the opening part of the empty `graphic` tag that tells the parser that a graphics file is about to be referenced.
- ✔ `image="figure1.gif"` is the first name-value pair for the `image` attribute, which is associated with a file named `figure1.gif` in the same directory as the current XML document.
- ✔ `alt="Book cover"` associates the text `"Book cover"` with the `alt` attribute, and thereby defines text for alternate display. If an XML application can't find or can't display the file named in the `image` attribute, or if the user has turned off graphics display in the application, the text associated with this attribute is shown instead of the graphic.
- ✔ `/>` closes the empty graphic tag because the tag is an empty tag that encloses no content.

Thus, the purposes of the attributes to the `graphic` tag are to define a source for a graphic, and to provide alternate text to display in place of that graphic if display is impossible or disabled. Another way to look at this information is that it provides a pointer to specific content — namely, the graphic file where a picture of a book cover is stored — along with text to show in place of that graphic if the graphic is not shown.

Please note that closing tags (such as `</title>`, drawing again from the book catalog DTD from Chapter 6) may not take attributes. Therefore, markup such as

```
</title name="Frank Boumphrey">
```

is illegal, even though the name attribute is indeed valid for the `<title>` tag.

Please note further that whereas most attributes take values, some do not (and therefore, have meaning by themselves without any modifiers). In XHTML, the ismap attribute that describes the file associated with the `<img />` tag as a clickable image map is a good example of an attribute that takes no value.

Appropriate Use of Attributes

XML applications are entirely open to the human imagination when it comes to creating elements — and by extension, are open to whatever attributes a designer might deem necessary. Because there are no technical limits on whatever attributes you might decide to create, we think it's a good idea to provide some guidelines as to what kinds of circumstances might justify using attributes for XML elements. By the same token, it's also a good idea to talk about some things that might not justify using attributes, but could perhaps be handled better in other ways.

Common HTML 4.0 attributes: The plus side

To begin with, you might take a look at how certain common attributes are used in HTML 4.0. There, you'll find such common attributes such as:

- ✔ id="name" is a document-wide identifier that uniquely identifies any element instance within the document.

- ✔ lang="name" specifies the language in which the element and its contents appear, usually according to RFC 1766, which specifies two-letter language codes like those used in the XML prolog. Also, be sure to reference the xml:lang namespace in your document prolog; doing so will resolve language references more or less automatically.

- ✔ dir=("ltr" | "rtl"): In text, languages parse either from left to right (the default) but some also parse from right to left (such as Hebrew). This attribute is often used with the lang attribute to indicate which direction to read when text-to-speech, Braille, or other nonvisual renderings might be applied to a document.

- ✔ title="text" associates advisory text with an element that is displayed as balloon help when mouseover events occur. This is how HTML provides balloon help for hyperlinks and graphics, for instance. Obviously, XML markup can support this same functionality, if desired.

In all of these cases, the attributes provide additional information that tells a browser how to interpret or present the content that may also be associated with such tags. The attributes provide additional information to help guide or control the way that the parser will identify or handle content associated with the tags wherein they occur.

Other perfectly valid examples of HTML attributes used appropriately include:

- ✔ method=("post"|"get") describes how a <form> tag will pass its input data to a server-side process for further handling.

- ✔ action="URI" describes which executable to invoke to handle server-side processing of form data.

- ✔ src="URI" describes where the source file for an img resides.

Here, these attributes provide processing instructions on how data should be handled, or describe the kinds of actions that should take place when that data is passed to a server. The preceding lists are neither exhaustive nor complete. The lists are meant to illustrate appropriate uses for attributes.

Common HTML 4.0 attributes: The minus side

Unfortunately, not everything you find by way of attributes in HTML 4.0 qualifies as a proper modifier for describing, locating, managing, or handling content. Many, many of its attributes aim to control how content is presented. More modern thinking on markup languages is that this job — that is, handling presentation — is not a job for a markup language that handles content. Rather, this is a job for a related style sheet or style language that offers more succinct and powerful ways to manage how content presentation may be handled. Furthermore, using separate controls for style and presentation allows content developers to concentrate on content, and allows design professionals to handle matters of appearance.

In HTML 4.0, the kinds of attributes that we suggest you stay away from in your XML applications include the following common attributes:

- ✔ class="text" is used for a comma-separated list of class names for styles to which an element may be associated.
- ✔ style="text" provides a way to embed style definitions within individual tags within a document.
- ✔ hspace="number" defines vertical space around an image or a text box.
- ✔ vspace="number" defines white space above and below a graphic or a text box.

On the other hand, you might be tempted to lump these kinds of attributes into the same category:

- ✔ height="number" defines the height of an image or a text box in pixels.
- ✔ width="number" defines the width of a graphic or a text box in pixels.

Although you would be justified in thinking of these attributes as presentation related, if you do plan to convert your XML into HTML for display on the Web, these particular attributes are incredibly useful for driving page displays when graphics are involved. If you find this troubling, think of these two attributes as "necessary evils" for capturing presentation data in XML element attributes.

Here, the governing concept is that these attributes are included entirely to manage how elements appear when displayed within a browser. Although it's entirely possible to make XML do this job directly, we suggest that you relegate presentation controls to separate handling using Cascading Style Sheets (CSS) or a separate XSL document. For one thing, the work of defining and handling such style markup is already finished and is already a standard (or becoming one). For another thing, we think it's better to defer such work to somebody else, if you don't absolutely have to do it yourself.

Based on these examples and on our experiences in defining our own XML markup, here are some do's and don'ts to consider when adding attributes to XML markup:

Do

Do use attributes to

- Indicate where data, links, or external resources reside.
- Describe how data or content is typed, encoded, measured, or represented.
- Identify or invoke external processing facilities, such as server- or client-side executables, applets, and so forth.
- Identify instances of elements within documents (this makes it easy to find them if you must ever search or navigate through a document programmatically).
- Provide additional information about content and external elements, along the lines of a built-in help system.

Thus, attributes are good for providing information about where data resides, what kind of data it is, how that data should be processed, and so forth.

Don't

Don't use attributes to

- Capture data that must always be displayed as part of a document's content.
- Position, pad, or put white space around elements.
- Specify font faces, font sizes, or font treatments (bold, italic, and so forth).
- Specify background colors or images, text colors, and so forth.
- Manage white space around page displays (margins, gutters, and so forth).

The first item in the list deserves an additional comment because the idea behind an attribute is to modify, control, type, or otherwise identify the content associated with the element to which it belongs. If an attribute captures data that will always appear when a document's content is displayed, you might want to consider creating another element to capture that data, and make that element a child of the current element instead. On the other hand, if certain combinations of attributes tend to occur predictably, you might want to create an element type for each such combination instead of relying on repeated use of the same attributes.

It's more efficient to search for element content directly than it is to search for specific attribute values for given elements. The distinction might be understood along the lines of an operation that requires two lookups (get the element; check the attribute value) instead of just one (get the element). Performing the two lookups might be hard to justify when such attributes occur rarely, but when they always occur, their values should be represented as content for an element instead.

In general, observing the primary don'ts for attributes means leaving presentation controls to whatever style sheet mechanisms you decide to use for your XML documents. Although the temptation to include such controls may sometimes be slightly overwhelming, please don't give in! You have access to other, better ways of controlling how your XML documents will look when presented to users.

Adding Attributes to DTDs

When it comes to adding attributes to DTDs, the primary rule to remember is one of ordering: Always declare your elements first using the <!ELEMENT declaration. Next, follow those declarations with as many <!ATTLIST declarations as you need — you can create one per attribute, or lump multiple entries together in a single <!ATTLIST declaration if you like — to describe as many attributes as your analysis shows you that each such element needs.

Returning to the book catalog DTD that appears in Chapter 6, take a look at those elements that include attributes (for brevity's sake, we show only those elements and their related attribute list markup):

```
<!ELEMENT Title (#PCDATA)*>
<!ATTLIST Title ISBN CDATA #REQUIRED>
<!ELEMENT Author (#PCDATA)*>
<!ATTLIST Author Status CDATA #IMPLIED>
```

In English, you could decode the four lines in this DTD fragment as follows:

1. Create a `<Title>...</Title>` element that may contain zero or more strings of character data. The content for this tag defines the title of a book.

2. The `<Title>` element must contain an attribute named `ISBN` that consists of a string of character (actually, numeric) data. Here, `ISBN` stands for "International Standard Book Number," and represents a unique 10-digit numeric code assigned to books scheduled for publication. An ISBN number makes it possible to identify any book, even when — as is sometimes the case — multiple books share identical titles.

3. Create an `<Author>...</Author>` element that may contain zero or more strings of character data. The content for this tag defines an author's name or names.

4. The `<Author>` element may (or may not) contain an attribute named `Status`, which consists of a string of character data. If the `Status` attribute is not defined for a tag, a null default value for the Status attribute (which equals something like "undefined" in human terms) is defined.

As a reminder of the general syntax for the `<!ATTLIST` declaration, here is how it may be expressed:

```
<!ATTLIST element-name attribute-name attribute-type
          attribute-default>
```

First, we tackle and explore this declaration item by item; after that, you will be ready to hear more about the final two items: attribute types and attribute defaults:

- `<!ATTLIST` opens the attribute declaration with a reserved keyword to identify the type of statement under construction.

- `element-name` names the element to which the attribute will apply. The earlier example shows this association quite clearly because `<!ELEMENT` declarations precede related `<!ATTLIST` declarations.

- `attribute-name` names the attribute that will apply to `element-name`. The earlier example shows how `<!ATTLIST` declarations follow related `<!ELEMENT` declarations.

- `attribute-type` names one of ten predefined types that attributes may take. (These are discussed further in the next section of this chapter.) In general, `attribute-type` serves to label what kind of string or string selection may appear as the value for the attribute.

✔ `attribute-default` defines how the attribute is to be handled — whether it appears or not. In general, this defines how the attribute's value is determined (or left alone) when the attribute does not appear or when no value is explicitly assigned (if that is permitted). Instead of using a reserved word to define how an attribute's value is handled by default, you may simply state that default by enclosing the desired value in quotes in the DTD.

The ten types of attributes in DTDs

In an XML DTD, the string supplied for the `attribute-type` field must belong to one of the ten following named types. These attributes are presented here more or less in alphabetical order for convenience; the examples use an ellipsis (. . .) to separate the DTD portion from actual content markup.

✔ CDATA: Character data supports a string of arbitrary length that can include any characters except an apostrophe, double quotes, ">", "<", or "&". This is a commonly used data type that accommodates all kinds of string data. CDATA is parsed, so you can use character entities in CDATA value to produce these invalid characters if they must be part of a value string (those entities are ', ", >, <, and &, respectively). For the same reason, you can also use general entities — those you define in your own DTD — in CDATA as well.

Example:

```
<!ELEMENT Square EMPTY>
<!ATTLIST Square Side CDATA #REQUIRED>
...
<Square Side="4&apos; 2&quot;"/>
<!-- Note: use &apos; for the feet symbol -->
<!--       use &quot; for the inches symbol -->
```

✔ ENTITY: Allows an attribute to take the value of an entity declared or referenced elsewhere in the DTD.

Example:

```
<!ELEMENT Bookcover EMPTY>
<!ATTLIST Bookcover source ENTITY #REQUIRED>
<!ENTITY X-cover SYSTEM "xml4dumcovr.tif" NDATA tif>
<!NOTATION tif "Tagged Image File Format">
...
<Bookcover source="&X-cover;"/>
```

✔ ENTITIES: This takes multiple entities as its value, where individual ENTITY references are separated by white space. Use this to point to a list of entities, such as various Uniform Resource Identifiers (URIs) to try when accessing external data resources, for instance.

Example:

```
<!ELEMENT Res-list EMPTY>
<!ATTLIST Res-list sources ENTITIES #REQUIRED>
<!NOTATION htm "HTTP 1.1">
<!ENTITY Site1 PUBLIC
  "http://www.yahoo.com" NDATA htm>
<!ENTITY Site2 PUBLIC
  "http://www.excite.com" NDATA htm >
<!ENTITY Site3 PUBLIC
  "http://www.askjeeves.com" NDATA htm >
...
<Res-list sources="&Site1; &Site2; &Site3"/>
```

✔ **Enumerated**: Strictly speaking, enumerated is not the name of an attribute type. However, you can create a list of legal values for any attribute you wish that takes the form `(option1|option2|...)` where each option is separated by a vertical slash, and the entire set is enclosed in parentheses. This means that the value for that attribute can only come from the set defined in the DTD. This mechanism provides a great way to control the values that a validating parser will accept when reading documents that claim to conform to some specific DTD. The names that appear in the list of legal values must be defined elsewhere in the DTD, or match input strings exactly from a document.

Example:

```
<!ELEMENT Primary EMPTY>
<!ATTLIST Primary Color (Red|Green|Blue) #REQUIRED>
...
<Primary Color="Red"/>
```

✔ ID: This is the identifier type, and must be unique for all such values in an entire XML document. This attribute value is used to search an XML document to locate a particular instance of some element. It comes in handy when you must find specific parts of documents, especially when programs handle such search activities. IDs must conform to the rules that govern XML names and name tokens.

Example:

```
<!ELEMENT Section (#PCDATA)>
<!ATTLIST Section SecID ID #REQUIRED>
...
<Section SecID="Section8">
  The topic of this section is wombats.</Section>
```

✔ IDREF: This too is an identifier type, and must also point to only one element, but points at some other element in an XML document. Hence, such an attribute acts as an "identifier reference," as the name of the type is meant to suggest. Use this to point to related elements elsewhere in an XML document. IDREFs must also conform to the rules that govern XML names and name tokens.

Example:

```
<!ELEMENT Section (#PCDATA)>
<!ATTLIST Section SecID ID #REQUIRED>
<!ATTLIST Section Prev IDREF #IMPLIED>
<!ATTLIST Section Next IDREF #IMPLIED>
...
<Section SecID="Section8"
        Prev="Section7" Next="Section12">
<!-- Please note that sections 9-11 are missing -->
  The topic of this section is wombats.</Section>
```

✔ IDREFS: This takes multiple element IDs as its value, where individual IDREF values are separated by white space. Use this to point to a list of related elements elsewhere in an XML document (handy when indexing elements that contain multiple occurrences of a term or a phrase, for instance).

Example:

```
<!ELEMENT Section (#PCDATA)>
<!ATTLIST Section SecID ID #REQUIRED>
<!ATTLIST Section Prev IDREF #IMPLIED>
<!ATTLIST Section Next IDREF #IMPLIED>
<!ATTLIST Section Xrefs IDREFS #IMPLIED>
...
<Section SecID="Section8"
        Prev="Section7" Next="Section12"
        Xrefs "Section1 Section2 Section4">
<!-- Please note that sections 9-11 are missing -->
  The topic of this section is wombats.</Section>
```

✔ NMTOKEN: XML restricts how strings that are to be used for names or name tokens may be constructed. An attribute value of type NMTOKEN must conform to these rules, and a validating parser will check any string of this type against those rules when parsing any XML document written to a DTD that uses this attribute type. Illegal characters include initial periods, numbers, white space characters (space, tab, line break, and so forth), most punctuation, and most higher-order ASCII characters, plus any initial string that takes the form "xml" in any combination of uppercase and lowercase. Use attributes of this type when they must identify other XML elements or attributes. The example allows DOS-style 8.3 file names, but won't allow names with embedded blanks or improper punctuation characters.

Example:

```
<!ELEMENT DOSname (File*,Variable*,Version)>
<!ELEMENT File EMPTY>
<!ATTLIST File name NMTOKEN #REQUIRED>
...
<File name="config.sys">
```

✔ NMTOKENS: This takes multiple name tokens as its value, where individual NMTOKEN references are separated by white space. Use this to point to a list of element or attribute names that must conform to XML naming conventions.

✔ NOTATION: The name of a particular notation — which may be a file type for graphics or other nontextual data, some type of data format for dates or timestamps, and so forth — defined elsewhere in a DTD in a <!NOTATION declaration.

Example:

```
<!ELEMENT video EMPTY>
<!ATTLIST video source ENTITY #REQUIRED>
<!ATTLIST video playback NOTATION #REQUIRED>
<!ENTITY CEO-msg SYSTEM "/multim/ceo120400.avi" NDATA cm>
<!NOTATION cm SYSTEM "realvideo.exe">
...
<video source="&CEO-msg;" playback="cm"/>
```

Next, we cover how default values for attributes may be handled.

Attributes and their defaults

The final field in the <!ATTLIST declaration deals with attribute defaults. Whereas you can provide a default value for an attribute by including it here enclosed in double quotes, you can also use one of three keywords to control how defaults are handled for the attribute:

✔ #FIXED: If this reserved word appears ahead of an explicit default, it means that the specified value must appear any time this attribute is used. But if the attribute or the related value does not occur, that value will be used by default. Thus, a declaration like

```
<!ATTLIST Author Status CDATA #FIXED "alive">
```

would mean that if the attribute or its value is omitted, the construct Status="alive" would be assumed for all such records. Unfortunately, alive would also be the only valid value for the status attribute (which is why this approach wasn't used in the actual book catalog DTD in Chapter 6). For similar reasons, the #FIXED reserved word is seldom used when declaring attributes, except when attribute values cannot change.

✔ #IMPLIED: When there is no reasonable default value for an attribute default, but there's also no reason to force a document's creator to include this attribute in every element to which the attribute belongs, the #IMPLIED reserved word comes in handy. This makes it possible for document authors to use the attribute when it's required, but to ignore it when it's not required. Thus, the #IMPLIED reserved word is a way to make an attribute optional, with a null or undefined value when the attribute is left out.

✔ #REQUIRED: Use the #REQUIRED reserved word to force any document's creator who seeks to conform to a DTD to supply that attribute and a value to go along with it. You can't control what value gets entered through the DTD, but you can require that the attribute be present and have a value by using this reserved word. If an author omits a required attribute-value pair, the parser will flag this as an error and require that this information be supplied to validate the document.

Unfortunately, you cannot define a default value when you use the #REQUIRED keyword, so if you want authors to use some kind of value as a default for such an attribute, be sure to document that information in a comment in your DTD!

A little practice with these reserved words, and some judicious reading of "other people's DTDs" should help you obtain a good understanding of how and when they should be used, beyond what we've noted here.

Predefined XML Attributes

There's a special class of XML names that qualifies as predefined attributes for XML markup. These names begin with the string xml: and help explain why valid XML names or name tokens cannot begin with the characters "xml" in any mixture of uppercase and lowercase.

The implications of this class of names is that there's a collection of special attributes related to XML that have been predefined for use with any kind of XML markup. Over time, we expect this class of names to become more fully populated, and to help define a core set of attributes that developers can invoke any time they create XML markup. At present, however, this set is limited to exactly two terms:

✔ xml:space
✔ xml:lang

The xml:space attribute describes what an application should do when white space occurs within an element. This reflects the notion that for XML itself, all white space is preserved and passed to the processor that handles an XML application. Although many such processors take the same tack as HTML, and treat all sequences of white space as a single space, the preservation of white space during parsing makes it possible for an application to take other approaches, and handle white space in its own way. Such a processor can elect to accept only certain valid white space characters (spaces, non-breaking spaces, tabs, and so forth) and replace them with specific sequences of spaces or preserve them as-is. This facility can be programmed in whatever way a developer wishes to handle white space. (See Elliotte Rusty Harold's excellent IDG book, *XML: Extensible Markup Language*, pp. 222-223, for further discussion of the details.)

The xml:space attribute is an enumerate type that accepts the values of default or preserve, which suggests syntax as follows:

```
<!ATTLIST element xml:space (default|preserve) "preserve">
```

Where element is the name of the XML element to which the xml:space attribute must be associated. (Usually, this will be the name of the executable element that acts as the XML processor for the application.) Notice that an enumerated type of (default|preserve) establishes the two legal values for xml:space, and that the quoted presence of "preserve" at the end of the declaration sets the default for xml:space to that value.

The xml:lang attribute indicates the language used to represent the parent element's content. The value of this attribute may be of type CDATA, NMTOKEN, or set equal to an enumerated list of language codes. These language codes are described in RFC 1766, as well as in ISO standard 639 (country codes appear in ISO standard 3166). To obtain the related details, simply use a search engine to locate the text for one or more of these standards documents.

Use of the xml:lang attribute is normally limited to cases where documents contain multiple languages (where its use overrides the language declaration in the XML prolog itself), or where computer-based translation of documents might be required. This attribute can also help to invoke the right spelling- and grammar-checking tools, and can help search engines decide which content to index and present to a document's readers.

A school of thought in the XML development community proposes that DTDs should take a similar approach when naming elements, so all elements in a DTD might begin with a two- or three-character code followed by an underscore before the actual element name occurs. That way, when you include multiple DTDs in a single document, you can be guaranteed that no two elements will have the same name. Likewise, use of XML namespaces helps to avoid name conflicts as well.

Over time, we expect the W3C to define additional xml: attributes, to make more general functionality available. It will be interesting to see what other kinds of attributes this will allow document designers to use in their DTDs!

Chapter 8

Putting Your DTD to Work

- -

In This Chapter

▶ Managing XML markup

▶ Using DTD definitions to control document structure

▶ Creating book descriptions

▶ Presenting multiple address orderings

▶ Understanding the trade-off between structure and flexibility

- -

*I*n Chapter 5, you discover how to use Document Type Definitions (DTDs) with XML documents. In Chapter 6, you build your own DTD to capture the precise nuances of whatever markup you want to create. In Chapter 7, you explore the ins and outs of using attributes as part of defining XML markup in a DTD. In this chapter, your ongoing DTD adventures continue!

In fact, if you're working with XML, it's nearly impossible to escape the need to modify or update (if not build) a DTD from time to time, especially when it comes to building documents that adhere to the markup and structure that a DTD can define. In this chapter, you explore what's involved in working with a DTD as you investigate the process of constructing markup according to a DTD's rules and regulations. In addition, you find out how to use DTDs to help control document structure.

Eliciting Markup from the DTD

To begin, we revisit the book catalog DTD introduced in Chapter 6. We use it to explore the nuances of the legal markup that this DTD can produce. Then, in the following section, we elaborate on that DTD a bit to demonstrate some of the ways that DTDs can help to manage a document's structure.

First, here's the book catalog DTD:

```
<!-- Begin bookcatalog.dtd last updated
     January 1, 2000  -->
<!ENTITY loc "Library of Congress">
<!ELEMENT Catalog (Book+)>
<!ELEMENT Book (Title,Author*,Publisher*,Pub_Date*)>
<!ELEMENT Title (#PCDATA)*>
<!ATTLIST Title ISBN CDATA #REQUIRED>
<!ELEMENT Author (#PCDATA)*>
<!ATTLIST Author Status CDATA #IMPLIED>
<!ELEMENT Publisher (#PCDATA)*>
<!ELEMENT Pub_Date (#PCDATA)*>
<!-- End of bookcatalog.dtd  -->
```

The primary element in this DTD is the `Catalog` element. As defined, the `Catalog` element must contain one or more `Book` elements because its definition uses the plus sign (+) occurrence indicator:

```
<!ELEMENT Catalog (Book+)>
```

Therefore, a valid `Catalog` must contain at least one or more `Book` elements to be properly constructed.

The `Book` element is the primary data structure in this DTD, and its definition is worth some additional exploration and explanation:

```
<!ELEMENT Book
     (Title,Author*,Publisher*,Pub_Date*)>
```

According to this definition, a `Book` element must be structured as follows:

- ✔ The definition of the `Book` element precedes a list of element names (separated by commas), some of which include occurrence indicators. This parenthesized list is called *element content* because it consists entirely of element names. The structure of this list defines the sequence for those elements that must or may compose a valid `Book` element.

- ✔ The content for a `Book` element must begin with one and only one `Title` element, as signified by the appearance of the `Title` element in the first position of the element content specification. In plain English, you could choose to view this as a declaration that "any book must have a title."

- ✔ Following the `Title` element, a `Book` element may include zero or more `Author` elements. This means the `Author` element is optional in `Book` elements and that an arbitrary number of such elements may be part of a valid `Book` element definition. This fits most typical books, which sometimes have no attributed author or a half-dozen authors.

✔ Following the optional `Author` element, a `Book` element may then include zero or more `Publisher` elements. Therefore, the `Publisher` element is optional as well and represents cases where no publisher is named for a book, where one publisher is named for a book or, as is common, where a publisher and one or more imprints are named for a book.

✔ Following the optional `Publisher` element, a `Book` element may include zero or more `Pub_Date` elements. (Notice the underscore between `Pub` and `Date` in the element name — this technique is required to avoid including white space.) This declaration means that a book might have no publication date, a single publication date, or multiple publication dates, with no limit on the total number of dates allowed.

Each of the constituent elements that may appear within the `Book` element is defined, including the `Title` and `Author` elements. Each of these consists of parsed character data (`#PCDATA`) and each takes a single attribute (`ISBN` and `Status`, respectively). `Publisher` and `Pub_Date` are defined to consist of parsed character data as well.

That's it for the re-cap of the `bookcatalog.dtd` file. Next, you can chew on its implications. . . .

Understanding the implications

As element content structures go, the model inherent in the `Book` element's declaration is flexible. Based on that single declaration, all of the following structures are legal:

```
<Catalog>
<!-- The minimal catalog contains a single book -->
  <Book>
<!-- The minimal book includes only a title -->
    <Title>Sample Title</Title>
  </Book>
</Catalog>
```

A catalog with only a single book is pretty useless, so assume that additional examples have multiple books, symbolized by an ellipsis between the first closing `</Book>` tag and the closing `</Catalog>` tag. In the interests of brevity, we omit that additional markup here.

Here's an example that includes a title plus multiple other elements within a single `Book` element:

```
<Catalog>
<!-- A book element can contain multiple non-title
     entries -->
  <Book>
    <Title>XML For Dummies, 2nd Edition</Title>
    <Author>Ed Tittel</Author>
    <Author>Frank Boumphrey</Author>
    <Publisher>IDG Books WorldWide</Publisher>
    <Publisher>Dummies Press</Publisher>
    <Pub_Date>3/17/2000: 1st Printing</Pub_Date>
    <Pub_Date>9/22/2000: 2nd Printing</Pub_Date>
  </Book>
...
</Catalog>
```

Legal Book elements can include more than two Author, Publisher, or Pub_Date tags. Book elements can also omit any or all of these tags because the DTD's occurrence indicator specifies that these tags may occur zero or more times. We think you should be able to figure this kind of markup out for yourself, so we don't do it for you here.

Instead, we'd like to write about what other things this particular structure makes illegal. It's as important to understand what a DTD does *not* allow — especially one with an element as flexible as the Book element — as it is to understand what *is* allowed. Therefore, here's a list of what's illegal, according to the structure of the declaration for the Book element (with examples, where appropriate):

✔ Any Book element can have one and only one Title element, and it must occur first within that element. Therefore, the following markup is illegal (for reasons noted in its comments):

```
<!--Two Title elements may not occur in a Book element -->
<Catalog>
  <Book>
    <Title>Concluding Unscientific PostScript</Title>
    <Title>Or, The Sickness Unto Death</Title>
  </Book>
<!-- The Title element must always occur first in a Book
        element -->
  <Book>
    <Author>Elliotte Rusty Harold</Author>
    <Title>XML: Extensible Markup Language</Title>
    <Publisher>IDG Books Worldwide</Publisher>
    <Pub_Date>9/98: 1st Printing</Pub_Date>
  </Book>
...
</Catalog>
```

✔ Whenever other optional elements follow the `Title` element in a `Book` element, they can appear only in the order specified in the element content declaration: `Author`(s) follow `Title`, `Publisher`(s) follow `Author`(s), `Pub_Date`(s) follow `Publisher`(s). Therefore, the following code is invalid because it breaks the element order requirements inherent in the declaration:

```
</Catalog>
<!-- Elements may only appear in the order specified in
        the element content declaration -->
  <Book>
<!-- This markup reverses the required order for elements,
        and is wrong, wrong, wrong. -->
      <Pub_Date>9/99</Pub_Date>
      <Publisher>IDG Books Worldwide</Publisher>
      <Author>Elliotte Rusty Harold</Author>
      <Title>XML: Extensible Markup Language</Title>
  </Book>
...
</Catalog>
```

✔ Where elements — such as `Title` and `Author` — take attributes, only declared attributes may appear and all values must be enclosed in quotation marks (which may be either single or double quotes but must be the same whenever attribute values are quoted). Therefore, the following markup is also illegal:

```
</Catalog>
  <Book>
<!-- Mismatched quotation marks are illegal, as are
      missing quotation marks -->
    <Title ISBN="0-7645-3199-9'>
        XML: Extensible Markup Language</Title>
<!-- The name of the correct attribute value is Status,
        not State -->
      <Author State="Alive">Elliotte Rusty Harold</Author>
  </Book>
</Catalog>
```

Thus, although the structure for a `Book` element is somewhat loose in terms of the number and kinds of component elements that can occur after the required lead-in `Title` element, plenty of structure is here to enforce. This leads into the next discussion, in which you grapple with the tradeoffs inherent between structure and flexibility when building XML DTDs.

Trading flexibility against structure

DTDs are quite flexible; you can "mix things up" in them. For instance, element declarations in DTDs can use parentheses to create multiple levels of structure. DTDs also support a way of specifying that one item from a set of possible choices can be chosen to appear. And finally, DTDs permit element choices to be combined with open-ended constructs such as ANY or #PCDATA, thereby opening the door to just about any conceivable kind of content.

To help you understand what this means, we play some games with the bookcatalog.dtd definition for the Book element, which appears as follows:

```
<!ELEMENT Book
        (Title,Author*,Publisher*,Pub_Date*)>
```

For example, you want each Publisher entry to be associated with a specific Pub_Date, and these must occur in pairs, if they occur at all. A second level of parentheses (and corresponding structure) makes this easy:

```
<!ELEMENT Book
        (Title,Author*,(Publisher,Pub_Date)*)>
```

Notice that we separated the Publisher and Pub_Date elements with a comma, enclosed both of them in parentheses, and added an asterisk as an occurrence indicator outside the parentheses. What this means in English might be stated as follows:

- ✔ A Book may contain zero or more paired sets of Publisher and Pub_Date elements.
- ✔ If a Book contains a Publisher element, that Publisher element may be associated with one, and only one, Pub_Date element.
- ✔ If a Book contains one or more paired sets of Publisher and Pub_Date elements, the Publisher element must always precede the Pub_Date element in each such a pair.

Please note that if your catalogs permitted individual publishers to be associated with multiple publication dates within book descriptions, you might change the element declaration to read:

```
<!ELEMENT Book
        (Title,Author*,(Publisher,Pub_Date*)*)>
```

In that case, zero or more Pub_Date elements could follow any particular Publisher element. As before, any Book element could include zero or more such pairs of subelements.

Add levels to simplify structure

DTDs are easier to read if you don't have to try to follow too many levels of structure in any single element declaration. That's why you might choose to create an intermediate-level element, perhaps named Pub_Record, to capture the nuances of how publisher and publication date entries need to be handled. This might lead you to create the following DTD:

```
<!--  Begin bookcatalog.dtd last updated
      January 2, 2000  -->
<!ENTITY loc "Library of Congress">
<!ELEMENT Catalog (Book+)>
<!ELEMENT Book (Title,Author*,Pub_Record*)>
<!ELEMENT Title (#PCDATA)*>
<!ATTLIST Title ISBN CDATA #REQUIRED>
<!ELEMENT Author (#PCDATA)*>
<!ATTLIST Author Status CDATA #IMPLIED>
<!ELEMENT Pub_Record (Publisher,Pub_Date)*>
<!ELEMENT Publisher (#PCDATA)*>
<!ELEMENT Pub_Date (#PCDATA)*>
<!--  End of bookcatalog.dtd  -->
```

This approach lets you concentrate on one level of element structure at a time and helps make your DTD easier for others to read and understand.

A matter of selection

DTDs also support what might be called a *selection technique*. This selection technique allows DTD designers to define sets of potential elements in ELEMENT declarations from which authors must choose one when implementing some particular element. This probably sounds a bit mysterious, so we present an example to show what we mean.

Given the following DTD fragment:

```
<!ELEMENT Address (Name, Company*, Street*, City, State?,
          Code?, Country*)>
<!ATTLIST Address Type (home|office|other) "office">
<!ELEMENT Name (#PCDATA)>
<!ELEMENT Company (#PCDATA)>
<!ELEMENT Street (#PCDATA)>
<!ELEMENT City (#PCDATA)>
<!ELEMENT State (#PCDATA)>
<!ELEMENT Code (Zip|Postal_Code)>
<!ELEMENT Zip (#PCDATA)>
<!ELEMENT Postal_Code (#PCDATA)>
<!ELEMENT Country (#PCDATA)>
```

The following XML markup is all legal. (Please read the comments for an explanation of each Address entry.)

```
<Address Type="home">
<!-- This Address element follows U.S. address syntax,
     including Zip, and designates no country -->
  <Name>Ed Tittel</Name>
  <Street>2207 Klattenhoff Drive</Street>
  <City>Austin</City>
  <State>TX</State>
  <Code>
     <Zip>78728-5480</Zip>
  </Code>
</Address>
<Address>
<!-- This Address element follows U.K. address syntax,
     including Postal Code, multiple street/location
     terms, and a country designation. Also because no
     type attribute appears, default = office -->
  <Name>George Worst</Name>
  <Street>204 Formans Road</Street>
  <Street>Sparkhill</Street>
  <City>Birmingham</City>
  <Code>
     <Postal_Code>B11 3AX</Postal_Code>
  </Code>
  <Country>U.K.</Country>
<Address>
```

The key lines in the DTD that allow you to select among a defined set of Address Types and that allow designation of a Zip or Postal_Code are

```
<!ATTLIST Address Type (home|office|other) "office">
...
<!ELEMENT Code (Zip|Postal_Code)>
...
```

The first attribute list indicates that for any Address that takes a Type attribute, the value of that attribute must be either "home", "office", or "other", and the default value for this attribute is "office" if an explicit assignment is not supplied. The second element declaration indicates that an address may include a Code element of some kind and this Code element will be either a Zip or a Postal_Code element (which corresponds to the difference between U.S.- and U.K.-derived postal coding schemes).

Two good ways to use DTD selection clauses are

- ✔ To choose one value from a set of possible values for attributes
- ✔ To choose one element from a set of possible elements when building an element hierarchy

Either way, you can use this syntax to limit an author's choices yet still provide alternative elements or attribute values.

Mixing up the order

These DTD selection clauses can be used also to permit the definition of alternative orders. To explain how this might come in handy, take a look at these two addresses:

Ed Tittel

2207 Klattenhoff Drive

Austin, TX 78728-5480

USA

George Worst

204 Formans Road

Sparkhill

B11 3AX

Birmingham

U.K.

Notice that in the U.S. address, the `City` follows the `City` and `State` entries. In the U.K. address, the `Postal_Code` precedes the `City` and the `State` seldom appears. If you wanted to be able to handle data in either order, you might consider building a DTD such as the following:

```
<!ELEMENT Address (Name,Company*,Street*,Locator,Country*)>
<!ATTLIST Address Type (home|office|other) "office">
<!ELEMENT Name (#PCDATA)>
<!ELEMENT Company (#PCDATA)>
<!ELEMENT Street (#PCDATA)>
<!ELEMENT Locator ((City,State?,Code?) |
                   (Code?,City,State?))>
<!ELEMENT City (#PCDATA)>
<!ELEMENT State (#PCDATA)>
<!ELEMENT Code (Zip|Postal_Code)>
<!ELEMENT Zip (#PCDATA)>
<!ELEMENT Postal_Code (#PCDATA)>
<!ELEMENT Country (#PCDATA)>
```

By creating an intermediate element named `Locator`, you create a placeholder in the original `Address` element. Then, when you define the `Locator` element, you can use a selection clause to stipulate that either of these two orders is valid: (`City, State, Code`) or (`Code, City, State`). In either case, the `State` and `Code` elements remain optional, where only one instance of each is allowed if those elements appear.

A close look at the `Locator` syntax, however, shows one of the problems with selection clauses. Please note that you must repeat the occurrence indicators that apply to each instance of the structure when the syntax allows an author to select from multiple orders. This increases the amount of work (and thinking) that you must do; therefore, use selection clauses sparingly.

Mixing Up Your Content Models

XML supports several ways to allow DTD creators to manage structure to some degree yet still leave themselves an out if they can't absolutely determine in advance how to structure the elements that go into such DTDs. In the DTD code throughout this book, there are elements that consist entirely of child elements or that contain parsed character data (#PCDATA).

To leave yourself an out when you can't define everything in advance, declare tags that contain both child elements *and* parsed character data. In DTD-speak, such elements are called *mixed content* to indicate that the content that might occur within the parent element might *not* be of the same type or follow a fixed sequence of child elements.

For instance, if the Locator element that we declared in the DTD example in the preceding section might have to accommodate other, arbitrary text data, we could make its declaration read as follows:

```
<!ELEMENT Locator (#PCDATA|City|State|Code)*>
```

This means that the ordering options for City, State, and Code elements disappear, although it would also be legal to provide a sequence of parsed character data as the content for the Locator element. Unfortunately, using mixed content means giving up most of the controls over sequence and structure that a DTD can provide.

Trading Control for Flexibility

In the end, the content to be captured using XML markup dictates how much structure you might seek to impose using a DTD. The more regular the content, the easier it is to represent a document's structure in a DTD. The less regular or predictable that document's content, the lower the probability that a DTD can enforce meaningful rules for content structure anyway.

Therefore, a text-oriented database such as a book catalog or an address book is more likely to present enforceable rules for structure than a free-form work such as a poem or a novel. That's because record-oriented content, such as a catalog entry or an address, has a much more regular and predictable structure than the prose that makes up a poem or a novel. Those guys weren't joking when they said, "Form follows function!" This is especially true for XML.

Chapter 9

Combining Multiple DTDs

*I*n Chapters 6 through 8, you explore the ins and outs of Document Type Definitions (DTDs) by dealing with them one at a time. In this chapter, you find out what happens when multiple DTDs interact. You also examine how to mix and match pieces of DTDs in a way that will make it much easier for you to build and use individual chunks of markup.

It's almost impossible to avoid the occasional interaction with a DTD when working with XML. Because you can't avoid DTDs, you might as well utilize them. There's a lot to be said for mixing and matching multiple DTDs when creating or customizing individual documents. In the same vein, it's good to know how to start from a standard DTD (or namespace) and customize from there. In this chapter, you find out how to do all these things.

Working with Entities in DTDs

Chapter 5 introduces the concept of an entity in a DTD — specifically, a name to which some value corresponds. In fact, a document entity is the root element in any document type declaration and provides the name by which a document is known in XML.

Most of the time, when XMLers discuss entities, it's not document entities that they mean — it's these other freaky things. These other freaky types of entities occur within the context of a DTD's or document prolog's `<!ENTITY ...>` declaration. These other types of entities take the general form

```
<!ENTITY name "replacement text">
```

where `name` represents the name of an entity, and `replacement text` represents the text that replaces each occurrence of the entity when that name string appears in the form `&name;` in an XML document body.

The following declaration and XML code show an `ENTITY` declaration in DTD code (which might be inside either an internal or external reference), followed by its invocation in the document body:

```
<!-- the following line occurs in DTD code -->
<!ENTITY loc "Library of Congress">
...
<!-- the following lines occur in document text -->
<Book>
<Title ISBN="0316769533">Catcher in the Rye</Title>
<Author Status="alive">J.D. Salinger</Author>
<Publisher>Little Brown and Company</Publisher>
<Pub_Date>1951</Pub_Date>
<Listing>&loc;</Listing>
</Book>
...
```

When an XML processor reads internal or external DTD subsets, it "learns" to replace all occurrences of the string `&loc;` with the string `Library of Congress`. In this way, document authors can create abbreviations for commonly used strings and save keystrokes when using those abbreviations in document bodies.

In XML-speak, these kinds of entities are called *general entity references*. Although they're quite handy, they are subject to three important limitations:

✔ No general entity reference may occur within a document before it's been declared, nor may entities use circular references. In other words, before you can use an entity, you have to declare it.

✔ You can't create circular entity references, where one entity declaration mentions a second entity, and the second entity declaration mentions the first. Here's an example of a circular reference:

```
<!ENTITY loc "Library of Congress &US;">
<!ENTITY US  "&loc; United States">
```

The problem with this pair of declarations is that neither one defines a plain, simple string by itself. Each declaration depends on the other, yet neither is completely defined. Avoid this in your designs at all costs!

✔ General entity references can't handle text that is only part of a DTD that is not used as document content. You might be tempted to create abbreviations for common DTD reserved words, such as (#PCDATA), as shown in this example:

```
<!ENTITY PCD "(#PCDATA)">
<!ELEMENT Title &PCD;*>
<!ELEMENT Author &PCD;*>
```

But alas, that is illegal for general entity references! General entities can define only text that will ultimately appear in the body of an XML document. That's why DTDs allow you to use another kind of entity, called a *parameter entity*, which can define substitutable text that can be used in DTDs. This serves as the subject of the next section in this chapter.

Parameter Entities Work in DTDs

General entities that take the form &name; become part of a document but can't function as part of a DTD's internal structure or markup. For that purpose, you must use parameter entities in your markup. Here's the general syntax of a parameter entity declaration:

```
<!ENTITY % name "replacement text">
```

As with general entity references, name represents the name of the entity, and replacement text represents the text that replaces each occurrence of the entity. But for a parameter entity, the name string must take the form %name; in an XML document when that entity is referenced. If we return to our previous example and correct it, it would have to take this form to be legal in a document prolog or standalone DTD:

```
<!ENTITY % PCD "(#PCDATA)">
<!ELEMENT Title %PCD;*>
<!ELEMENT Author %PCD;*>
```

Because we're using the right kind of entity in this code fragment, it will work as advertised. But replacing a simple string with a parameter entity falls far short of what parameter entities can really do.

Parameter entities really shine in two special cases:

✔ When complex collections of markup occur repeatedly in a DTD, the repeated text can become the subject of a parameter entity declaration. Then, you can replace each occurrence of the repeated text with the parameter entity. This not only speeds data entry but also means if that markup ever has to change, only the parameter entity needs to be altered and all other occurrences are updated automatically. Cool beans!

✔ You can use parameter entities to carve DTDs into significant chunks of code and then put each chunk in its own file. Then, you can make a parameter entity in a master DTD point to each individual file where the necessary code resides. This lets you mix and match meaningful pieces of DTD code to customize DTDs for specific kinds of markup as needed.

For an example of the first case, where we use parameter entities to replace complex collections of markup, consider the following markup, which recognizes only primary colors:

```
<!ENTITY % Colors "(Red|Green|Blue)">
<!ELEMENT Foreground EMPTY>
<!ATTLIST Foreground Color %Colors; #REQUIRED>
<!ELEMENT Background EMPTY>
<!ATTLIST Background Color %Colors; #REQUIRED>
<!ELEMENT Textcolor EMPTY>
<!ATTLIST Textcolor Color %Colors; #REQUIRED>
...
```

Now, what if you wanted to update this code to accommodate the CMYK color model? It's easy to change the <!ENTITY ...> declaration as follows:

```
<!ENTITY % Colors "(Cyan|Magenta|Yellow|Black)">
```

This replaces the pure primary colors (red, green, and blue) with the richer, more accurate CMYK colors for every attribute list definition for the Foreground, Background, and Textcolor tags. That's a lot easier and less tedious than having to replace each instance of (Red|Green|Blue) with (Cyan|Magenta|Yellow|Black).

In general, if you need to repeat complex markup more than twice in a DTD, consider taking time out to create a parameter entity, and use that entity reference instead of repeating code. This ultimately simplifies document maintenance, for you or those who follow behind you!

For an example of the second instance, where parameter entities show their stuff by allowing you to build custom DTDs, let's say you build a DTD that includes markup to deal with book descriptions, author biography information, and publisher contact information. You might benefit from separating these three disjoint types of markup into separate files and using parameter entities to tie those files into the master DTD for your book database information. To create a list of author biographies or a publisher contact list, you could create other master DTDs where only the author biography markup or the publisher contact information markup is invoked.

These kinds of parameter entities are called *external parameter entity references* because they refer to information that's external to the DTD or document prolog in which they appear. Thus, if you created three DTD files for the markup mentioned in the preceding paragraph named `bookdsc.dtd`, `authbio.dtd`, and `pubinfo.dtd`, respectively, you could use the following markup to create a single DTD to combine their contents:

```
<-- Master DTD for book descriptions,
    author bios, and publisher info -->
<!ENTITY % Bookdsc SYSTEM "bookdsc.dtd">
<!ENTITY % Authors SYSTEM "authbio.dtd">
<!ENTITY % Pubinfo SYSTEM "pubinfo.dtd">
%Bookdsc;
%Authors;
%Pubinfo;
```

Using this technique to mix and match chunks of DTD code is easy, simple, and powerful. In fact, we think this tip is almost worth the price of admission!

As with general entities, parameter entities must be declared before they can be used. We hope that's intuitive: Without a definition, an XML parser can't know what to substitute for the `%name;` symbol when it appears in a document prolog or in a standalone DTD!

Calling All DTDs!

By now, you should understand that it's possible to include an entire DTD as the prolog to any XML document. But it's also possible to refer to an external DTD in a prolog, so you can incorporate the same kind of information from one or more external sources. (The "or more" part comes into play if the DTD that's called uses parameter entities to incorporate multiple chunks of DTD markup from multiple files, as shown in the preceding section.)

Using external DTDs is a great idea because you can then share a single DTD among any group of XML documents. As long as all those documents use the markup described in the DTD, you can manage that markup by operating on a single common DTD instead of having to change the same prolog information across an entire set of XML documents. We like to think of this as a divide-and-conquer approach — namely, one where you divide the DTD information common to all documents and manage it separately from the content unique to each document (which must be managed separately).

If you're creating a standalone DTD, such a file consists of everything from the opening declaration of the root document element — for example, the Catalog element in the DTD at the end of Chapter 6 that follows the `<!DOCTYPE Catalog [` in the prolog — through all of the root element's children, grandchildren, and so forth, up to the `]>` markup that closes the prolog. Given the document from Chapter 6, here's what a standalone DTD based on that markup would look like:

```
<!ENTITY loc "Library of Congress">
<!ELEMENT Catalog (Book+)>
<!ELEMENT Book (Title,Author*,Publisher*,Pub_Date*)>
<!ELEMENT Title (#PCDATA)*>
<!ATTLIST Title ISBN CDATA #REQUIRED>
<!ELEMENT Author (#PCDATA)*>
<!ATTLIST Author Status CDATA #IMPLIED>
<!ELEMENT Publisher (#PCDATA)*>
<!ELEMENT Pub_Date (#PCDATA)*>
```

If this were stored in a file named catalog.dtd that resides in the same directory as the XML document itself, the prolog to the original XML document could be condensed into this single line:

```
<!DOCTYPE Catalog SYSTEM "catalog.dtd">
```

Also, the related XML document must change because it's no longer a stand-alone document; it now requires access to the external DTD. Thus, the initial line of the document, which reads like this in Chapter 6:

```
<?xml version="1.0" standalone="yes"?>
```

must change to

```
<?xml version="1.0" standalone="no"?>
```

to instruct the XML parser to seek its DTD information from an external source. It's really simple, don't you think?

When DTD Definitions Collide

In computer science jargon, a *name collision* occurs when more than one definition for a named object exists. This always poses the problem of how such conflicts can be resolved. Speaking generally, resolving such conflicts first requires that a developer — that's you! — understands what it means when such conflicts occur.

For XML documents, name collisions can occur when multiple definitions of the same markup appear in multiple DTD fragments or between references to an external DTD and internal DTD markup within a single document. This might sound like a recipe for chaos, and such collisions can be problematic if you don't watch what you're doing. But understanding how such collisions are resolved in an XML document can sometimes work to your advantage. Read on for all the gory — er . . . glorious — details!

In the "Parameter Entities Work in DTDs" section earlier in this chapter, we explain how you can break DTD markup into discrete chunks, put each chunk in a file, and then assemble those chunks in a single master DTD. As a consequence, you might wonder what happens if more than one chunk contains a definition of the same markup.

Likewise, it's possible to combine a reference to an external DTD within a standalone DTD or inside the prolog of an XML document with internal DTD markup. This also introduces the possibility of a name collision. In that case, what happens when external and internal definitions collide?

The answers are surprisingly simple, if not what you might want or hope to hear:

✔ Allowing name collisions across external DTDs is a no-no. It may work anyway, as long as you're not trying to validate XML documents using a validating XML processor or parser. If you try to validate a document (or documents) where there's an irresolvable conflict between external definitions, that document (or documents) will likely be declared invalid. In some cases, this might mean that the documents will display improperly or not at all. This can be a real problem for your users.

Whenever you assemble multiple DTDs to create a single master DTD, you will be served best if you structure them to avoid name collisions across whatever collection of component DTDs you use. In some cases, you might be able to get away with collisions, but we recommend that you avoid them between external DTDs just like you avoid them on the road!

✔ If you're not sure that there are no collisions, try a validating XML parser or editor, and see what kinds of error messages you find. (For example, both Clip and Adept Editor can ferret out this kind of information for you, if properly instructed. See Chapter 21 for more information about these and other XML tools.)

✔ When name collisions occur between an external DTD and internal DTD markup within a document, the internal markup always wins. This might sound confusing, until you stop to consider that this provides a mechanism whereby you can incorporate standard, external markup into an XML document, yet still customize that markup to your heart's content for special purposes.

Because we want you to avoid collisions between external DTDs, we also avoid explaining how to make them happen. But because adding internal DTD markup after an external DTD reference is a valuable customization tool, here's how to make that happen:

1. **Start your document with a <!DOCTYPE declaration that invokes your external DTD.**

   For example:

   ```
   <!DOCTYPE Catalog SYSTEM "catalog.dtd"
   ```

   Note that we do not close this declaration just yet!

2. **Follow this with standard internal DTD markup.**

   For this example, we assume you wanted to redefine the order of elements in the Book element so Pub_Date precedes Publisher:

   ```
   [  <!-- This bracket opens internal DTD code -->
   <!ELEMENT Book
      (Title.Author*.Pub Date*.Publisher*)>
   ]> <!-- This bracket closes internal DTD code -->
   ```

   Although this is a trivial example of customization, as long as you remember that you can redefine any entity or attribute declarations that appear in the external DTD (or any DTDs that it references in turn), you have the right idea. Because the internal markup section trumps the markup in the external DTD, customization is possible. Change the order, add new entities, or redefine old attributes — it's all up to you!

Wandering outside XML's Boundaries

Although XML documents include mostly XML data as content, you'll occasionally want to include other kinds of data — such as graphics, video, streaming multimedia, and programs — in your XML documents as well. Within an XML document, any data that's not explicitly XML is called an *unparsed entity* and can appear only as the value associated with an attribute. Thus, non-XML data can be referenced from within an XML document but isn't really part of that XML document.

Simply put, this means that when an entity is labeled as non-XML, it's ignored by the XML parser as it chunks its way through the document. The parser then returns control over that non-XML data object back to whatever application called the parser. As with modern Web browsers, this provides an opportunity to call a helper module or plug-in that knows how to handle such data, so it can be rendered or displayed within the XML document.

To invoke an unparsed entity in an XML document, you have to include an external general entity reference to that data. The inclusion of the NDATA keyword in that declaration, followed by a notation type name, clues the parser into what's going on — and allows the application to invoke the right kind of help. Then, you must also create a <!NOTATION declaration to identify the NDATA type, and provide the application with the necessary identification to

call the correct helper or plug-in. A notation declaration represents a set of rules that describes how an identifiable class of non-XML data behaves, which is usually different from how XML data behaves.

For example, let's assume we want to extend our `Catalog` object to include a reference to a GIF file that contains a digitized image of a card catalog. Here's the DTD markup that this would require:

```
<!-- This DTD fragment is incomplete. -->
<!-- It shows only new markup -->
<!NOTATION gif SYSTEM "PSP.exe">
<!-- Associates .gif files with PaintShop Pro -->
<!ELEMENT Book
  (Title,Author*,Publisher*,Pub_Date*)>
<!ELEMENT Title (#PCDATA)*>
<!ATTLIST Title ISBN CDATA #REQUIRED>
<!ELEMENT Author (#PCDATA)*>
<!ATTLIST Author Status CDATA #IMPLIED>
<!ELEMENT Publisher (#PCDATA)*>
<!ELEMENT Pub_Date (#PCDATA)*>
<!ENTITY Cclog SYSTEM "cclog.gif" NDATA gif>
<!-- Include &Cclog; in content to call image -->
```

The `ENTITY` definition for `Cclog` ties the `NOTATION` declaration to the unparsed entity through the value that follows the `NDATA` attribute.

Turning DTD Content On or Off

When documents can take multiple forms of display, or when they're under construction, it's sometimes necessary to turn parts of a DTD on or off to enable or disable particular types of markup. One way to do this is to manually wrap DTD text in comment tags (`<!--` and `-->`) to turn text off, and remove an unwanted comment wrapper to turn DTD text back on.

Another way to handle this is to use the XML `IGNORE` directive to turn text off, which works like this:

```
<![IGNORE[
  all text ignored up to closing brackets on
  the next line in this example
]]>
```

As with most other XML markup, white space is not significant. But if you keep the opening `<![IGNORE[` and closing `]]>` text on separate lines, they'll be easy to find and remove as necessary.

You can use this directive to skip over any text in a DTD (either a standalone DTD or an internal DTD in a document's prolog). It's important to make sure that you bracket entire chunks of code inside the directive, though. Otherwise, you'll create nonsense out of your DTD. In other words, make sure that you ignore complete declarations, and don't leave incomplete bits of code outside the brackets.

Likewise, an INCLUDE directive for XML lets you explicitly include text in a DTD as well. The syntax is the same as for IGNORE, but uses the keyword INCLUDE instead. Please note that if an INCLUDE directive occurs inside an IGNORE directive, it is ignored because the parser always ignores everything it sees until the IGNORE directive is closed.

An even better way to use the INCLUDE and IGNORE directives is to use one or more parameter entities in your DTDs to control what gets included or ignored in those DTDs. If you use the parameter entity name around a section of code, whatever value you assign to that entity as you parse the document determines whether the code is included or ignored. For example, editing the %Case1; entity definition as follows:

```
<!ENTITY % Case1 "IGNORE">
```

will cause any code bracketed like the following to be ignored:

```
<![%Case1;[
  any complete section of DTD code
]]>
```

To include that code in a subsequent pass through the document, you'd only need to edit the DTD to read

```
<!ENTITY % Case1 "INCLUDE">
```

Not only can you flip-flop the values for %Case1; references as you like, you can also create as many such ignore/include case values as you like (Case2, Case3, and so on), so you can arbitrarily include and ignore related sections of your DTD at will. This function is especially helpful when you use a modular design to create DTDs, and build them piecewise for inclusion in what we call master DTDs earlier in this chapter. A master DTD can then control the behavior of its component DTDs by making the right settings for the various include/exclude parameter entities that component DTDs use.

Chapter 10

Adding Character to XML

*A*lthough experts estimate that about 80 percent of the Web's current content is in English, that doesn't mean English is the only language that the Web supports. As Web technology becomes increasingly global in scope, the ability to use character sets beyond the traditional Roman alphabet will help you reach a truly global audience in their native languages.

Early computers used 7-bit strings to represent simple alphabetical characters; modern computers use a mix of 8- and 16-bit strings to represent a broad range of characters, depending on the application and the location. Often, use of 16-bit characters depends on whether users require access to non-Roman alphabets, such as those for Hebrew or Japanese. In keeping with its intent to be friendly to all Web users, XML is designed to support 16-bit character encoding. This encoding already includes character strings for most of the world's known alphabets, plus all kinds of symbols for disciplines from genetics to mathematics. It even has room left over to accommodate more character sets and symbols as need for them arises.

About Character Encodings

Many modern computers still use 8-bit encodings to represent most character data, especially in English. But the most powerful and modern character encodings use 16 bits' worth of data to represent individual characters.

Clearly, the trend is toward longer bit strings to encode character data. Thus, size does matter when representing character data. Here's why:

- A 7-bit string can represent a maximum of 2^7, or 128, different characters. This is enough for the 26-character basic Roman alphabet in uppercase and lowercase ($A – Z$ and $a – z$), plus a modicum of symbols, punctuation characters, and so forth. In short, it works fine for simple Roman alphabets and related characters, but just barely.

- An 8-bit string can represent a maximum of 2^8, or 256, different characters. This captures everything a 7-bit encoding can handle and leaves room for what some experts call higher-order characters. (Those with encoding values greater than 127 must all have a 1 in the first bit position.) This permits computer character sets to add all kinds of control characters and a modest set of diacritical marks that English doesn't use much but languages such as German (with its umlauts), French (with its diacritical marks), and other European languages use quite frequently.

- A 16-bit string can represent a maximum of 2^{16}, or 65,536, different characters. This captures everything an 8-bit encoding can handle and allows for another 65,280 character codes (or more than 99.6 percent of the available character space). This leaves room for all the major human alphabets, from ancient Aramaic and Greek to modern Mandarin and Hangul (Korean), plus all kinds of symbols and other special characters.

In short, where international representation is concerned, 16-bit character encodings provide the space necessary to cover a full range of known character sets, with room left over for future expansion. That's why XML supports 16-bit character encodings. That's also why experts expect XML to enable universal access to online character data to any human being who can read almost any language!

Introducing Unicode

An industry group called the Unicode Consortium was formed in January, 1991 to promote an open, standard, fully international, 16-bit character encoding technology. Not surprisingly, this encoding is also known as Unicode. Today, Unicode 3.0 (the current, standard version of Unicode) represents the third generation of the consortium's work in defining a single character encoding technology that can accommodate nearly every known human character set under a single representational scheme. Pretty amazing stuff.

In addition, the Unicode Consortium has maintained an ongoing relationship with the International Organization for Standardization, or ISO. This produced an organized, international ISO standard (how's that for redundant?), known as ISO 10646, that represents the same information as the Unicode standard. By 1993, the ISO working group responsible for incorporating Unicode as an official ISO standard had completed its initial work, and ISO 10646-1:1993 came into being. The *-1* after the number indicates that it is the first draft of the standard; the *1993* indicates that it was approved in 1993. ISO has updated 10646 to stay synchronized with the most current Unicode standards.

Today, Unicode defines just over 40,000 different character codes. Of this range, 20,000 characters are defined for the Han ideographs used for Mandarin and other Chinese languages, whereas over 11,000 characters are defined for Hangul (Korean). The nearly 9,000 remaining characters represent most other written languages. For convenience, the Unicode character code for 0 through 255 (8-bit character codes, in other words) match the character set defined for ISO-8859-1, also known as the ISO-Latin-1 character set. This is the default character set that's used to encode HTML documents on the Web.

Many people — including numerous XML experts — refer to the XML character set as "Unicode" (and we think there's good reason to do so). However, if you ever spend any time perusing the XML specifications from the W3C, you will observe that THEY refer to character sets by their ISO designations. Thus, you will see plenty of references to ISO 10646 but only scant mention of Unicode. Go figure!

Note that XML 1.0 references Unicode 2.0, not Unicode 3.0. The W3C is working on the upgrade as we write this book, in the wake of Unicode 3.0's recent release.

For more information about Unicode characters, symbols, history, and the current standard, you can find a plethora of information at the Unicode consortium's Web site at www.Unicode.org.

You can even join a Unicode-oriented mailing list that operates at unicode@unicode.org by sending an add request in the Subject: field of an e-mail message to unicode-request@unicode.org. For those seeking a definitive reference to Unicode, the Unicode Consortium has authored a book entitled *The Unicode Standard, Version 3.0* (published by Addison-Wesley Developers Press). Although it lists for $50, it's a worthwhile reference if you want to be able to check that what your browser is showing for a character matches its correct representation.

Of Character Sets, Fonts, Scripts, and Glyphs

Although XML can represent just about any kind of character data imaginable, that's just the beginning of what's involved to make exotic character data appear on a computer's display. The raw character data — which XML can handle just fine, thank you very much — represents a set of written characters, called a *script*, which may or may not use a conventional Roman alphabet.

To see what's in XML scripts that 7- or 8-bit character encodings can't cover — which means special symbols or non-Roman alphabets — you'll need a few extra local ingredients:

- ✔ **A character set that matches the script you're trying to read and display.** For the purposes of this discussion, a *character set* represents a collection of 16-bit values that maps to some specific symbol set or alphabet.

- ✔ **Software that understands the character set for the script (or at least the general encoding type).** Such software includes the underlying operating system on your computer. Fortunately, most modern operating systems — including various flavors of UNIX, Linux, and Windows 9*x*, NT, and 2000 — can handle 16-bit character codes. The Mac OS has some minor problems, but conversion tools are readily available. Likewise, that character set must be interpreted an application (such as your Web browser or a word processor; today, some browsers can handle 16-bit character codes; others can't).

- ✔ **An electronic font that allows the character set to be displayed on screen (and in print, and so forth).** A *font* contains graphical bitmaps that correspond to character codes that appear in a character set, so that each character has its own unique bitmap. These bitmaps are scaled (to create font sizes) and styled (to create font appearances, such as bold and italic) to create bitmaps for display on-screen or in print image files. Each individual bitmap in a font is known as a *glyph*.

All these ingredients are necessary to work with alternate character sets because humans understand scripts, computers understand numbers (or bit patterns, if you prefer), and displays require images. Character sets represent a mapping from a script to a set of corresponding numeric character codes. Fonts represent a collection of glyphs for the numeric character codes in a character set. All three elements are necessary to represent and render characters on-screen.

Finally, to create text to match the alphabet used in a script, you need an input tool — such as a text or XML editor — that can work with the character set and its corresponding font to create additional text that uses that character set. This will allow you to use the alternate alphabet in your document and to see what you're doing!

For Each Character, a Code

In the ISO 10646 character set, individual characters correspond to specific 16-bit numbers. For convenience, most character sets occur in the form of sequential ranges of such numbers, where uppercase and lowercase characters as well as characters for the digits 0 through 9 are in sequence. To determine the code that represents a character, you have to look it up in the Unicode or ISO 10646 specification. (This is where the Unicode book we mentioned earlier in this chapter comes in handy.)

Even if you don't have access to an editor or text entry tool that understands a particular character set, you can always use numeric entities to represent its characters. In general, numeric entities take one of two forms:

```
&#4096;  <!-- &#  id is a decimal number -->
&#x0F00; <!-- &#x id is a hexadecimal number-->
```

Each of these two entities represents the first character in Tibetan script; 4096 in decimal is the same as 0F00 in hexadecimal (base 16) notation.

Key Character Sets

Around the world, computers use a variety of character sets, depending on the languages (or scripts, if you prefer) that their users employ to represent text. Most computers today use some variant of ASCII (American Standard Code for Information Interchange), an 8-bit character set that handles the basic Roman alphabet used for English, along with punctuation, numbers, and simple symbols. To augment this meager character set, extensions to support additional characters or diacritical marks are added on a per-language basis. Most European languages match standard ASCII values from 0 to 127 and define alternate mappings between character codes and local script characters for the code from 128 to 255.

Non-Roman alphabets, such as Hebrew, Japanese, and Thai, depend on special character sets that include basic ASCII (0–127, or 0–255, depending on the implementation) plus the character sets for the script that corresponds to the "other alphabet" in use. The number of bits in such character encodings depends on the size of the other alphabet. It's not uncommon for such encodings to use 16-bit values to accommodate a second character and symbol set along with the ASCII set. A listing of character sets built around the ASCII framework appears in Table 10-1.

Table 10-1		ISO 8859 Character Sets
Charset	*Script*	*Languages*
ISO-8859-1	Latin-1	ASCII plus most Western European languages, including Albanian, Afrikaans, Basque, Catalan, Danish, Dutch, English, Faroese, Finnish, Flemish, Galician, German, Icelandic, Irish, Italian, Norwegian, Portuguese, Scottish, Spanish, and Swedish. Omits certain Dutch, French, and German characters
ISO-8859-2	Latin-2	ASCII plus most Central European languages, including Czech, English, German, Hungarian, Polish, Romanian, Croatian, Slovak, Slovene, and Serbian
ISO-8859-3	Latin-3	ASCII plus characters required for English, Esperanto, German, Maltese, and Galician
ISO-8859-4	Latin-4	ASCII plus most Baltic languages, including Latvian, Lithuanian, German, Greenlandic, and Lappish; now superseded by ISO-Latin-6
ISO-8859-5		ASCII plus Cyrillic characters for Slavic languages, including Byelorussian, Bulgarian, Macedonian, Russian, Serbian, and Ukrainian
ISO-8859-6		ASCII plus Arabic characters
ISO-8859-7		ASCII plus Greek characters
ISO-8859-8		ASCII plus Hebrew
ISO-8859-9	Latin-5	Latin-1 except that some Turkish symbols replace Icelandic ones
ISO-8859-10	Latin-6	ASCII plus most Nordic languages, including Inuit, non-Skolt Sami, and Icelandic
ISO-8859-11		ASCII plus Thai
ISO-8859-12	Latin-7	ASCII plus Celtic
ISO-8859-13	Latin-8	ASCII plus the Baltic Rim characters
ISO-8859-14	Latin-9	ASCII plus Sami (Finnish)
ISO-8859-15	Latin-10	Variation on Latin-1, including Euro currency sign, plus extra accented Finnish and French characters

A careful reading of Table 10-1 shows that most character sets can render English and German, plus a collection of other, sometimes related languages. When choosing a variant of ISO-8859, remember that all the languages you want to include must be part of that variant; otherwise, you must use Unicode.

In fact, XML goes beyond such idiosyncratic or customized character sets and uses Unicode because it can house character codes for the vast majority of known human scripts in a single encoding. Even if an XML processor can't display certain character codes — because necessary fonts are not be present, for instance — such processors must be capable of handling any valid character code in the Unicode range from 0 to 65,535.

In fact, each text entity in XML has an associated text encoding. If some specific encoding is not defined in a text entity's definition, the default is an encoding called UTF-8, which stands for Unicode Transformation Format, 8-bit form. UTF-8 matches all 7-bit ASCII code values for character encodings 0 through 127, and matches ISO-8859-1 for values 128 through 255. But even though UTF-8 represents code in 8-bit chunks, a single character code can be as long as three such chunks. UTF-8 uses a mathematical formula to convert standard Unicode encodings into more compact forms; please consult Appendix A, section A.2, of *The Unicode Standard, Version 3.0* for details. For our discussion, the important thing to remember is that UTF-8 represents the Roman alphabet efficiently, requiring only a single byte for common characters.

Unicode itself has been dinged because it fails to represent the Han ideographs fully. Unicode defines encodings for 20,000 such ideographs out of a possible lexicon of 80,000 needed to completely represent Chinese, Japanese, Korean, and historical Vietnamese. For that reason, ISO-10646 specifies a character encoding called UCS, or Universal Character System, that combines four 8-bit values for each character encoding. 31 bits of this total string may be used to represent characters, for over 2.1 billion unique codes. In addition to providing space for every character in every known written language , UCS permits complete and distinct character sets to be assigned to each language. At this point, UCS is mostly of theoretical interest because its only defined encodings match Unicode's. But UCS certainly leaves plenty of room for more characters in everyone's future!

Using Unicode Characters

Any software that supports XML files directly, including the XML tools and editors included on the *XML For Dummies* CD, supports Unicode or UTF-8 formats. So do many modern word processors — for instance, Word 97 and later versions support a format called encoded text that uses Unicode encoding.

If you don't have ready access to such tools and want to save XML files in Unicode format, you must make use of a conversion tool, probably to convert ASCII to Unicode or to UTF-8. Sun Microsystem's free Java Development Kit (JDK) is available at

```
http://java.sun.com/products/jdk/1.2/
```

This material includes a command-line utility named `native2ascii` that converts between numerous localized character sets and Unicode. Please consult the associated help file to understand the syntax for and options that work with this utility.

If you can't convert your XML text into UTF-8 or straight Unicode encodings, you can tell the XML processor what kind of character encoding you're using. If you do this, however, you're taking a chance because not all XML processors can handle arbitrary encodings. However, widely used tools such as Netscape Navigator (Version 4.1 or newer) and Internet Explorer (Version 5.0 or newer) can handle most ISO-8859 variants. To use an alternate character encoding, you must identify that encoding in your XML document's prolog as follows:

```
<?xml version="1.0" encoding="ISO-8859-9" ?>
```

In addition to the encoding names that appear in Table 10-1, you can use other encoding names as well. For other possible encodings, check the official Internet Assigned Numbers Authority (IANA) list at

```
www.isi.edu/in-notes/iana/
        assignments/character-sets
```

Please note that XML parsers are required to support only UTF-8 and UTF-16 (native Unicode) encodings, so the `encoding` attribute in an XML document prolog might not work with all such tools. If you try using an ISO-8859 variant or some other character set and don't get the results you want, you might have to figure out how to translate the document into Unicode. Ouch!

Finding Character Entity Information

Elsewhere in this chapter, we mention one excellent source for obtaining information about character entity assignments for Unicode — namely, the Unicode Consortium's book entitled *The Unicode Standard, Version 3.0*. You can also find plenty encoding information online. For example, here's the site of the Unicode Character Database:

```
ftp://ftp.unicode.org/Public/UNIDATA/
        UnicodeCharacterDatabase.html
```

Likewise, the W3C has information about Unicode character ranges and encodings in Appendix B "Character Classes," for the XML 1.0 Recommended Specification, at

```
www.w3.org/TR/REC-xml#CharClasses
```

You will also find the XHTML entity lists useful in this context:

- ✔ **Latin-1:** www.w3.org/TR/xhtml1/DTD/xhtml-lat1.ent
- ✔ **Special:** www.w3.org/TR/xhtml1/DTD/xhtml-special.ent
- ✔ **Symbols:** www.w3.org/TR/xhtml1/DTD/xhtml-symbol.ent

A bit of judicious poking around in your favorite search engine, using search strings such as "Unicode encodings" or "XML character encodings" can turn up other interesting sources of this information online. Happy hunting!

Part IV
The Sense of Style
for XML

The 5th Wave   By Rich Tennant

Cleopatra
Carpet Cleaners

Cleopatra
Carpet Cleaners

"So far our Web presence has been pretty good.
We've gotten some orders, a few inquiries and
nine guys who want to date our logo."

In this part. . .

By itself, XML doesn't look like much in a Web browser. But couple an XML document with some kind of style sheet and — presto! — you have something to see. Part IV delves into the mysteries of combining presentation directives with XML content, starting in Chapter 11 with a description of how style information applies to XML. Chapter 11 also covers how CSS (Cascading Style Sheets), a current standard endorsed by the World Wide Web Consortium for both HTML and XML, works with XML.

Chapter 12 goes native as it examines the state and capabilities of the Extensible Stylesheet Language (XSL), an XML-based alternative to CSS that is still under construction. Chapter 13 outlines the details involved in applying styles to XML documents, and Chapter 14 explains how to use such applications to manage how XML documents present themselves to their readers. When you get through this part of the book, you'll really be stylin'!

Chapter 11

How Style Really Works

*1*f you've jumped straight to this chapter, you most likely know all you ever wanted to know — and more — about building XML documents. Heck, you can probably even build your own DTDs. But after all that hard work, slaving over an XML editor all day, you don't seem to have much to show for your efforts except for a bunch of, frankly, pretty plain text. Perhaps you're wondering "What? That's it? There has to be more to XML than this."

You're right. There's more to XML than just text, tags, and DTDs. In Parts I through III, we hammer home the importance of separating content from formatting, and we concentrate entirely on content. Now it's time to give formatting and display issues their due.

In this first of four chapters devoted to *style sheets* — the mechanism you use to guide the format and display of your XML documents — we introduce you to the basics of using style sheets with XML (and even HTML, just for fun). Our primary focus in this chapter is Cascading Style Sheets (CSS): the first style sheet tool you can use with XML documents and the only one you can use with HTML documents. When you're finished with this chapter, you'll be able to create your own style sheet and apply it to the XML or HTML document of your choice. Nifty, huh?

Stylin' XML and HTML

If you've worked extensively with HTML, you might be wondering why you need style sheets for XML. After all, you don't have to use a style sheet with an HTML document to make it display in a Web browser (although you *can* use style sheets with HTML). Why is XML limited in this way?

Remember that HTML includes a more-or-less static set of tags. You don't make up your own HTML tags as you go along and expect the browser to know what to do with them. This means Web browsers can anticipate all the tags you'll use and prepare to deal with them. Believe it or not, you're actually using a style sheet with HTML documents, but that style sheet is built into the browser itself.

Because XML gives you the power to create your own markup tags — so you can describe your content in the best possible way — the XML tag set is literally unlimited. There's no way XML browsers or processing applications can possibly identify every single tag you could come up with and be prepared to deal with them in advance. Even if they could, how could you be sure that those browsers and processing tools would treat your content in the way you want? You can't — that's where style sheets come into play.

Adding form to function

XML (and the DTDs created according to its specification) is a highly functional language. But XML isn't intended to describe *how* content should be formatted. Instead, it's designed to describe the *roles* that content plays in a document.

We all know that form is often as important as function and that, more often than not, form supplements function. Take a look at Figure 11-1. It's a plain line of text: 12-point Times New Roman with no bells or whistles. As far as anyone can tell, it's just a bunch of characters.

Now take a look at Figure 11-2. It's the same line of text, but now it's in 28-point Times New Roman and centered on the page. Its function becomes clearer: Most likely, this line of text isn't just some text but is instead a title for the page.

If you intend to display an XML document in any way — be it on a printed page, a computer screen, an overhead, or some other display device — you must define formats that best represent the functions of the various kinds of content in your document.

One document, many uses

One of the best things about XML is that it's highly portable. You can send one XML document from system to system, and even application to application, without changing it. This means you don't need to create multiple versions of your content.

Figure 11-1:
Plain text
doesn't tell
you much
about its
function.

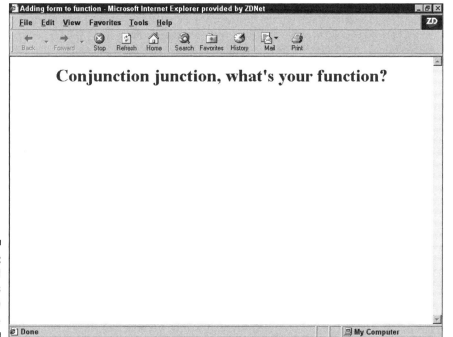

Figure 11-2:
Formatted
text gives
clues as to
its function.

The separation of form from function makes XML documents even more portable. You can write one XML document and then write multiple style sheets for it. Why would you want more than one style sheet? To take advantage of the particular mediums you're designing for. For example, you could prepare one style sheet for putting the XML document on the Web and another style sheet for printing the XML document. Best of all, you don't need to change the XML document at all!

Flip to Chapter 3 and take a quick peek at our bean burrito recipe written in our own Recipe Markup Language (RML). We can display that recipe in two ways: on a countertop recipe system and on a recipe Web site. One document, two displays, as we show in Chapter 3 in Figures 3-1 and 3-2.

By using XML to describe a document's content and style sheets to drive its display, you need only make changes to one document to change all forms of display. After the XML document is updated, your content is also updated in whatever forms it can be displayed. This means less work for you and improved consistency of content. It's a win-win situation. In fact, it seldom gets much better than this in the wild and wooly world of markup languages!

When a document doesn't need a style sheet

Occasionally, an XML document won't need a style sheet. "What?" you gasp. "No style sheet? After all the cheering that's taken place?" Yes, it's true. Some XML documents can function perfectly without a style sheet. And what documents are these? It's simple: Documents that aren't meant for human consumption (or readable displays) don't need style sheets.

Remember, XML isn't limited to describing content meant only for display. Indeed, you can use XML to send instructions to computer systems and applications. When you use XML to create such documents, you have an easy yet consistent way to set up groups of instructions for an application that any non-programmer can use. You can even create a pretty interface for building such XML documents. But we digress.

XML documents designed to guide the actions of a computer or an application and whose content isn't displayed by that computer or application don't need style sheets because, well, honestly, the computer doesn't care if the content is pretty or not. It just reads data.

Documents that use the Channel Definition Language (CDF) to define channels of Web information are good examples of XML documents that don't need style sheets. CDF documents simply define a channel and its parameters. The content the channel spits out is described using HTML or another markup language. For this reason, you'll never see a style sheet for a CDF document. Chapter 18 examines CDF in detail. In that chapter, you can see why you wouldn't want to build a style sheet for a CDF document.

When Style Sheets Cascade

If you're not convinced by now that style sheets are cool, we can't write much more that will change your mind. So we jump straight into the show and tell!

To begin, take a look at the first of two style sheet mechanisms you can use with XML documents: Cascading Style Sheets (CSS). (The other method is the Extensible Stylesheet Language, or XSL, which we cover in the "Meet XSL" section later in this chapter.) The CSS specification was created for use with HTML documents and is its de facto style tool. Therefore, what you find out in the next several pages can be used with HTML documents as well. Think of it as a bonus.

CSS1: The original master of Web style

Cascading Style Sheets 1 (CSS1) was the first version of CSS developed for use with HTML. Released as a W3C recommendation in 1996, CSS wasn't adopted quickly in the Web community because — we're ashamed to admit — developers were happy with their convoluted tables and `<font>` tags. Support for CSS1 was limited as well. Now, however, the newest versions of the big browsers (namely, Internet Explorer and Netscape Navigator) support all elements in CSS1.

With CSS1, you can control the format and display of

- Colors and backgrounds
- Fonts and text
- Spacing
- Element positioning and sizing
- Element visibility

Most style sheets of the CSS variety that you see at work on the Web today use the CSS1 specification simply to make them backward compatible. If you want to see how a simple CSS1 document can affect the look and feel of a page, visit the W3C's CSS page, shown in Figure 11-3, at `www.w3.org/Style/css`.

Notice how the text overlaps at the top of the page and how whole chunks of text are indented beneath headings. This is not a trick made possible by convoluted HTML but rather a good style sheet at work. (And it's a lot easier to build, after you get the hang of the underlying markup conventions.)

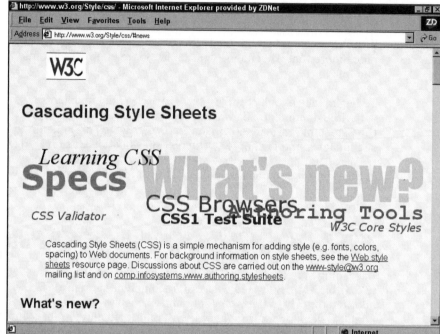

Figure 11-3:
The W3C's
CSS Web
page.

CSS2: The current style master

Cascading Style Sheets 2 (CSS2) was published as a W3C recommendation in 1998. Once again, developers and browser vendors have been slow to adopt CSS2 even though it provides added page layout controls. The latest big browsers support parts of the CSS2 specification but definitely not all of it.

Additions to CSS1 in CSS2 include the following:

- Support for paged media
- Tables
- Aural style sheets
- Support for system colors and fonts
- Counters and automatic numbering

We look forward to the day when CSS2 is fully supported because CSS2 makes life so much easier for both XML and HTML designers.

What does cascading mean?

You're probably wondering what the *C* in *CSS* is about. What does cascading mean in the context of a style sheet? *Cascading* refers to the capability to apply multiple style sheets to any document in a way that handles conflicting style definitions gracefully. Each cascading style sheet attached to any document carries a weight that identifies how important it is in the grand scheme of style. If one style sheet conflicts with another, the style sheet with the heavier weight — in other words, the one that's higher on the style sheet food chain — takes precedence.

For example, if an individual Web page implements CSS, three style sheets apply to it: the cascading style sheet, the browser's built-in style sheet, and the individual user's preference settings, such as font sizes, styles, and colors. These three style sheets cascade — are applied to — the Web page in this order:

1. **User's preferences**

2. **Cascading Style Sheet**

3. **Browser's style sheet**

Therefore, if the cascading style sheet indicates that the font size should be 10-point Times but the user has set his or her preferences so all text is displayed in 12-point Garamond, the user's style sheet wins. More often than not, cascading style sheets override a browser's default settings.

That's it for the basics of the *C* in *CSS*. Of course, if you start to apply multiple cascading style sheets to a document, things can get interesting. CSS incorporates a host of mechanisms to handle such an occurrence. If your curiosity gets the better of you, check out the CSS1 specification at

```
www.w3.org/TR/REC-CSS1
```

The Basics of CSS

Enough talk already. It's time to roll up your sleeves and get your hands dirty building a style sheet. Working on the principle that you should jump right into the deep end, we show you a fully functional style sheet for a bean burrito recipe (also used in Chapter 3) written in the Recipe Markup Language (RML). The recipe looks like this:

```xml
<?xml version="1.0" standalone="yes"?>
<Recipe cook="The XML Gourmet">
    <Title>Bean Burrito</Title>
    <Category name="tex-mex" />
    <Ingredients>
        <Item>1 can refried beans</Item>
        <Item>1 cup longhorn colby cheese, shredded</Item>
        <Item>1 small onion, finely chopped</Item>
        <Item>3 flour tortillas</Item>
    </Ingredients>

    <CookingInstructions>
        Empty can of refried beans into medium saucepan.
        Heat over medium-high heat until beans are smooth
        and bubbly.
        Warm tortillas in microwave for 30 seconds.
    </CookingInstructions>

    <ServingInstructions>
        Spread 1/3 of warm beans on each tortilla.
        Sprinkle with cheese and onions.
        Roll tortillas and serve.
    </ServingInstructions>
</Recipe>
```

This recipe includes the following elements:

- `<Recipe>. . .</Recipe>` holds everything in the document (much like the `<html>. . .</html>` element in an HTML document.) Therefore, its style rule should include margin information for the entire document as well as background color and base font information.

- `<Title>. . .</Title>` identifies the recipe's title, so perhaps it should use colored text in a sans-serif font that's centered on the page and a bit larger than the text around it.

- `<Ingredients>. . .</Ingredients>` works with the `<Item>. . . </Item>` element to create a bulleted list.

- `<Item>. . .</Item>` works with the `<Ingredients>. . . </Ingredients>` element to create a bulleted list.

- `<CookingInstructions>. . .</ CookingInstructions>` should be formatted like a regular paragraph.

- `<ServingInstructions>. . .</ ServingInstructions>` should be formatted like a regular paragraph.

We could do quite a bit more with this style sheet to create an impressive layout and design, but that only adds more lines of code to our examples. For these purposes, simple is beautiful. Simple examples can also teach you all you need to know about style sheets without going overboard. Feel free to enhance and build on this style sheet, however, as you find out more about CSS.

A truly simple cascading style sheet for XML

Keeping our elements and their appearance requirements in mind, we create this truly simple cascading style sheet for our XML recipe:

```
Recipe {margin-top: .5in;
        margin-bottom: .5in;
        margin-left: 1.5in;
        margin-right: 1in;
        color: navy;
        background-color: white;
        font-family: serif;
        display: block
        }

Title {text-align: center;
       font-size: 120%;
       font-family: sans-serif;
       color: maroon;
       display: block
       }

Ingredients.Item {margin-left: 2in;
                  display: list-item;
                  list-style-type: circle;
                  }

CookingInstructions, ServingInstructions {display: block}
```

Dissecting a simple cascading style sheet

Isn't our style sheet pretty? As you can see, a style sheet is nothing more really than a collection of style rules that govern the formatting of the various elements in a document. All style rules use the same syntax, so even if you've never seen a cascading style sheet, you can probably guess how to build a basic style rule.

The magic formula for building CSS style rules

All style rules in a cascading style sheet follow the same syntax — or magic formula if you prefer:

```
selector {declaration}
```

The `selector` identifies the tag to which the style rule applies. The `declaration` holds all the specifics that the style rule applies to the selector.

We can even break this basic syntax down a bit further:

```
selector {property: value}
```

All declarations consist of `property: value` pairs. Some of the ones from our RML style sheet include

- ✔ `{font-family: sans-serif}` to display tag content using a sans-serif font, such as Arial or Geneva
- ✔ `{margin-left: 1.5in}` to set the left margin to 1.5 inches for tag content
- ✔ `{color: navy}` to display tag content using the color navy

All specific CSS properties — and the values they can take — are predefined in the CSS1 and CSS2 specifications. The hardest part of learning CSS is remembering specific property names and their values.

CSS includes a variety of property categories. Because property categories are so central to the mastery of style sheets for XML and CSS, we devote most of Chapter 12 to a discussion of CSS1 property families and their proper usage.

A quick note about another important CSS term: inheritance. Did you note that when we set style rules for the `<Recipe>. . .</Recipe>` element and specified margins, background color, font, and text color, we didn't set them again for each of the other document elements? That's because the recipe element is the document element and contains all other elements inside it. Thus, the style rule we create for the recipe element is *inherited* by all other elements that nest within it. This means that after you create a style rule for an element, any other elements it contains are also subject to that style rule.

And that's really all there is to creating a style sheet. You put together a whole bunch of selectors and declarations and poof! — there's a style sheet.

Variations on the magic: Selector specifications

But wait, it can't really be that simple. Not all our selectors in our truly simple style sheet look the same. What about `Ingredients.Item`? It has an extra period that none of the other selectors use. This syntax tells the application processing the style sheet to look for `<Ingredients>` tags followed by `<Item>` tags. If those tags don't appear in that specific order, the style rule doesn't apply to the `<Item>` tag.

The example in the previous paragraph is just one of the many variations on the selector portion of the magic formula. You can link selectors to different tags based on attribute values, context, type, parent-child relationships, and a variety of other options.

The specifics of selectors are too detailed to discuss here, but they are covered brilliantly in the CSS1 specification at

```
www.w3.org/TR/REC-CSS1
```

and the CSS2 specification at

```
www.w3.org/TR/REC-CSS2/
```

Efficiency is good: Combining selectors and declarations

What if you want to assign the same style rule to two different elements? You could retype the declaration or cut and paste it. But then, if you change one instance of that declaration, you must change it in each and every selector where that declaration appears. It's much easier to simply apply one declaration to several selectors. To do so, simply list all of your selectors separated by commas, as in:

```
selector, selector. . . {declaration}
```

Our sample style sheet combines selectors this way in its last style rule:

```
CookingInstructions, ServingInstructions {display: block}
```

Along these same lines, you can also combine declarations in a style rule to include a collection of property/value combinations in a single selector. The syntax for this neat trick is to separate your `property: value` combinations with semicolons, as we did in most of our style rules, including this one:

```
Title {text-align: center;
      font-size: 120%;
      font-family: sans-serif;
      color: maroon;
      display: block
      }
```

CSS is nothing if not efficient; but sometimes, you have to strive to grasp that efficiency!

Punctuating CSS rules

Punctuation plays a large role when creating CSS style rules. If you accidentally use a colon instead of a semicolon to separate `property: value` pairs in a declaration, your style sheet will break. Table 11-1 provides a short, but helpful, guide to punctuating CSS properly.

Table 11-1		Punctuation in CSS
Character	*Name*	*What It Does*
.	period	Identifies selector context
,	comma	Separates multiple selectors in a style rule
;	semicolon	Separates multiple property/value combinations in a style rule
:	colon	Separates a property and its value in a declaration

Applying a truly simple cascading style sheet to HTML

Because CSS is designed to work with HTML documents, you can use what you discover in this chapter to write cascading style sheets for HTML documents. The major difference when using CSS with HTML is that all selectors refer to HTML tags instead of custom tags from an XML DTD.

If we convert our burrito recipe to HTML, it looks something like this:

```
<html>
   <head>
      <title>Bean Burrito</title>
   </head>

   <body>
   <h1>Bean Burrito</h1>
   <ul>
      <li>1 can refried beans</li>
      <li>1 cup longhorn colby cheese, shredded</li>
      <li>1 small onion, finely chopped</li>
      <li>3 flour tortillas</li>
   </ul>

   <p>
      Empty can of refried beans into medium saucepan.
      Heat over medium-high heat until beans are smooth
      and bubbly.
      Warm tortillas in microwave for 30 seconds.
   </p>

   <p>
      Spread 1/3 of warm beans on each tortilla.
      Sprinkle with cheese and onions.
      Roll tortillas and serve.
   </p>
   </body>
```

The style sheet for this HTML document takes the following form:

```
body {margin-top: .5in;
      margin-bottom: .5in;
      margin-left: 1.5in;
      margin-right: 1in;
      color: navy;
      background-color: white;
      font-family: serif;
      display: block
      }

h1 {text-align: center;
      font-size: 120%;
      font-family: sans-serif;
      color: maroon;
      display: block
      }

ul.li {margin-left: 2in;
                display: list-item;
                list-style-type: circle;
                }

p {display: block}
```

Linking CSS to HTML and XML

So you've built some style sheets and now you want to use them with XML —
or even HTML — documents. It's pretty easy to do so, but the method varies
between XML and HTML. To reference a cascading style sheet in an XML document, use a processing instruction that takes this format:

```
<?xml-stylesheet href="url" type="text/css"?>
```

So, for a style sheet named rml_web, saved in the style folder, use this processing instruction to reference it in the burrito recipe:

```
<?xml-stylesheet href="style/rml_web" type="text/css"?>
```

An entire W3C recommendation governs how style sheets link to XML
documents. The recommendation is updated frequently, so it always includes
the most current information about this topic. We suggest you give it a once-
over at

```
www.w3.org/TR/xml-stylesheet
```

To link a cascading style sheet to an HTML document, use one of the
following methods:

- Reference an external style sheet with the `<link>` tag, for example:

  `<link rel="stylesheet" href="`*`url`*`" type="text/css">`

  where `rel="stylesheet"` specifies that the link is to a style sheet; `href="url"` points to the style sheet's location; and `type="text/css"` identifies the style sheet as a cascading style sheet.

- Include style rules (known as an internal style sheet) directly within an HTML document between `<style>. . .</style>` tags in the document's header (between the `<head>` and `</head>` tags, in other words).

- Import style rules from an external style sheet into an internal style sheet (between `<style>. . .</style>` tags in the document header) using `@import url(url)`.

- Place directly within an HTML tag using the `style=` attribute, for example, `<p style="color: teal; font-family: Garamond; margin-right: 1in;">. . .</p>`.

The Best of CSS on the Web

There's much more to CSS than we can cover in this book, so we provide you with additional resources. Some of the very best resources for discovering more about CSS appear — where else? — on the Web itself. Before you build any serious, complex cascading style sheets, take the time to peruse one or two of them. Our favorites include

- The W3C's CSS pages at `www.w3.org/style/css`

- The Web Design Group's CSS tutorials and resources at `www.htmlhelp.com/reference/css/`

- WebMonkey's CSS tutorials and resources at `http://hotwired.lycos.com/webmonkey/reference/stylesheet_guide`

- Webreview's CSS articles at `webreview.com/wr/pub/Style_Sheets`

Meet XSL

As you know by now, CSS isn't the only option for styling XML documents. XSL, the Extensible Stylesheet Language (XSL) is a style sheet application created specifically for XML. We'll warn you right now that XSL isn't as easy to learn as XML. In the end, XSL style sheets are simply XML documents — and you're already well on your way to knowing the many ins and outs of XML.

XSL is needed because XML is more complex and powerful than HTML. Out of necessity, XML requires a more robust and dynamic style tool. Unlike many W3C technologies, XSL has undergone drastic changes as it has moved through its development phase. The first XSL working draft looks nothing like the XSL we discuss in this chapter and Chapter 12.

XSL currently works in two different capacities:

- As a transformation language (XSLT, the *T* stands for transformation) for converting documents written in one XML DTD into another DTD
- As a formatting language (XSL) for defining how XML documents should be displayed

Current usage of XSL focuses on the transformation function. XML developers use XSL to convert XML documents into HTML and then apply cascading style sheets to the resulting HTML documents for display on the Web. The formatting part of XSL is still in flux, and only a few applications can read and interpret XSL style sheets for display. XSL will take a while to become "fully cooked." The good news is that XSLT is actually a recommendation and as close to "fully cooked" as you can get when dealing with Web technologies.

XSL has as many facets as XML, so we've had to pick and choose those aspects that we cover in this book. We decided that the most practical and useful information about XSL involves using it to convert XML documents into HTML. This allows XML documents to be displayed on the Web with cascading style sheets.

Consequently, in Chapter 12, we describe the different CSS property families so you can get up to speed on using CSS to format Web documents. Also in Chapter 12, you find out how to write an XSL style sheet that converts an XML document into an HTML equivalent. The last chapters of Part IV (Chapters 13 and 14) look at specific XSL issues, such as packaging styles into macros, using styles directly with XML tags, and an introduction to something fondly called the XML object model. Sounds peachy, yes?

Because XSL is in flux and because it's so complex and powerful, please visit the W3C's XSL page at www.w3.org/Style/XSL/. If you drop in on a regular basis, you can keep up with this important area in the wacky, wonderful world of XML. When you've finished this book, you'll have the background you need to read and understand the various articles and discussions of XSL you'll find, and you'll be well on your way to writing your own XSL style sheets. Bon voyage!

Chapter 12

The Building Blocks of CSS

XML separates form from function, where style sheets provide the form and XML defines the functions. In Chapter 11, you find out why we think style sheets are way-cool and how to build style rules to create Cascading Style Sheets (CSS). You also discover that CSS is not your only option for adding style to XML documents — you can also use XSL, the Extensible Stylesheet Language. Thus, your XML style sheet options are pretty broad.

In this chapter, we take a much closer look at the properties you can use to build style sheets according to the CSS1 and CSS2 specifications. Properties are the keys to style rules. Because style properties and their values are pre-defined by the specifications, it's important for you to understand them. This will help you determine, from the get-go, what you can and can't do with CSS.

CSS: Today's Style of Choice

You're probably wondering why we're devoting an entire chapter to CSS — a style language originally designed for HTML — when this is an XML book and XSL is available. Appearances to the contrary notwithstanding, there's a good reason for this move on our part. Actually, there are several good reasons. . . .

There's more than one version of CSS — like that's a big surprise. Version 2 of CSS, aptly named CSS2, is the most recent version. Not all Web browsers that support CSS support CSS2. Once again, this should not be a big surprise. Because we want to give you the most recent information, all our discussions in this chapter refer to CSS2. Note that some CSS2 properties, such as the display property, might not work in your browser if it supports only CSS1.

The realities of the Web must intrude

We all like to play with the latest and greatest technologies and visualize the effect they can have on the delivery of information to the world. But at the same time, we must also step back and look at the realities of the here and now. Although XML is a great tool for storing data for all kinds of stuff, it's not exactly Web-compatible yet. But because the Web is hot, hot, hot, content developers — like you — want to deliver their data through the Web. So if you want to transmit XML through the Web, your best style choice is CSS because XSL ain't completely cooked yet.

XSL is an emerging standard and has changed substantially from its initial definition to its current state. Most experts, including your humble authors, believe that XSL will continue to change some more before it finally becomes a standard. This makes it difficult for browser vendors to create a browser that works with XSL. So, rather than support a way of doing things that might not work in a few months, most browser vendors are waiting for XSL to become a standard before they implement it. However, the 4.0 versions (and later) of most major browsers do support CSS.

What this means to you is that the best and quickest way to create style sheets for your XML documents is to use CSS. That way, your content will have the largest support base for Web delivery. The good news is that lots of CSS resources — and even a few software packages designed to create CSS — are available on the Web. Check out `www.w3.org/style/css` for the latest info on CSS resources and tools.

CSS is easy to use

CSS is really, really, really easy to use — even if you're building style sheets from scratch. This is a huge plus when you're trying to get a solution of any kind up and running quickly. We don't dispute that XSL is much more power-ful than CSS and robust enough to support the many uses of XML. But XML isn't stable yet, and may, at times, be overkill.

We like CSS because it is human-readable and uses a simple but flexible syntax. To understand CSS, you need only remember this magic formula:

```
selector {property: value}
```

If you're new to CSS and would like a little help creating your first style sheets, we recommend you visit the W3C Core Styles page at `www.w3.org/StyleSheets/Core/`. The W3C's core styles are a collection of style sheets you can immediately use with HTML documents. Although you can't simply hook them up to your XML documents, they do provide a complete style solution that you can easily alter to fit your XML document needs. It's the old method of learning by example — one that we've found to be very effective time after time.

Style sheets for tomorrow

So the question is, "With the emergence and eventual settling of XSL, will your style sheets written according to CSS be useful in the long run?" We are happy to report that the answer is yes. CSS isn't going anywhere; in fact, the W3C is currently working onCSS3. We also have it on good authority that CSS will continue to work with XML.

XSL and CSS pack a powerful 1-2 punch

Just because CSS and XSL are competing technologies, don't think that you have to choose one over the other. CSS and XSL play very well together — so much that one of the most powerful uses for both style mechanisms involves using them together.

In Chapter 11, we note that XSL has two primary purposes: to apply style to XML documents and to convert documents written according to one DTD to documents that use another DTD. The conversion process is called *transformation,* and many XML developers use XSL to transform documents written using any XML vocabulary — such as the Chemical Markup Language (CML) and the Genealogical Markup Language (GedML) — into HTML documents.

They then style their newly transformed XML documents with CSS for display on the Web. By using XSL to convert XML documents to HTML and then using CSS to control the display of the resulting HTML, developers can use the power of XML for data storage yet still deliver content to users through standard Web browsers.

Because XSL is such a complex and detailed style mechanism — and because it's still in flux — we don't discuss it in-depth in this book. In Chapter 13, we look at XSL's basic syntax and how you can use it to write style sheets to convert XML documents to HTML. You'll get a good idea of how this new style tool functions, be able to follow discussions and updates, and be ready to dig further into XSL when it stabilizes. For now, we're convinced that this approach will do everyone the most good.

All about CSS Properties and Values

In this section, you get down to the nitty-gritty of CSS: properties and values. CSS properties and the values they take are the keys to creating style sheets. Until you know the rules, you won't really know what you can and can't do with CSS.

Despite the fact that CSS is simple to use, it's a topic of some depth. Entire books have been written on the subject. We try to distill the pertinent information about CSS properties and their values into a solid core of information in this chapter. However, we encourage you to read further about CSS and style issues if you plan to develop lengthy or complex style sheets of your own.

We divide most CSS properties into groups based on the particular part of an element's display that they affect. Those groups are

- ✔ Text style and formatting
- ✔ Element display
- ✔ Margins
- ✔ Borders and backgrounds
- ✔ Padding
- ✔ Layout

For each group of properties, we tell you a bit about how they work as a group and include any important information you need to use those properties. We then provide a table with the values that each property can work with, briefly describe that property, indicate whether the property is inherited or not, and include an example of that property in use.

Before we can launch into a discussion of property groups, we need to tell you a bit about the different ways to set measurements — such as font sizes, line heights, and colors — in your style rules. We also give you a bit of insight into the standard syntax we use when describing different CSS properties and values.

Inheritance defines a property's staying power. Inherited properties pass from one element to any other elements that may be nested inside it.

Units of measure in CSS

Units of measure are extremely important in CSS, and they refer to more than just pixels and inches. When measuring style, you can measure a variety of things, including lengths, URLs, and colors. When referring to a unit of measure, CSS uses this collection of keywords:

- ✔ length
- ✔ percentage
- ✔ uri
- ✔ color
- ✔ absolute-size
- ✔ relative-size
- ✔ border-style
- ✔ border-width
- ✔ margin-width
- ✔ padding-width
- ✔ shape

A keyword represents a specific way to define a value and usually covers a wide range of possible values or a specific way to state a value. For example, CSS supports different length measurements, as shown in Table 12-1.

Table 12-1		CSS Length Measurement Units	
Name	*Abbreviation*	*What It Is*	*Type*
centimeter	cm	Unit of measure in the metric system	Absolute
inch	in	Unit of measure in the English system	Absolute
millimeter	mm	Unit of measure in the metric system	Absolute
pica	pc	Equal to 12 points	Absolute
point	pt	Equal to 1/72 of an inch	Absolute
pixel	px	Size of a dot on a display device (screen, printer, etc.)	Relative
em	em	Font's height	Relative
ex	ex	Height of a font's letter x	Relative

If you want to specify that a paragraph's right margin should be one inch, use this style rule, which includes the abbreviation for inches:

```
P {margin-right: 1in}
```

When you specify a length, you can use any integer in combination with any of these measurement units. Therefore, 12cm is just as acceptable as 12pc. CSS also supports percentages and uses the standard percent sign (%) after any integer to represent a percentage value.

CSS uses a specific notation for defining a URL as a value for a property. To specify a URL, use the syntax:

```
url(url)
```

For example, to refer to the W3C's home page in a style sheet, type

```
url(http://www.w3.org/)
```

Style sheets support a variety of ways to refer to color. You can use standard color names, such as navy, red, white, and teal, or you can use hexadecimal color codes. CSS also supports red-green-blue (RGB) color notation. The specifics of color and CSS are a bit detailed, so if you want to go beyond conventional Web color syntax, visit

```
www.w3.org/TR/REC-CSS2/syndata.html#value-def-color
```

When you look at a style sheet property definition, a keyword reference looks something like this:

```
<length>
```

We know, we know, we didn't touch on absolute-size, relative-size, border-style, border-width, margin-width, padding-width, and shape keywords. Those are best explained in the context of the group of property values for which they are used, Therefore, we talk about them in the following sections. The length, percentage, color, and uri keywords cross over all categories, so we decided to get them out of the way right here and now.

Decoding property value definitions

The W3C uses a specific syntax in its CSS specifications to describe what values you can use with any given property. Because you will inevitably have to visit — and make sense of — a CSS specification one day, we use the same syntax in our property definitions. Table 12-2 includes a rundown of the different values you might see in a property definition, an example of each, and what each particular value represents.

Table 12-2		Syntax in Property Definitions
Value	*Example*	*What It Is*
Keyword	color	Specifies a keyword that must be used exactly as listed in the specification
\<type\>	\<url\>; \<length\>	Indicates that a specific kind of value must be used with the property
X|Y	\<length\> | \<percentage\>	A list of possible values that must be used with the property (not limited to two options)
X||Y	\<border-width\> || \<border-style\> || \<color\>	A list of possible values that can be used with the property (not limited to two options)
[items]	[thin | medium | thick | \<length\>]	Groups a set of value options
Value?	[\<font-style\> || \<font-variant\> || \<font-weight\>]?	An optional value
Value*	[[\<family-name\> | \<generic-family\>],]*	A value that can be repeated one or more times
Value{X,Y}	\<length\>{1,4}	A value that must be used *X* number of times and may be used as many as *Y* number of times

For example, the property definition for the background-position property combines several of these possible value types into one value definition:

```
[ [<percentage> | <length> ]{1,2} |
[ [top | center | bottom] || [left | center | right] ] ]
| inherit
```

What this seemingly convoluted property definition says is that the background-position property can take one of several values, including a percentage or a length, both of which must be used at least once and up to twice. The property can also take a combination of one value from [top | center | bottom] and one value from [left | center | right], like this: top center. Barring all these options, the value for background-position can simply be inherited. Luckily, most property definitions aren't this complex.

Enough with the syntax and the tech stuff; it's time to move on to the properties themselves.

Styling and formatting text

The CSS properties for styling and formatting text are pretty straightforward. They allow you to specify which font to use to display an element, how large or small you want that display to be, what color the text should be, and a host of other visual details.

The most important thing to remember when working with fonts is that if a user's system does not support a font you've included in a style definition, the system will not and can not display that particular font. The good news is that you can specify several fonts, and the browser will work its way down through the font list until it finds one it can display.

The `<absolute-size>` and `<relative-size>` keywords work with the font properties to specify font size. Your options for `<absolute-size>` are

- ✔ `xx-small`
- ✔ `x-small`
- ✔ `small`
- ✔ `medium`
- ✔ `large`
- ✔ `x-large`
- ✔ `xx-large`

Options for relative size are

- ✔ `larger`
- ✔ `smaller`

To specify that a heading's font size should be extra-extra large, use this style rule:

```
H1 {font-size: xx-large}
```

A quick experiment with these settings will show you how they appear by default in your Web browser.

Table 12-3 lists the text styling and formatting properties.

Table 12-3 **Text Styling and Formatting Properties**

Property	Values	What It Is	Inherited?	Example
color	`<color>` | `inherit`	Sets the text color	Yes	`color:teal`
font-family	`[[ <family-name> | <generic-family> ],]* [<family-name> | <generic-family>)] | inherit`	Specifies the font	Yes	`font-family: Verdana`
font-size	`<absolute-size> | <relative-size> | <length> | <percentage> | inherit`	Specifies the font size	Yes	`font-size: 12pt`
font-stretch	`normal | wider | narrower | ultra-condensed | extra-condensed | condensed | semi-condensed | semi-expanded | expanded | extra-expanded | ultra-expanded | inherit`	Specifies how text should be stretched	Yes	`font-stretch: narrow`
font-style	`normal | italic | oblique | inherit`	Specifies the font style	Yes	`font-style: italic`
font-variant	`normal | small-caps | inherit`	Identifies a variation on the standard font display	Yes	`font-variant: small-caps`

(continued)

Table 12-3 (continued)

Property	Values	What It Is	Inherited?	Example
font-weight	normal | bold | bolder | lighter | 100 | 200 | 300 | 400 | 500 | 600 | 700 | 800 | 900 | inherit	Specifies how dark text should appear	Yes	font-weight: bolder
font	[['font-style' || 'font-variant' || 'font-weight']? 'font-size' [/ 'line-height']? 'font-family'] | caption | icon | menu | message-box | small-caption | status-bar | inherit	Shorthand for combining font style information	Yes	font: italic Courier 12pt
letter-spacing	normal | <length> | inherit	Sets the amount of space between letters	Yes	letter-spacing: 2em
line-height	normal | <number> | <length> | <percentage> | inherit	Sets the amount of space between lines	Yes	line-height: 10pt
text-align	left | right | center | justify | <string> | inherit	Specifies how text should be aligned	Yes	text-align: center
text-decoration	none | [underline || overline || line-through || blink] | inherit	Identifies a decoration for text	No	text-decoration: blink

Property	Values	What It Is	Inherited?	Example
text-indent	\<length\> | \<percentage\> | inherit	Identifies by how much text the first line of text should be indented	Yes	text-indent: .5in
text-transform	capitalize | uppercase | lowercase | none | inherit	Transforms text regardless of its original case	Yes	text-transform: uppercase
vertical-align	baseline | sub | super | top | text-top | middle | bottom | text-bottom | \<percentage\> | \<length\> | inherit	Aligns text vertically	No	vertical-align: middle
word-spacing	normal | \<length\> | inherit	Sets the amount of space between words	Yes	word-spacing: 10ex

CSS shorthand expedites styles

The developers of CSS wanted to make it as easy as possible for you to build style sheets. They recognized early on that although individual properties address specific portions of an element's display, such as font face, color, and size, it might be nice to quickly and easily assign similar properties in one fell swoop. To set font color, face, and size, you can use these three properties:

```
font-size: 100%
font-face: Helvetica
color: navy
```

However, that's three lines of code, and three different declarations to keep track of. Instead, you can use the shorthand property font to set the same values more quickly:

```
font: 100% Helvetica navy
```

Throughout our property definitions, you'll see descriptions that start with *Shorthand for.* These properties combine the functionality of several other properties and are always the way to go when you're building complex style sheets.

The following style rule creates a paragraph whose text should be teal in color, bold, and displayed in the Arial font. This same rule also specifies that the paragraph's text should be centered:

```
P {text: teal;
    font-weight: bold;
    font-family: Arial;
    text-align: center;
    }
```

Defining display

The display properties affect the most basic aspects of an element's display. Use these properties to specify that an element should be displayed

- ✔ As a block element (paragraphs and headings)
- ✔ As an inline element (citations and boldface text)
- ✔ As a list (bulleted, numbered, or otherwise)

The display properties allow you to take lists to a higher level. You may not only decide whether something is a bulleted list or a numbered list but also specify an image to act as a bullet or choose from one of several different numbering systems for a numbered list. Table 12-4 lists the CSS display properties and their values.

Most display properties are in the CSS2 specification, not the CSS1 specification. Therefore, don't be surprised if the 3.0 and 4.0 versions of most browsers don't support them very well.

Table 12-4		Display Properties		
Property	**Values**	**What It Is**	**Inherited?**	**Example**
display	inline | block | list-item | run-in | compact | marker | table | inline-table | table-row-group | table-header-group | table-footer-group | table-row | table-column-group | table-column | table-cell | table-caption | none | inherit	Specifies how an element should be displayed	No	display: block
list-style-image	<uri> | none | inherit	Identifies a graphic to be used as bullets in a list	Yes	list-style-image: url(/graphics/bullet1.gif)
list-style-position	inside | outside | inherit	Indicates that list item text should wrap under the list marker (outside) or to the right of the marker (inside)	Yes	list-style-position: inside

(continued)

Table 12-4 (continued)

Property	Values	What It Is	Inherited?	Example
list-style-type	disc | circle | square | decimal | decimal-leading-zero | lower-roman | upper-roman | lower-greek | lower-alpha | lower-latin | upper-alpha | upper-latin | hebrew | armenian | georgian | cjk-ideographic | hiragana | katakana | hiragana-iroha | katakana-iroha | none | inherit	Identifies a marker (number or bullet) to use with list items	Yes	list-style-type: upper-alpha
list-style	['list-style-type' || 'list-style-position' ||'list-style-image'] | inherit	Shorthand for combining list style information	Yes	list-style: url(/graphics/ bullet1.gif) inside
white-space	normal | pre | nowrap | inherit	Specifies how white space should be treated when an element is displayed	Yes	white-space: nowrap

Living inside the box

The box model is a key concept in the development of style sheets with any real flavor. To put it simply, any block element, such as a paragraph, a heading, or a list, occupies a chunk of space in a display. That chunk of space is referred to as the *element's box*. Such a box has several different aspects, including margins, the padding between the margins and its content, and the border around the box.

In a standard HTML page, boxes can't overlap and you can't control box margins or padding. Using style sheets, however, you can set the exact size for an element's display box, use margins to position it on the page, add padding between the outside edges of a box and its content inside, add a border and define that border's style, and much more.

The CSS2 specification has a great explanation of the box model at `www.w3.org/TR/REC-CSS2/box.html` that is a must-read if you're going to play with your element display boxes. After you understand how the box model works, its margin, padding, background, and position properties will be much more useful to you.

This style rule creates a list item in a numbered list that uses lowercase Greek letters for markers. The style rule also indicates that the item's text should wrap inside — to the right — of the list marker:

```
li {display: list-item;
    list-style-type: lower-greek;
    list-style-position: inside;
    }
```

Setting margins

The margin properties dictate how the margins are defined for an element's display box. If you're not certain what we mean by an element's display box, take a quick look at the sidebar titled "Living inside the box."

When you look at the property definitions for the margin properties, you'll see the keyword `<margin-width>`. This keyword indicates that a margin width can be defined as a length or a percentage or set to auto so the browser can choose a width for itself. Table 12-5 lists the margin properties.

Table 12-5	Margin Properties			
Property	*Values*	*What It Is*	*Inherited?*	*Example*
margin-bottom	<margin-width> | inherit	Sets the width of the bottom margin	No	margin-bottom: 1in
margin-left	<margin-width> | inherit	Sets the width of the left margin	No	margin-left: .5in
margin-right	<margin-width> | inherit	Sets the width of the right margin	No	margin-right: 1.5in
margin-top	<margin-width> | inherit	Sets the width of the top margin	No	margin-top: 1in
margin	<margin-width> {1,4} | inherit	Shorthand for setting all four margin widths at once	No	margin: 1in 1in .5in 1.5in

To add one-inch margins to the top and bottom of an element and half-inch margins to the left and right of the same element, use this style rule:

```
p {margin-top: 1in;
   margin-bottom: 1in;
   margin-left: .5in;
   margin-right: .5in;
   }
```

Applying backgrounds and borders

CSS works wonders with backgrounds and borders. With CSS, you can apply a different background to each element on a page and even specify whether the background should scroll with the element's content on a screen or stay in one place. You can specify also how a background should tile. You can set the background to not tile at all, to tile only horizontally or vertically, or tile to fill the entire page. We're excited about the design implications associated with CSS backgrounds — and you should be, too.

Borders in CSS are cool because you can access and modify the border around each box on a page that has been — until now — invisible to both users and designers. The two keywords associated with borders are `<border-style>` and `<border-width>`.

Your options for border style follow:

- none
- hidden
- dotted
- dashed
- solid
- double
- groove
- ridge
- inset
- outset

The none option means no border. This value forces the computed value of `border-width` to be 0.

For border width, your options are

- thin
- medium
- thick
- `<length>`

The background and border properties are listed in Table 12-6.

Table 12-6   **Background and Border Properties**

Property	Values	What It Is	Inherited?	Example
background-attachment	scroll | fixed | inherit	Specifies whether an element's background should scroll with it or remain stationary on a screen	No	background-attachment: fixed
background-color	<color> | transparent | inherit	Defines a background color for an element	No	background-color: teal
background-image	<uri> | none | inherit	Defines a background image for an element	No	background-color: url(/graphics/background1.gif)
background-position	[[<percentage> | <length>]{1,2} | [[top | center | bottom] || [left | center | right]]] | inherit	Specifies how a background image should be positioned relative to the element content	No	background-position: center center
background-repeat	repeat | repeat-x | repeat-y | no-repeat | inherit	Specifies how a background image should be tiled	No	background-repeat: repeat-x
background	'background-color' || 'background-image' || 'background-repeat' || 'background-attachment' || 'background-position'] | inherit	Shorthand for setting all background properties	No	teal url(/graphics/background1.gif) repeat-x fixed center center
border-bottom-width	<border-width> | inherit	Sets the width for the bottom of an element's border	No	border-bottom-width: .25in

Property	Values	What It Is	Inherited?	Example
border-bottom	['border-bottom-width' || 'border-style' || <color>] | inherit	Shorthand for setting the properties of a border's bottom	No	border-bottom: .25in dashed navy
border-left-width	<border-width> | inherit	Sets the width for the left side of an element's border	No	border-left-width: .25in
border-left	['border-left-width' || 'border-style' || <color>] | inherit	Shorthand for setting the properties of a border's left side	No	border-left: .25in dashed navy
border-right-width	<border-width> | inherit	Sets the width for the right of an element's border	No	border-right-width: .25in
border-right	['border-right-width' || 'border-style' || <color>] | inherit	Shorthand for setting the properties of a border's right side	No	border-right: .25in dashed navy
border-top-width	<border-width> | inherit	Sets the width for the top of an element's border	No	border-top-width: .25in
border-top	['border-top-width' || 'border-style' || <color>] | inherit	Shorthand for setting the properties of a border's top	No	border-top: .25in dashed navy
border-color	<color>{1,4} | transparent | inherit	Shorthand for defining color for all four sides of a border	No	border-color: navy
border-style	<border-style>{1,4} | inherit	Shorthand for defining style information for all four sides of a border	No	border-style: dashed
border-width	<border-width>{1,4} | inherit	Shorthand for defining the width of all four sides of a border	No	border-width: .25in
border	['border-width' || 'border-style' || <color>] | inherit	Shorthand for defining all border style settings	No	border: .25in dashed navy

This nifty style rule attaches to the very center of an element a graphic named sun.gif stored in the graphics directory. The graphic remains fixed on the page and doesn't scroll even when the element it is attached to does scroll:

```
h1 {background-image: uri(/graphics/sun.gif);
    background-attachment: fixed;
    background-position: center;
    }
```

Padding the box

Padding is the amount of white space between the content inside an element's box and its outside border. Using the CSS properties listed in Table 12-7, you can closely control padding on all sides of a box. The <padding-width> keyword indicates that you can specify padding as a percentage or a length.

Table 12-7		Padding Properties		
Property	*Values*	*What It Is*	*Inherited?*	*Example*
padding-bottom	<padding-width> | inherit	Sets the amount of white space between an element's content and its bottom margin	No	padding-bottom: 10px
padding-left	<padding-width> | inherit	Sets the amount of white space between an element's content and its left margin	No	padding-left: 10px
padding-right	<padding-width> | inherit	Sets the amount of white space between an element's content and its right margin	No	padding-right: 10px
padding-top	<padding-width> | inherit	Sets the amount of white space between an element's content and its top margin	No	padding-top: 10px
padding	<padding-width> {1,4} | inherit	Shorthand for setting white space for all sides of an element	No	padding: 10px 20px

To set a padding of 20 pixels on all four sides of an element, use this short-and-sweet style rule:

```
p {padding: 20px}
```

Controlling layout

The CSS layout properties enable you to control how your element boxes are laid out on the screen. You can overlap boxes using the z-index property, prohibit boxes from sitting next to each other using the clear property, specify the height and width for a box, and control how boxes are laid out relative to each other when one box contains another. Table 12-8 lists the layout properties.

Before you work with these properties to create a complex style sheet, we recommend that you read through the visual formatting model information in the CSS2 specification at

```
www.w3.org/TR/REC-CSS2/visudet.html
```

This style rule creates a paragraph that is two inches by two inches and that can't have other elements sitting to either side of it. The rule also specifies that a scroll bar should appear within the paragraph's box if the paragraph's content is too big to fit in a two-inch-by-two-inch area.

```
p {width: 2in;
   height: 2in;
   clear: none;
   overflow: scroll;
   }
```

Other cool CSS properties

Our list of properties and values is neither exhaustive nor all-inclusive. Instead, we listed the most often used properties and those that have the best support among Web browsers. CSS2 also includes properties that control

- ✔ User interface
- ✔ Paged media
- ✔ Tables
- ✔ Aural style sheets
- ✔ Generated content

After you've worked with CSS for a while, we suggest you take the time to investigate these other properties.

From CSS to XSL

Now that you know what a style sheet is, how it works with XML and HTML documents, and how to create your own style sheets, you can move on to the next piece in the puzzle: XSL. XSL is more complicated than CSS but offers a much more powerful set of tools for styling XML documents.

Table 12-8

Layout Properties

Property	Values	What It Is	Inherited?	Example
position	static | relative | absolute | fixed | inherit	Identifies what kind of box an element occupies	No	position: fixed
bottom	\<length\> | \<percentage\> | auto | inherit	Specifies how far one box's bottom edge should be from the bottom edge of the box that contains it	No	bottom: 10px
left	\<length\> | \<percentage\> | auto | inherit	Specifies how far one box's left edge should be from the left edge of the box that contains it	No	bottom: 10px
right	\<length\> | \<percentage\> | auto | inherit	Specifies how far one box's right edge should be from the right edge of the box that contains it	No	bottom: 10px
top	\<length\> | \<percentage\> | auto | inherit	Specifies how far one box's top edge should be from the top edge of the box that contains it	No	bottom: 10px
clear	none | left | right | both | inherit	Indicates which sides of a box may not have other elements float beside them	No	clear: both
clip	\<shape\> | auto | inherit	Specifies how an element's content should be clipped if the content doesn't fit in the box specified for it	No	clip: auto

(continued)

Table 12-8 (continued)

Property	Values	What It Is	Inherited?	Example
float	left | right | none | inherit	Determines whether the box should float to the left or right, if at all	No	float: right
height	<length> | <percentage> | auto | inherit	Defines the height of the box	No	height: 5in
width	<length> | <percentage> | auto | inherit	Defines the width of the box	No	width: 5in
max-width	<length> | <percentage> | none | inherit	Defines the maximum width of a box	No	max-width: 5in
min-width	<length> | <percentage> | none | inherit	Defines the minimum width of a box	No	min-width: 1in
overflow	visible | hidden | scroll | auto | inherit	Specifies how content that doesn't fit within a box should be displayed	No	overflow: scroll
visibility	visible | hidden | collapse | inherit	Controls the visibility of the content within a box	No	visibility: hidden
z-index	auto | <integer> | inherit	Identifies the place a box has in a stack of boxes	No	z-index: 3

Chapter 13

Applying Style to XML with XSL

In This Chapter

▶ Choosing your style poison

▶ Transforming XML documents with XSLT

▶ Dissecting a simple XSLT style sheet

▶ Embedding transformation instructions in an XML document

*W*e would be remiss if we didn't devote some coverage to a discussion of XSL — the style sheet language developed specifically for XML. Just as XML is a robust and flexible tool for describing data, XSL is a robust and flexible tool for applying style to the data described using XML. And XSL isn't just for describing data, either.

The Two Faces of XSL

XML's style needs are extensive. Clean XML document structures aren't always in the form you need for presentation, but outside tools can help manage the transformation. In addition, to truly take advantage of XML's power as a tool for sharing data across systems, there should be an easy way to convert documents from one Document Type Definition (DTD) to another.

The architects of XML decided that the responsibility for display and for document conversion should be handled by a style mechanism, so they developed XSL. During development, these same architects realized that creating one mechanism for display and conversion was a Herculean task. Put simply, there had to be a better way. It turns out that the better way was to split the style and conversion mechanisms into two different but related mechanisms: the Extensible Stylesheet Language (XSL) and XSL Transformations (XSLT). That's why we cover these topics separately, too!

XSL

XSL is the display arm of the XML style mechanism and is an XML vocabulary that describes how to present information. XSL as we know it now — as a developing W3C specification — is quite different from XSL's conception. The current XSL working draft focuses on using XSL to control the display of XML documents.

The key to an XSL style sheet is a critter known as a formatting object. A *formatting object* represents a piece of a document. These pieces can be as large as a page or as small as a list item. When you build an XSL style sheet, you take each part of a document that you want to display, fit it into a formatting object, and then describe how that formatting object should appear.

Just like Cascading Style Sheets (CSS), XSL has a host of formatting properties to help you control every aspect of a formatting object's display — from its text color to the amount of space between letters and words. And just like CSS, after you find out how to build style rules — as well as what properties you have at your disposal when you're building style rules — you're well on your way to building XSL style sheets.

If XSL really isn't that hard to master, why do we avoid serious discussion of this topic? The answer is twofold. Whereas the basic concepts behind XSL are fairly straightforward, the syntax for building XSL style sheets is complex. It has to provide a flexible, extensible mechanism to add style to documents that can be described in just about any way.

More importantly, the development of the XSL specification has been a roller coaster ride — and we're not talking about a kiddie roller coaster either. We're talking about a big, scary, inverted, looping roller coaster. The original working draft for XSL looks nothing like the current XSL implementation, and we're not convinced that the ups and downs and other gyrations are over.

Because the XSL working draft is unstable, it isn't well supported in any mainstream development or browsing tools. This makes it hard to develop and display XSL style sheets. Rather than spend tons of time on what might be or what was, we'd rather talk about stuff you can use today.

The most current version of the XSL working draft as of this writing was released on April 21, 1999. The best way to keep up with changes in the XSL specification is to keep a close watch on the W3C's XSL page at www.w3.org/Style/XSL/. After the specification becomes a recommendation, it will be stable — well, as stable as anything on the Web can be — and ready for use as an XML styling tool.

XSLT

The second face of XSL is a conversion tool, known as XSLT. The *T* stands for *transformation,* and that's exactly what this part of XSL is designed to do. XSLT provides a set of rules to convert documents described by one set of tags to documents described by another set of tags. The two sets of tags don't even have to look anything alike.

To write an XSLT style sheet, you simply identify an element in one document and specify how it should be described using a different tag or set of tags. You can grab entire elements or just an element's content. You can even reference attribute values and turn them into tag content or vice versa. All in all, it's really kind of cool.

The primary use of XSLT in the here and now is to transform documents described using XML tags to HTML for display in a Web browser. This nifty trick overcomes the dilemma created by a lack of stability in XSL and an overall lack of consistency in browser support for XML. HTML is also much more backward compatible than XML; therefore, you can describe and store your data in XML, and still display it in HTML. This means a wide variety of users can see it using their everyday Web browsers. Because XSLT is actively being used to transform XML documents to HTML, we focus our coverage of XSL on this particular issue: XSLT.

XSLT is an official recommendation, unlike XSL, which is still a working draft. XSLT also doesn't share XSL's turbulent past. You can visit the current XSLT recommendation at

```
www.w3.org/TR/xslt
```

XSL style sheets are XML documents

The good news about any flavor of XSL is that XSL style sheets are really just XML documents. They use tags, attributes, and all the other standard XML syntax tools. This means that when you master XSL, you're really just mastering yet another DTD. Cool, huh?

Because XSL style sheets are just XML documents, technically, any XML parser can process them. For a style sheet to be useful, however, the parser has to be part of a larger system that knows what to do with the results of the parsed style sheet.

Specialized XSL tools are under development and some already exist. But beware, XSL processing tools that have been around for a while may have been written before the current XSL working draft was released and may not support style sheets written using the most current XSL or XSLT syntax.

The best way to keep up with new XSL tools is to visit the W3C's XSL page we told you about previously (www.w3.org/Style/XSL/). Another great XSL resource on the Web is XSL Info, which you can find at www.xslinfo.com. This site is a sibling site to www.xmlinfo.com, www.schema.net, and www.xmlsoftware.com — all run by James Tauber, a knowledgeable and well-respected member of the Web community.

A Simple Transformation Using XSLT

The best way to show you how XSLT works is by example. In this section, we look at an XML document we want to transform, the HTML document we want to transform it into, and the XSLT style sheet that manages the transformation. After you know where you are, where you're going, and how you're going to get there, we break our XSLT style sheet into its component parts so you can see what's really going on and how the transformation occurred.

The bean burrito recipe

If you read other chapters in this book, you probably recognize the bean burrito recipe. If you plan on reading the entire book, by the time you're finished, you won't be able to look at another bean burrito recipe. But then again, how often do you come face to face with a bean burrito recipe?

Here's our now-classic bean burrito recipe, which is described using our very own Recipe Markup Language (RML):

```
<?xml version="1.0" standalone="yes">

<Recipe cook="XML Gourmet">
  <Title>Bean Burrito</Title>
  <Category name="tex-mex" />

  <Ingredients>
    <Item>1 can refried beans</Item>
    <Item>1 cup longhorn colby cheese, shredded </Item>
    <Item>1 small onion, finely chopped</Item>
    <Item>3 flour tortillas</Item>
  </Ingredients>
```

```
<CookingInstructions>
     Empty can of refried beans into a medium saucepan.
     Heat over medium heat until beans are smooth
     and bubbly.
     Warm tortillas in microwave for 30 seconds.
   </CookingInstructions>

   <ServingInstructions>
     Spread 1/3 of warm beans on each tortilla.
     Sprinkle with cheese and onions.
     Roll tortillas and serve.
   </ServingInstructions>

</Recipe>
```

If we feed this file into Internet Explorer, it ignores all the tags it doesn't rec-ognize — which is all of them — and simply displays the text within the markup, as shown in Figure 13-1.

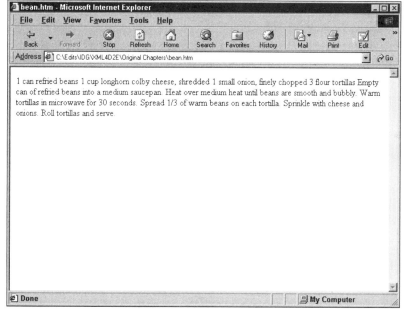

Figure 13-1:
Internet
Explorer
ignores all
the XML
tags.

So, if we want to display the bean burrito recipe in a useful and meaningful way in a Web browser, we have to describe it with something that the Web browser can work with — namely HTML.

Describing the bean burrito recipe with HTML

Although HTML markup doesn't describe the pieces and parts of the bean burrito recipe as well as RML does, Web browsers speak HTML and display HTML described content in a nice, pretty way. Based on the different roles each bit of content in our XML document plays, we can build a set of HTML markup to display the content that looks something like this:

```html
<html>
  <head>
    <title>Bean Burrito</title>
  </head>

  <body>
    <h1>Bean Burrito</h1>

    <h2>Ingredients</h2>

    <ul>
    <li>1 can refried beans</li>
    <li>1 cup longhorn colby cheese,shredded</li>
    <li>1 small onion, finely chopped</li>
    <li>3 flour tortillas</li>
    </ul>

    <h2>Cooking Instructions</h2>
    <p>
    Empty can of refried beans into a medium saucepan.
    Heat over medium heat until beans are smooth
    and bubbly.
    Warm tortillas in microwave for 30 seconds.
    </p>

    <h2>Serving Instructions</h2>
    <p>
    Spread 1/3 of warm beans on each tortilla.
    Sprinkle with cheese and onions.
    Roll tortillas and serve.
    </p>

  </body>
</html>
```

Simple and to the point, Figure 13-2 shows what this HTML looks like displayed in a Web browser.

So the question becomes: How do we convert our XML to HTML for display in a Web browser? Enter XSLT.

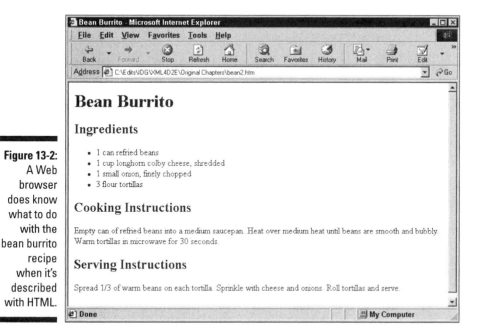

Figure 13-2:
A Web
browser
does know
what to do
with the
bean burrito
recipe
when it's
described
with HTML.

An XSL style sheet for converting XML to HTML

A fairly simple XSLT style sheet manages the conversion of our bean burrito recipe from XML to HTML:

```
<xsl:stylesheet version="1.0"
 xmlns:xsl="http://www.w3.org/1999/XSL/Transform"
 xmlns="http://www.w3.org/TR/xhtml1/strict">

<xsl:output
    method="xml"
    encoding="iso-8859-1" />

<xsl:template match="Recipe">
  <html>
    <head>
      <title>
        <xsl:value-of select="Recipe/Title" />
      </title>
    </head>
```

```
      <body>
        <xsl:apply-templates />
      </body>

    </html>
  </xsl:template>

  <xsl:template match="Recipe/Title">
    <h1>
      <xsl:apply-templates />
    </h1>
  </xsl:template>

  <xsl:template match="Recipe/Ingredients">
    <h2>Ingredients</h2>
    <ul>
      <xsl:for-each select="Item">
        <li>
          <xsl:apply-templates />
        </li>
      </xsl:for-each>
    </ul>
  </xsl:template>

  <xsl:template match="Recipe/CookingInstructions">
    <h2>Cooking Instructions</h2>
    <p>
      <xsl:apply-templates />
    </p>
  </xsl:template>

  <xsl:template match="Recipe/ServingInstructions">
    <h2>Serving Instructions</h2>
    <p>
      <xsl:apply-templates />
    </p>
  </xsl:template>

</xsl:stylesheet>
```

In a nutshell, this style sheet specifies how each element in RML should be changed to HTML. Each style rule identifies one element from RML and provides instructions on how to convert it to a similar or equivalent HTML element or set of elements. We discuss how the style sheet does this in more detail shortly.

When style takes a name, it's not in vain

Looking at the XSLT style sheet that converts our bean burrito recipe from XML to HTML, you probably noticed that it does indeed look like a good ol' XML document — tags and all. You probably also noticed a strange addition to each and every tag — `xsl:`. The `<template>. . .</template>` element in this style sheet is expressed as `<xsl:template>. . .</xsl:template>`. So what's that all about?

The use of the `xsl:` identifier is part of an addition to XML called namespaces. A *namespace* is a unique identifier that links an XML markup element to a specific DTD. So the `xsl:` portion of `<xsl:template>` indicates that the template element is defined by the XSL specification. But why all the extra work?

Because anyone can build their own tags using XML, it's possible — and most likely probable — that two DTDs or documents will use the same elements. For example, our RML markup language uses `<Title>. . .</Title>` in much the same way as HTML uses `<title>. . .</title>`.

Remember that a parser can deal with just about any set of XML tags. And a well-formed XML document can use tags from any DTD. However, a special processor designed to work with documents written with one or two specific DTDs might not know what to do with a document that combines tags from several different DTDs, some of which may conflict, just like the RML `<Title>` tag conflicts with the HTML `<title>` tag.

Namespaces prevent conflicts in markup by identifying which DTD a tag comes from. Before you can use a namespace marker such as `xsl:`

or `xhtml:` — or `rml:` — you have to identify it, like this:

```
<html:ul
    xmlns:html='http://www.w3.o
    rg/TR/REC-html40'>
<html:li>List item</html:li>
<html:li>List item</html:li>
<html:li>List item</html:li>
</html:ul>
```

In this example, the DTD the namespace references is the DTD for the HTML 4.0 specification. The `xmlns` attribute, which stands for XML namespace, indicates that the element (`<ul>` in this case) belongs to a namespace other than the one that belongs to the current DTD. The value for `xmlns` — `http://www.w3.org/TR/REC-html40` — points to the DTD that defines the namespace.

Namespaces let the processing application know which DTD you're using, so you may utilize the markup from several different DTDs in one document. In the end, namespaces permit efficient sharing of vocabularies across documents and help eliminate possible confusion when two or more vocabularies use the same tags.

If you want to know more about namespaces, check out the XML Namespaces recommendation, which lives at

```
www.w3.org/TR/REC-xml-names
```

In addition, James Clark, the developer of one of the more popular XML parsers, put together a note on XML namespaces at

```
www.jclark.com/xml/xmlns.htm
```

that provides a good explanation of how they work and why you might want to use them.

An XSLT Style Sheet in Detail

It's time to break an XSLT style sheet into its component parts and see what makes it go. XSLT is a robust conversion tool and has many facets. We won't attempt to describe them all here. Instead, we focus on the most basic structures that make up an XSLT style sheet.

An XSLT style sheet is made up of a set of instructions to convert documents described using one DTD into documents described using a second, different DTD. Each instruction focuses on one element in the source document and specifies how it should be changed to fit the second DTD. The style sheet doesn't replace or change the elements in the source file, but instead builds a new file to hold the results of the transformation.

Remember that an XSLT style sheet is an XML document. Because XML documents are created using vocabularies, this ultimately means that XSLT is simply a vocabulary to convert a document from one vocabulary to another. Therefore, when you're learning XSLT, all you're really learning is what XSLT tags you can use to transform a document using one set of tags to a document that uses another set of tags. XSLT is nothing more than tags for changing tags to tags. Whew!

In this section, we look at the most fundamental elements of XSLT and how they work to transform documents.

Templates

The instructions in an XSLT style sheet that control how an element and its content should be converted are called templates. A *template* identifies which element in a document should be changed and then specifies how the element should be changed. The template element is `<xsl:template>`. . . `</xsl:template>`.

Looking back at the XSLT style sheet in the section "An XSL style sheet for converting XML to HTML," notice that it's comprised of a series of template elements, like this one:

```
<xsl:template match="Recipe">
  <html>
    <head>
      <title>
        <xsl:value-of select="Recipe/Title" />
      </title>
    </head>
</xsl:template>
```

Patterns

A template in an XSLT style sheet focuses on a single element in a document. To identify the element to which the template applies, XSLT uses the `match=` attribute with the `<xsl:template>` tag to point to a specific element. The value of `match=` is called a *pattern*. The XSLT processor looks at the pattern, works its way through the source document to find the pattern, and applies the template to every element that matches the pattern. In this example, the pattern to match is the `<Recipe>` element:

```
<xsl:template match="Recipe">
  <html>
    <head>
      <title>
        <xsl:value-of select="Recipe/Title" />
      </title>
    </head>
</xsl:template>
```

In this slightly more complex example, the pattern to match is any instance of the `<Title>` element found nested in the `<Recipe>` element:

```
<xsl:template match="Recipe/Title">
  <h1>
    <xsl:apply-templates />
  </h1>
</xsl:template>
```

Although these two examples use fairly simple patterns, the syntax for specifying patterns, called XPath, is complex and allows you to specify detailed patterns that can point to a specific element on a page based on its context, its content, or other criteria. The XPath mechanism isn't limited to working with XSLT and is so important that it has its own specification. We discuss XPath in detail in Chapter 16.

Results

In addition to using a pattern to identify which element in the source document to transform, the template also specifies how to transform the element itself. These transformation instructions guide the XSLT processor through content transformation. This template looks for the `<CookingInstructions>` element nested in the `<Recipe>` element and converts it to an HTML paragraph (`<p>`) — with a second-level heading that reads *Cooking Instructions* attached for good measure:

```
<xsl:template match="Recipe/CookingInstructions">
  <h2>Cooking Instructions</h2>
  <p>
    <xsl:apply-templates />
  </p>
</xsl:template>
```

Processing element content

In addition to changing the cooking instructions element to an HTML paragraph element, the cooking instructions template also specifies that any content within `<CookingInstructions>`. . .`</CookingInstructions>` should have the same template applied. The style sheet does this with the empty `<xsl:apply-templates>` element. Because the `<CookingInstructions>` element doesn't have any other content that matches any template patterns in the style sheet, the XSLT processor simply moves the content within `<CookingInstructions>`. . .`</CookingInstructions>` as-is from the source document to the results document, which locates this XML:

```
<CookingInstructions>
    Empty can of refried beans into a medium saucepan.
    Heat over medium heat until beans are smooth
    and bubbly.
    Warm tortillas in microwave for 30 seconds.
  </CookingInstructions>
```

The template specifies that the XML should be transformed to

```
    <h2>Cooking Instructions</h2>
    <p>
    Empty can of refried beans into a medium saucepan.
    Heat over medium heat until beans are smooth
    and bubbly.
    Warm tortillas in microwave for 30 seconds.
    </p>
```

You'll see the `<xsl:apply-templates />` element used frequently in XSLT style sheets.

In this example, the `apply templates` element simply moves the text within `<ServingInstructions>`. . .`</ServingInstructions>` from the source document to the results document when `<ServingInstructions>`. . . `</ServingInstructions>` is transformed to a paragraph:

```
<xsl:template match="Recipe/ServingInstructions">
  <h2>Serving Instructions</h2>
  <p>
    <xsl:apply-templates />
  </p>
</xsl:template>
```

The apply-templates element doesn't always move text from one document to another. In many cases, there are other templates to apply to the content of an element. Look at the first template in our sample XSLT style sheet:

```
<xsl:template match="Recipe">
  <html>
    <head>
      <title>
        <xsl:value-of select="Recipe/Title" />
      </title>
    </head>

    <body>
      <xsl:apply-templates />
    </body>

  </html>
</xsl:template>
```

This template looks for the recipe's document element (<Recipe>) and replaces it with the basic building blocks of an HTML document (<html>, <head>, <title>, and <body>). Notice the <xsl:apply-templates /> tag within the <body>. . .</body> tags. The placement of the apply-templates element here tells the XSLT processor to apply all the remaining style sheet templates to all the content within the <Recipe> element — that's the rest of the recipe — and places the results within the <body>. . . </body> tags of the results document.

So, when you create style rules, you have to think about how you're going to not only transform an individual element but also deal with its content. Does the content from the source document need its own transforming? Does it need to be nested in a particular set of markup in the new document? Or do you even want to transform the content at all? If you don't specify <xsl:apply-templates>, the results document won't include any of the content from within an element — text, markup, or otherwise.

Just the text, please

What if you want to only grab the content of an element and not deal with the element itself? There's nothing simpler. The <xsl:value-of> element extracts the content from a tag without taking the tag along. In the preceding template for the recipe element, you find this bit of code:

```
<title>
   <xsl:value-of select="Recipe/Title" />
</title>
```

This portion of the template indicates that the content within the `<Recipe><Title>. . .</Title></Recipe>` tags should be enclosed in the `<title>. . .</title>` elements in the resulting HTML document. The template points to this part of the RML document:

```
<Recipe cook="XML Gourmet">
  <Title>Bean Burrito</Title>
```

The resulting HTML looks like this:

```
<head>
   <title>Bean Burrito</title>
</head>
```

Dealing with repeating elements

A single list might have 50 items, and you want each of those items to be transformed the same way. You could write a pattern that looks for each item in the list — yes, you really can do that; XPath is that powerful. It makes much more sense, however, to write a template that loops through each item and applies the same transformation to each instance of the element, as in this style rule:

```
<xsl:template match="Recipe/Ingredients">
  <h2>Ingredients</h2>
  <ul>
    <xsl:for-each select="Item">
      <li>
        <xsl:apply-templates />
      </li>
    </xsl:for-each>
  </ul>
</xsl:template>
```

The `<xsl:for-each>` element points at a specific tag that is repeated and applies the same transformation to each instance. In this template, every `<Item>` element nested within `<Recipe><Ingredients>. . . </Ingredients></Recipe>` is changed to an HTML list item (`<li>`) within an unordered list (`<ul>`). The style rule points to this portion of the recipe:

```
<Ingredients>
    <Item>1 can refried beans</Item>
    <Item>1 cup longhorn colby cheese, shredded </Item>
    <Item>1 small onion, finely chopped</Item>
    <Item>3 flour tortillas</Item>
</Ingredients>
```

The transformation to HTML looks like this:

```
<ul>
  <li>1 can refried beans</li>
  <li>1 cup longhorn colby cheese, shredded </li>
  <li>1 small onion, finely chopped</li>
  <li>3 flour tortillas</li>
</ul>
```

A Different Approach

There's more than one way to skin the proverbial cat. This saying holds true for XSLT as well. There's more than one way to create XSLT style rules for transforming documents. You can write a separate style sheet, or you can use the XSLT abbreviated syntax and build the conversion style rules right into the results document, as we did here:

```
<html xsl:version="1.0"
      xmlns:xsl="http://www.w3.org/1999/XSL/Transform"
      lang="en">

  <head>
    <title>
      <xsl:value-of select="Recipe/Title" />
    </title>
  </head>

  <body>
    <h1>
      <xsl:value-of select="Recipe/Title" />
    </h1>

    <h2>Ingredients</h2>
    <ul>
      <xsl:for-each select="Recipe/Title/Item">
        <li>
          <xsl:value-of select=" /" />
        </li>
      </xsl:for-each>
    </ul>

    <h2>Cooking Instructions</h2>
    <p>
      <xsl:value-of select="Recipe/CookingInstructions" />
    </p>
```

```
      <h2>Serving Instructions</h2>
      <p>
        <xsl:value-of select="Recipe/ServingInstructions" />
      </p>

    </body>
</html>
```

This HTML document with XSLT style rules built in (let's hear it for name-spaces) coverts our recipe using techniques similar to those we used to create the series of templates. Instead of creating a template that converts the <CookingInstructions>. . .<CookingInstructions> element to a paragraph with a second-level heading attached, this document simply extracts the cooking instructions content and places it between the para-graph tags already in place in the document.

In some ways, this method is much easier than creating an entire set of tem-plates for converting a document from one DTD to the other. The down side to this method is that you can't process the content of an element as you can with the <xsl:apply-templates> element in an XSLT style sheet.

When you use this method, you also hard-code the results document and cram in the content. If you want to change the results document, you must change the hard coded HTML (or other markup). That's not a big deal if you only have one document to convert, but what if you have 500?

Just the Tip of the Iceberg

TheXSLT elements we discussed are only a few of the XSL elements you can use to transform an XML document from one DTD to another. You can sort through elements, point to attribute values, create attributes, and assign attributes values in the results document — and that's only the beginning. To take total advantage of XSLT, you need to be familiar with the XSLT recom-mendation, which you can find at www.w3.org/TR/xslt.

In Chapter 14, we take a look at some selected XSL topics that we think are both interesting and useful as you begin to find out more about the intrica-cies of building complex style sheets. We discuss the XML object model, the concepts of trees and nodes, and other fun — if not slightly hairy — subjects.

Chapter 14

Special Topics on XML Style

In This Chapter

▶ Using the XML object model

▶ Combining style sheets

▶ Adding style definitions directly in XML documents

*A*pplying styles to XML is a complex business. Chapters 11, 12, and 13 cover the two major XML style tools — Cascading Style Sheets (CSS) and Extensible Stylesheet Language Transformations (XSLT). This chapter covers some other key XML style issues that you should know about.

We touch on several different XML style issues that should help you if — or when — you delve deeper into your studies of XML style.

Objectifying XML

Throughout this book, we use an example bean burrito recipe described with the Recipe Markup Language (RML). In case you've managed to avoid it, here it is:

```
<?xml version="1.0" standalone="yes">

<Recipe cook="XML Gourmet">
  <Title>Bean Burrito</Title>
  <Category name="tex-mex" />

  <Ingredients>
    <Item>1 can refried beans</Item>
    <Item>1 cup longhorn colby cheese, shredded </Item>
    <Item>1 small onion, finely chopped</Item>
    <Item>3 flour tortillas</Item>
  </Ingredients>
```

```
<CookingInstructions>
    Empty can of refried beans into a medium saucepan.
    Heat over medium heat until beans are smooth
    and bubbly.
    Warm tortillas in microwave for 30 seconds.
</CookingInstructions>

<ServingInstructions>
    Spread 1/3 of warm beans on each tortilla.
    Sprinkle with cheese and onions.
    Roll tortillas and serve.
</ServingInstructions>

</Recipe>
```

This document can be described as a series of elements and their content. You can also describe the document as a series of objects. To put it simply, each element in the document is an individual object. This bit of the recipe includes five different objects:

```
<Ingredients>
    <Item>1 can refried beans</Item>
    <Item>1 cup longhorn colby cheese, shredded </Item>
    <Item>1 small onion, finely chopped</Item>
    <Item>3 flour tortillas</Item>
</Ingredients>
```

The objects are:

- ✔ Ingredients
- ✔ Item
- ✔ Item
- ✔ Item
- ✔ Item

Even though the individual <Item>. . .</Item> elements use the same tags, they are all individual objects in the document.

So what's the big deal about these individual objects? A Document Object Model (DOM) uses standard syntax to describe a document as a series of objects. Programming languages such as JavaScript, VBScript, C++, and Java can access the DOM for a document, reach out and grab a particular object, and manipulate it.

In addition to identifying each element in an XML document as an individual object, a DOM also shows how the elements relate to each other hierarchically. In fact, the DOM identifies each unique object in a document based on its position in the document's hierarchy.

As you might have guessed, the way a DOM is laid out adheres to a specific syntax, and that syntax is defined in a W3C recommendation. To find out all there is to know about the DOM 1.0 Recommendation, visit `www.w3.org/DOM/`.

Note that the DOM Level 2 is a recommendation. The DOM Level 2 adds more features without adding lots of detail.

The DOM Recommendation is divided into two different parts: Core DOM and HTML DOM. The Core portion of the recommendation specifies how to create DOMs for XML documents. The HTML portion specifies — yep, you guessed it — how to create DOMs for HTML documents. When you look for and study DOM references, be sure to identify which portion of the DOM the reference covers.

XML processors create a DOM each time they parse an XML document. Figure 14-1 illustrates how the DOM for the bean burrito recipe might look to an XML processor.

```
Bean Burrito Document
        ├──<? xml />
        │     ├ version
        │     │     └──1.0
        │     └ standalone
        │           └──yes
        │
        └──<Recipe>
              ├ cook
              │     └──XML Gourmet
              ├ <Title>...<1 Title>
              │     └──Bean Burrito
              ├ <Category 1>
              │     └──name
              │           └──tex-mex
              ├ <Ingredients>...<1 Ingredients>
              │     ├ <Item>...<1 Item>
              │     │     └ 1 can refried beans
              │     ├ <Item>...<1 Item>
              │     │     └ 1 cup longhorn colby cheese, shredded
              │     ├ <Item>...<1 Item>
              │     │     └ 1 small onion finely chopped
              │     └ <Item>...<1 Item>
              │           └ 3 flour tortillas
              ├ <Cooking Instructions...<1 Cooking Instructions>
              │     └ (text of cooking instructions)
              └ <Serving Instructions>...<1 Serving Instructions>
                    └ (text of serving instructions)
```

Figure 14-1:
The DOM describes an XML document as a hierarchical series of objects.

Of parents, children, and siblings

To understand how the DOM works and how applications use programming commands to access individual objects in a document, you need to have a good grasp of how document elements relate to each other. The terms *parent, child,* and *sibling* are all used to describe element relationships. For example, in this bit of the bean burrito recipe, the `<Title>. . .</Title>` and `<Category />` elements are children of the `<Recipe>. . .</Recipe>` element:

```
<Recipe cook="XML Gourmet">
  <Title>Bean Burrito</Title>
  <Category name="tex-mex" />
. . .
</Recipe>
```

`<Title>. . .<Title>` and `<Category />` are also siblings of each other and `<Recipe>. . .</Recipe>` is their parent.

The concept of parents and siblings doesn't extend past one level of nesting in this collection of objects, so there are no great-great-great grandchildren or grandparents. The concepts of nieces and nephews are absent as well. In general, the element family tree extends only to the immediate element family.

A forest of trees and nodes

The following discussion of trees and nodes is a bit on the techie side because it just can't be helped. If you don't plan to program an application that reads and processes XML documents, you can probably live the remainder of your life happily without knowing the first thing about trees and nodes. However, many XML resources — especially the more technical ones — tend to assume that you at least understand the basics of trees and nodes. So, although you can skip this section for now if you're not planning on programming applications for XML, you might want to revisit it later as you encounter more technical XML resources.

Speaking of trees, the concept of a hierarchical data tree is also important to the DOM. The DOM for any given XML document lays the objects out as a tree of elements. Figure 14-2 shows the objects in the bean burrito recipe displayed in a tree formation.

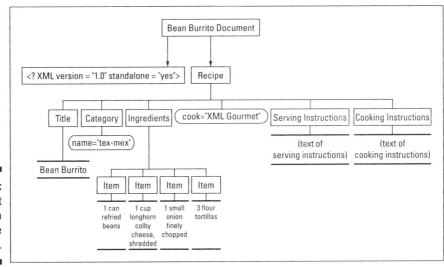

Figure 14-2: Document objects in a tree formation.

In the bean burrito recipe, the tree's root is the `<Recipe>. . .</Recipe>` element. All its children are branches in the tree, and the `<Ingredients>. . . </Ingredients>` element branches out one step further with its `<Item>. . . </Item>` children. Also notice that the tree includes things other than the elements in the document — attributes and element content, for example. The objects included in a DOM are more than just elements and are called *nodes* when displayed on the DOM tree.

Because the bean burrito recipe is such a simple document, we can't use it to illustrate all the parts a DOM tree can include. For that, you need to turn to Figure 14-3.

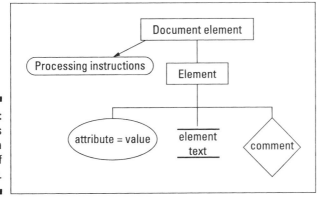

Figure 14-3: A DOM is really just a tree of nodes.

Each of the nodes you see in Figure 14-3 represents a type of node that a DOM's tree can include. If you're familiar with basic XML structures, you recognize the majority of node types because they're common XML elements. The ones in our bean burrito recipe are

- **The document's root element**: `<Recipe>. . .</Recipe>`
- **Elements**: Such as `<Item>. . .</Item>` and `<Category />`
- **Text**: The content of `<CookingInstructions>. . . </CookingInstructions>`
- **Attributes**: Such as `cook="XML Gourmet"`

Node types that aren't included in the bean burrito recipe but are discussed in other chapters of the book are

- Namespaces (Chapter 15)
- Processing instructions (Chapter 5)
- Comments (Chapter 5)

As you can see, there's not much in any given XML document that you can't access using the DOM. Not surprisingly, that's what the members of the W3C had in mind when they created the DOM specification.

The DOM and style sheets

This DOM stuff is all well and good, but you might be wondering why this is relevant to XML style sheets. Remember that the DOM opens a document to inspection and manipulation by programming languages. Software that processes XML documents first runs the document through a parser that generates a DOM. The application then uses programming commands to manipulate the different objects in the document.

XSL and XSLT style sheets are really just XML documents. Therefore, for most applications to be able to process style sheets and apply them to XML documents, both the style sheet and the document must be parsed, listed as individual DOMs, and then manipulated by programming commands.

Web browsers and the DOM

The best examples of applications that use XSLT style sheets and the DOM to process XML documents are Web browsers — Internet Explorer in particular. To display XML documents in Internet Explorer, you actually have to write a VBScript or JScript script to apply an XSLT style sheet to the XML document for conversion to HTML. This script accesses the DOM that's created when the Internet Explorer parser, Microsoft XML (MSXML), reads and parses both the XML document and the related XSLT style sheet.

The version of XSLT that Internet Explorer 5.0 supports isn't exactly like the XSLT standard. Before you use XSLT with Internet Explorer 5.0, be sure to read through the XML documentation at `http://msdn.microsoft.com` to get the complete scoop on the differences.

Before you can use the DOM, XSLT, and XML to browse Web pages, you must have a solid understanding of not only XML and its related technologies but also a scripting language. The Microsoft Developer Network Web site has extensive resources that provide detailed instructions for converting XML documents to HTML using the DOM and scripting languages. Visit `http://msdn.microsoft.com/xml/XSLGuide/` to find out more.

Combining Style Sheets

Style sheets provide form for function. In addition, you can apply more than one style sheet to any given XML document. Nifty, huh? Imagine the following scenario.

A corporate Web site has several sections, each devoted to a different corporate function or department. The powers-that-be in the corporation want the Web site to adopt a consistent look and feel. A reasonable request, don't you think? However, individual content providers want to create a look and feel that best matches their content and reflects their particular department's individual style. Yet another reasonable request. The question becomes, how can you accommodate a need for a consistent look and feel, while allowing owners of different pieces of the site's content some flexibility to define their own look and feel?

The answer is multiple style sheets. One style sheet sets the overall look and feel for all pages on the site. It might define basic color schemes and page layout, apply consistent headers and footers on each page, and help maintain continuity among all pages on a site. Other style sheets work with the base corporate style sheet to provide a customized look and feel for each individual department or group's area of the site. If the style sheets are designed to cooperate, they'll combine to create a consistent look and feel for the site that takes the different types of site content into account.

Another possible scenario for a combination of style sheets is to create multiple XSLT style sheets to guide the conversion of XML documents to HTML or some other type of markup. The base XSLT style sheet does many of the same things as the base corporate style sheet we describe in the previous paragraph: set color schemes, define basic layout, and add standard generated text, such as headers and footers. Other XSLT style sheets guide the conversion of document content. One might convert the content in a specific way for display as a press release, whereas another might convert the content for inclusion in a knowledge base.

Combining style sheets is a powerful tool for document styling and transformation. Following are the three ways you can combine XSL and XSLT style sheets:

✔ Import the style sheet into another style sheet

✔ Include the style sheet in another style sheet

✔ Embed a style sheet directly into an XML file

The next few sections look at each of these options in a bit more detail.

Importing one style sheet into another

The XSL specification includes this nifty little element for including style sheets directly in an XML document:

```
<xsl:import />
```

Nest this element in the `<xsl:stylesheet>`. . .`<xsl:stylesheet>` root element and use the `href=` attribute to point to the style sheet you want to import, like this:

```
<xsl:stylesheet version="1.0"
          xmlns:xsl="http://www.w3.org/1999/XSL/Transform">
   <xsl:import href="training.xsl" />
      . . .
</xsl:stylesheet>
```

This bit of code imports an XSL style sheet named `training.xsl` into the base style sheet contained in `<xsl:stylesheet>`. . .`<xsl:stylesheet>`. Because the contents of `training.xsl` become part of the document's base style sheet, if you make any changes to the style information contained in `training.xsl`, those changes automatically become part of the base style sheet.

If you're going to import one style sheet into another, you must list the `<xsl:import>` tag before you create any other style rules. Also, if any style rules in the imported style sheet conflicts with the ones in the base style sheet, the base style rules take precedence.

Including one style sheet within another

You won't be surprised when we tell you that the XSL tag to include one style sheet within another is `<xsl:include />`. This tag works exactly like the `<xsl:import/>` tag, as in this bit of code:

```
<xsl:stylesheet version="1.0"
          xmlns:xsl="http://www.w3.org/1999/XSL/Transform">
   <xsl:include href="training.xsl" />
   . . .
</xsl:stylesheet>
```

You might be wondering about the difference between imported and included style rules. They aren't too different, but they differ enough to have different names. *Imported styles* are treated by processing applications as a separate set of rules. As we've said, if imported style rules conflict with base style rules, the base style rules win.

Included styles are treated as part of the base style sheet by processing applications. All style rules, base or included, are treated as equals. If one style rule conflicts with another, the one listed first in the style sheet takes precedence.

Embedding a style sheet directly in an XML document

You can also stick style rules directly in the XML document that they apply to. The style sheet element (`<xsl:stylesheet>. . .</xsl:stylesheet>`) must be nested directly in the document element, as in this example:

```
<?xml version="1.0"?>
<?xml-stylesheet type="text/xml" href="#id(inline_style)"?>
<Recipe>

   <xsl:stylesheet version="1.0"
     xmlns:xsl="http://www.w3.org/1999/XSL/Transform"
     id="inline_style">
   . . .
   </xsl:stylesheet>
   . . .
</Recipe>
```

Notice how the style sheet ID specified in the `<?xml-stylesheet>` processing instruction (`href= "#id(inline_style)"`) matches the value of the `id` attribute of the `<xsl:stylesheet>` element (`id="inline_style"`). This convention allows you to use a processing instruction to include a style sheet and then refer to it later in the document. All things considered, it's kinda cool.

XML processors are not required to support the embedding of style rules in XML documents. Unless you know for sure that every processor that will parse your document knows what to do with embedded style rules, we suggest you avoid this method for assigning style rules to XML elements and simply link an external style sheet to your documents.

The process of combining and embedding style sheets is different than actually linking a style sheet to an XML document. You can combine style sheets using an `<xsl:include/>` or `<xsl:import/>` tag and then link the style sheet to an XML document. For all the gory details on how to link a CSS or XSL style sheet to an XML document, see Chapter 12.

Part V
XML's Lovely Linking Languages

The 5th Wave   By Rich Tennant

"Give him air! Give him air! He'll be okay. He's just been exposed to some raw XML code. It must have accidently flashed across his screen from the server."

In this part. . .

Some of XML's enduring appeal is that it can support all kinds of advanced capabilities that HTML can only dream of. XML's linking languages make a good case in point — they make it possible to create hyperlinks with multiple targets, reference points inside other XML documents without changing those document's innards, and control access to external resources of many kinds.

In Chapter 15, we explore and explain the XML Linking Language (XLink), which permits construction of all kinds of complex links. Chapter 16 covers the XML Path Language (XPath), which makes it possible to locate remote resources of many kinds, and explains the complex harmonies that XLink, XPointer, and XPath can deliver to those in the know. Finally, Chapter 17 tackles the XML Pointer Language (XPointer), which enables anchors and targets of many kinds and allows documents to point to specific locations without having to alter the destination's markup one whit.

Chapter 15

The XML Linking Language

*T*he XML Linking Language (XLink) allows you to bring the wonders of hyperlinking into your XML documents. In this chapter, you're introduced to the magic of XLink. You find out how to link elements in XLink and declare simple XHTML using namespaces. In addition, you gain an understanding of extended and out-of-line XLinks. Finally, you find out how to declare linking elements in a DTD. Sounds like more fun than a barrel of monkeys. (We like monkeys!) Time to get started!

XLink Explored and Explained

It's arguable that the chief reason for the success of the World Wide Web is the hyperlink. Long before the advent of Hypertext Markup Language (HTML), the Internet was a busy and active place with academics and others exchanging e-mails, conversing on e-mail lists, bulletin boards, and news groups, and exchanging files using the File Transfer Protocol (FTP).

The business of looking for files and materials was performed using various protocols and related services that included the Wide Area Information Server (WAIS, developed by a now-defunct company called Thinking Machines, Inc.) and Gopher (developed at the University of Minnesota, home of the "Golden Gophers" — hence, the name Gopher).

Then, along came HTML with its hyperlinks, which provided an instant *web* of connectivity. Suddenly, the Internet wasn't just a place for academics and nerds; it became accessible to everyone from Vice President Gore to aged Aunt Polly, who doesn't know the difference between computer RAM and the RAM pickup truck!

XLink brings the magic of hyperlinking to your XML documents. XLink, however, not only allows hyperlinking in the same ways that HTML delivers, but also allows all kinds of wonderful new types of links.

Before we get down to the nitty gritty of XLink, you must tackle some definitions. If you have some knowledge of HTML, most of these definitions will be familiar. On your mark, get set, go:

- **Resource:** Anything that can be retrieved over the Internet, such as a document, an image, a sound file, or even a list generated automatically in response to a query.

- **Link:** You might tend to think of a link as something you click on, but that's not necessarily what a link really is. A link represents a relationship between two or more objects.

- **Hyperlink:** Now this is something you usually do click on! A hyperlink is an object that usually causes a fresh display or presentation on-screen.

- **Linking element:** An element that contains a link. In HTML, `<img>` and `<a>` elements are examples of linking elements. In XLink, `<simple>` elements are examples of linking elements. See the "Types of linking elements" section later in this chapter for more details.

- **Locator:** Data that identifies a resource to which you can link.

- **Traversal:** The act of using a link. By following a link, you traverse from one resource to another.

- **Arc:** A symbolic representation of traversal behavior. It contains information about both ends of a link, the direction of traversal, and the timing of the traversal. XLink uses an `<arc>` element to capture such data. See the "Types of linking elements" section later in this chapter for more details.

Using Namespaces

It's impossible to get more than a superficial understanding of XLink without some knowledge of XML's namespace specification. So, before you go any further, you must understand XML namespaces.

Some of you might be following the news and discussions about the development of XML and might have seen XML gurus arguing about namespaces in much the same way medieval pundits argued over how many angels could dance on the head of a pin. Fear not, because the basics of namespaces are really quite simple. . . .

A namespace is a powerful tool. In XML, a *namespace* merely allows you to use the tags and semantics of one type of XML document in another type of XML document without going through the rigmarole of defining and declaring the other document's markup in a DTD.

For example, all HTML tags and elements are contained in the HTML namespace. This namespace requires a unique name to identify it — a name that won't be used for anything else. And what kind of name has been designed from the word go to be unique? Why, a Uniform Resource Locator (URL), of course. Therefore, a namespace usually has a URL as its name.

When a URL is used to identify a namespace, it's being used purely as a unique name. Nothing has to be at the other end of the URL. A URL is designed to be unique and, furthermore, the domain name is under somebody's control. This makes URLs ideal choices for use as unique names. For example, www.hypermedic.com is a domain that happens to be under our control, so we can make up a unique name for use as a namespace, such as www.hypermedic.com.xml.mynamespace, and be 100 percent sure that no one else can (legally) use the same name.

If you want to include in your own document type a tag from another XML document type, such as an XHTML document, you must tell the XML software that you're going to do this. You can do so in several ways, but the simplest way is to use the xmlns:somename attribute in the root element. The somename part of the name can be anything you care to call it.

Any element or attribute that contains a colon (:) is reserved for use by the W3C. The colon tells software that it's dealing with a special attribute.

Immediately after the colon, we put a name. Then we give the attribute the value of the namespace of tags we want to employ. For example:

```
<Clients xmlns:html="http://www.w3.org/html">
```

tells our software that we want to use the HTML tag set in our document. Therefore, the name of the HTML namespace is http://www.w3.org/html.

The namespace for XHTML was recently finalized. The previous code works with Internet Explorer 5.0 browsers, which have limited (and incorrect) support for namespaces.

We also added a name after the colon. This name tells our browser that whenever it comes across an element prefixed with this name, it belongs to the `http://www.w3.org/html` namespace. We could have used any name we wanted after the colon, such as `xmlns:junk` or `xmlns:myprefix`, but `xmlns:html` is more descriptive.

Now, if a namespace-conforming browser comes across any element with the following form, the browser knows that it denotes an element belonging to the XHTML namespace:

```
html:element-name
```

The following is a well-formed XML document, called clients.xml, which we could use to keep track of our clients:

```
<?xml version="1.0"?>
<?xml-stylesheet type="text/css" href="link1.css"?>
<Clients
  xmlns:html="http://www.w3.org/html">
 <Client>
   <Name>John Smith</Name>
   <Address> 123 Elm, Sometown, Ohio</Address>
   <Phone>123-456-7891</Phone>
   <Fax>123-456-7891</Fax>
   <Email>
    <html:a href="mailto:john@hypermedic.com">
            john@hypermedic.com</html:a>
   </Email>
   <Website>
     <html:a href="http://www.hypermedic.com">
            Hypermedic</html:a>
   </Website>
 </Client>
</Clients>
```

Type this and give it a suitable style sheet (see Part IV for the lowdown on style sheets), such as

```
Client,Name,Address,Phone,Fax,Email,Website{display:block;}
```

Now, run it in a namespace-enabled browser, such as Internet Explorer 5.0. If you run it in Internet Explorer 5.0, you'll see that the `html:a` element's content looks just like XHTML `a` element's content. In other words, it's blue and underlined (see Figure 15-1), the pointer turns to a hand when it hovers over the content, and when you click on it, it acts like a hyperlink.

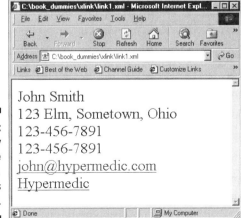

Figure 15-1:
The display
of the
`html:a`
element's
content.

When you run clients.xml, Internet Explorer 5.0 does the following:

✔ Reads the root element, `<Clients xmlns:html="http://www.w3.org/html">`, and sees that clients.xml uses a namespace.

✔ Looks at the name of the namespace, `"http://www.w3.org/html"`, and sees that this is the HTML namespace. Internet Explorer is quite familiar with HTML semantics.

✔ Looks at the abbreviation we have chosen and notes that it should use HTML semantics every time it sees the prefix `html:` before an element.

✔ Displays all `clients.xml` elements in accordance with the style sheet.

✔ Displays the `html:a` element using HTML semantics.

You might want to add an element such as `html:h1` to this document and see what happens!

Internet Explorer 5.0 doesn't handle the HTML namespace correctly. It displays your stuff only if you use the `html:` prefix — but theoretically, you should be able to use any prefix you want. The name of the namespace is what the browser should examine to figure out any applicable semantics. Internet Explorer 5.0 seems to have hard-wired this association instead.

If the browser sees a namespace it's not familiar with, it just displays the element using a default representation. You can find the namespaces recommendation at `www.w3.org/TR/1999/REC-xml-names-19990114/`.

Linking Elements in XLink

You've spent a little time looking at HTML namespaces because a basic understanding of namespaces is essential to understanding the XLink specification, which resides at `www.w3.org/TR/xlink`.

You've just seen how to use a namespace to add an XHTML link to a document. The `<a>` link is powerful and has withstood the test of time. However, XLinks not only have all the utility of XHTML links, but also promise to cause a revolution in linking practices at least as great as the original HTML hyperlink. To add an XLink to your XML document, you must do one of two things:

✔ Use the XLink namespace

✔ Declare the XLink in a DTD (see the "Creating Link Elements in DTDs" section later in this chapter)

The XLink namespace

The XLink namespace is

```
http://www.w3.org/1999/xlink/namespace/
```

To use an XLink namespace, you declare it in your document as described in the preceding section, "Using Namespaces." Here's clients.xml rewritten to use the `<simple>` linking element from the XLink namespace:

```
<?xml version="1.0"?>
<?xml-stylesheet type="text/css" href="link1.css"?>
<Clients
  xmlns:xlink="http://www.w3.org/1999/xlink/namespace/">
<Client>
   <Name>John Smith</Name>
   <Address> 123 Elm, Sometown, Ohio</Address>
   <Phone>123-456-7891</Phone>
   <Fax>123-456-7891</Fax>
   <Email>
    <xlink:simple href="mailto:john@hypermedic.com">
             john@hypermedic.com</xlink:simple>
   </Email>

   <Website>
     <xlink:simple href="http://www.hypermedic.com">
             Hypermedic</xlink:simple>
   </Website>
  </Client>
</Clients>
```

If you run this example in Internet Explorer 5.0, you won't see anything special because it's not wired to understand XLink's semantics. You need to use a more fully XML-enabled browser such as Amaya (covered in Chapter 21).

A conforming XML browser must be able to understand the semantics of XLink for correct results to occur. It's likely that most general-purpose browsers will support the linking semantics of XHTML as well as those of XLink for a while. We hope that support for XLink semantics will be added to the next generation of browsers.

Types of linking elements

The XLink specification describes four linking elements and a host of attributes. Here are the linking elements:

- ✔ <simple>...</simple> is a simple linking element that acts much like the HTML <a> link. It shares the href attribute with the HTML element but also has its own set of attributes.

- ✔ <extended>...</extended> is a new brand of link that allows all kinds of wonderful linking policies. We look at these kinds of links in the section entitled "Extending Basic Linking Behaviors" later in this chapter.

- ✔ <locator/> is always used as a child element in an extended link. We look at the <locator> in some detail in the section entitled "Extending Basic Linking Behaviors" later in this chapter.

- ✔ <arc/> is an empty element that's also used with extended links. It's covered in the "Creating Link Groups" section later in this chapter.

<xlink:simple> Links

The <xlink:simple> XLink element has almost the same type of functionality as an <a> link in HTML, except it supports several more attributes. The attributes for an <xlink:simple> XLink element are as follows:

- ✔ href, as in the <a> link of HTML, gives the location of the resource that the simple element is linking to. This is the only required attribute of the simple element. All other attributes are optional.

- ✔ `role` is a string that you can use to describe the element's role.

- ✔ `title` is the optional title of the simple link.

- ✔ `show` describes the behavior of the link when it fetches the resource at the other end. This is discussed further in the "What can we show you?" section later in this chapter.

- ✔ `actuate` takes one of two values: `onRequest` or `auto`. If the value is `onRequest`, some active event, such as a mouse click, must occur for the link to be activated. If the value is `auto`, the link loads automatically. The `<a>` link in HTML is an example of a link activated `onRequest`, and the `<img>` element in HTML is an example of a link that usually activates automatically. The default behavior is `onRequest`.

What can we show you?

The `show` attribute requires a little explanation. It's an enumerated attribute that can take one of three values: `new`, `embed`, or `replace`. The default value is `replace`.

If the `show` attribute is left with the default value of `replace` when a link is activated, the resource that contains the link is replaced with a new resource. This is what happens for most instances of an HTML link.

If given the value of `new`, the `show` attribute opens the requested resource in a new window. (To accomplish this in HTML, you must use a script.)

When given the value of `embed`, the `show` attribute embeds the requested resource in the existing document. Although you can do this with image resources in HTML using a script, you can do this with any resource in XLink.

Describing local and remote links

A link is usually a fresh resource — a completely new document. Of course, you can link to a place inside the same document that contains a `<simple>` link. To do this, the `href` attribute must be an XPointer of some kind. (XPointers are covered in Chapter 17.)

Typically, you use local links in a table of contents at the head of a document. It's possible to use a full URI (User Resource Identifier, a reference mechanism that works much like a URL) as the value of an `href` attribute. If you do this, the link is no longer local; it's considered remote.

A *remote resource* is a document, an image, a sound file, or any other kind of resource located somewhere besides in the document that contains the link.

Extending Basic Linking Behaviors

One of the most exciting things about XLink is the `extended` link, which allows you to associate a series of links. Whereas a simple link just takes the user of your document from one resource to another, an `extended` link gives users a bunch of selections.

The `extended` link requires helper elements to achieve full functionality. These elements are the `locator` element and the `arc` element.

The <xlink:extended> element

The `<xlink:extended>` element uses `<xlink:locator>` child elements to list the various links it may access and attributes to describe the group behavior of such child elements. Here are the attributes for the extended element:

- `role` is a string you can use to describe the element's role.
- `title` is the optional title of the extended link.
- `showdefault` is similar to the `show` attribute of the `simple` element but applies to the default behavior for all locator elements.
- `actuatedefault` is similar to the default behavior of the `actuate` attribute of the `simple` element and describes the default behavior for all child elements.

The <xlink:locator> element

The `<xlink:locator>` element defines the locations of all resources for an extended link. It takes an obligatory `href` attribute and optional `role` and `title` attributes. Here's a snippet from an XML document that uses both the extended and locator elements:

```
<Middle-ages
    xmlns:xlink="http://www.w3.org/1999/xlink/namespace /">
<!--The previous URL matches the draft specification -->
<!--Check the current spec for the current URL -->
<!--This is warfare.xml-->
[lots of text and markup here]
```

```
These <xlink:extended
       role="weapon list"
       title="Description of Weapons"
       showdefault="new"
       show actuate="onRequest">weapons
          <xlink:locator title="Longbow" href=
          "longbow.htm"/>
          <xlink:locator title="Crossbow"
          href="crossbow.htm"/>
          <xlink:locator title="Stirrup" href="stirrup.xml"/>

       <xlink:extended>
revolutionized medieval warfare, making it more lethal and
          bloody

[lots more text and markup here]

</Middle-ages>
```

Note again, that we declared the XLink namespace in the root element.

In this example, we have an extended link where the word weapons will be highlighted. Now, when the user lets the pointer hover over *weapons,* it's likely that a tip box will appear showing the title of the extended link: "Description of Weapons." When the user clicks your link, he or she is presented with a drop-down box with the titles of the optional pages as choices. Clicking any one of these selections displays a new window (because showdefault is set to new).

The XLink specification gives no detailed description of how a browser is supposed to behave; it just says that a browser must recognize the markup and act on it in an appropriate way. One form of behavior could be a drop-down box; another could be a pop-up box. Or perhaps links could be presented inline, which is what you must do today with HTML.

When Links Get Out of Line

Both the simple element and the extended element examples shown in previous sections are examples of inline links. An *inline link* is a link in one of the participating resources. Or in non-nerdy language, with an inline link, all the markup that describes the link must be on the page you click!

XLinks, however, give you the opportunity to take links out of line. In other words, you can place them in a different document. Here's how the example from the preceding section might look if you used an out-of-line link:

```
<Middle-ages
    xmlns:xlink="http://www.w3.org/1999/xlink/namespace">
<!-- This is warfare.xml-->
[lots of text and markup here]

These <xlink:extended
        role="xlink:external-linkset"
        title="Description of Weapons"
            <xlink:locator href= "weaponlinkset.xml"/> weapons
<xlink:extended>
revolutionized medieval warfare, making it more lethal and
            bloody

[lots more text and markup here]

</Middle-ages>
```

Through this simple change, potentially hundreds of locator elements together with descriptions of their behaviors are moved into an external document called weaponlinkset.xml.

This not only cleans up the document that contains the link, but also allows different show and actuate behaviors for different resources. Perhaps even more importantly, it allows a Webmaster to control all links for a site from a single location. Instead of editing thousands of documents when a link changes (yes, we know automated software can do this, but it's still a pain), a Webmaster can simply edit a single link document. When links are out of line, though, some thought must go into the external document to create the necessary link groups.

When we refer to an out-of-line link, the role attribute of an extended element must take a special value. As shown in the preceding example, it takes the following value:

```
role="xlink:external-linkset"
```

When you specify this second value, it means the browser should also follow up on any links referred to by the documents in a link document! As you can imagine, this can get out of hand quickly because it could lead to every single link on the Web! For this reason, it's always better to limit the links to those specifically declared in an external-linkset, which is what the first value does.

Creating Link Groups

When links are inline, it's pretty clear which is the originating document and which is the destination document. When links are out of line, this isn't always so clear, so you use the <arc/> element to spell it out.

Here's what the contents of `weaponlinkset.xml` might look like. The extended link description has two sets of child elements: the locator elements, which have all been given a unique `role` attribute value, and the `arc` elements, which describe the behavior of the links. Note also that the originating `warfare.xml` document is placed in its own locator element:

```
<WeaponLinks
     xmlns:xlink="http://www.w3.org/1999/xlink/namespace">
<!-- This is weaponlinkset.xml-->
<xlink:extended>
<!--begin locator elements-->
         <xlink:locator
              title="Middle Age Warfare"
              role="sourcedoc"
              href="warfare.xml"
         <xlink:locator
              title="Longbow"
              role="longbow"
              href= "longbow.htm"/>
         <xlink:locator
              title="Longbow Picture"
              role="longbowpic"
              href= "longbow.jpg"/>
         <xlink:locator
              title="Crossbow"
              role="crossbow"
              href= "crossbow.htm"/>
         <xlink:locator
              title="Stirrup"
              role="stirrup"
              href= "stirrup.xml"/>
<!--begin arc elements-->
         <xlink:arc
              from="sourcedoc"
              to="longbowpic"
              show="embed"
              actuate="auto"/>

         <xlink:arc
              from="sourcedoc"
              to="longbow"
              show="new"
              actuate="onRequest"/>
         <xlink:arc
              from="sourcedoc"
              to="crossbow"
              show="new"
              actuate="onRequest"/>
         <xlink:arc
              from="sourcedoc"
              to="stirrup"
              show="replace"
              actuate="onRequest"/>
```

```
        <xlink:arc
            from="stirrup"
            to="sourcedoc"
            show="replace"
            actuate="onRequest"/>

<xlink:extended>

</WeaponLinks>
```

The role of the `locator` elements in the preceding example is pretty straight-forward: They describe the locations of the resources! But the `arc` elements need a little more discussion.

An `<xlink:arc>` element describes what behavior a link in an out-of-line document should adopt. It defines which two resources to connect, the direction of the link, what to do when the link is activated, and when to activate that link. Here's a list of the `arc` element's attributes:

- The `to` and `from` attributes to define the two resources to be connected. Note that the preceding example references the `role` attribute of the locator elements to reference the two resources to be linked.

- The `to` and `from` attributes provide information about the direction of the link.

- The `show` attribute defines whether to embed the new resource in the old resource, replace the old resource with the new resource, or display the new resource in its own window.

- The `actuate` attribute defines whether the link should be activated as soon as it's recognized or await some kind of request.

Here's some additional information about the `arc` elements from the preceding example:

- The first `arc` element embeds a picture of a longbow (`longbow.jpg`) in the source document when it's loaded:

  ```
  <xlink:arc
              from="sourcedoc"
              to="longbowpic"
              show="embed"
              actuate="auto"/>
  ```

- The next three `arc` elements describe what the browser does when the `weapons` hyperlink in `warfare.xml` is clicked. The browser sees that the direction of the link is from `sourcedoc` to the other documents and creates a selection mechanism using the `title` attribute for the `locator` elements. When the browser fetches `stirrup.xml`, it replaces the current window and opens the two HTML documents in their own windows:

```
<xlink:arc
            from="sourcedoc"
            to="longbow"
            show="new"
            actuate="onRequest"/>
        <xlink:arc
            from="sourcedoc"
            to="crossbow"
            show="new"
            actuate="onRequest"/>
        <xlink:arc
            from="sourcedoc"
            to="stirrup"
            show="replace"
            actuate="onRequest"/>

        <xlink:arc
            from="stirrup"
            to="sourcedoc"
            show="replace"
            actuate="onRequest"/>
```

✔ The last arc element is for a link that exists in stirrup.xml, which also references weaponlinkset.xml. It tells the browser to link to warfare.xml and to show the page by replacing the contents of stirrup.xml:

```
<xlink:arc
            from="stirrup"
            to="sourcedoc"
            show="replace"
            actuate="onRequest"/>
```

Creating Link Elements in DTDs

In previous examples, we use the generic XLink elements with a namespace. Suppose that instead you want to designate a permanent linking element. Here again is clients.xml. We made the <Email> and <Website> elements into linking elements and added an empty element, <Picture />, that embeds a picture of the client in our document:

```
<?xml version="1.0"?>
<?xml-stylesheet type="text/css" href="link1.css"?>
<!DOCTYPE Clients SYSTEM "Clients.dtd>"
<Clients
   xmlns:html="http://www.w3.org/html">
  <Client>
    <Name>John Smith</Name>
    <Address> 123 Elm, Sometown, Ohio</Address>
    <Phone>123-456-7891</Phone>
```

```
    <Fax>123-456-7891</Fax>
    <Email
        xlink:href="mailto:john@hypermedic.com">
                john@hypermedic.com
    </Email>
    <Website
     xlink:href="http://www.hypermedic.com/jsmith.htm"
     xlink:role= "Clients web site"
     xlink:title= "Clients web site"
     xlink:show= "new"
     xlink:actuate= "onrequest"
     >
                Hypermedic
    </Website>
    <Picture
     xlink:href= "jsmith.jpg"
     xlink:role= "Clients picture"
     xlink:title= "John Smith"
     xlink:show= "embed"
     xlink:actuate= "auto"
    />
  </Client>
</Clients>
```

Here's how we declare these elements in the DTD:

```
<!ELEMENT  Email (#PCDATA) >
<!ATTLIST Email
     xmlns:xlink  CDATA  #FIXED " has
           http://www.w3.org/1999/xlink/namespace /"
xlink:href   CDATA   #REQUIRED
     xlink:type    (simple|extended|locator|arc)
     #FIXED "simple"
>


<!ELEMENT  Webpage (#PCDATA) >
<!ATTLIST Webpage
     xmlns:xlink  CDATA  #FIXED "
           http://www.w3.org/1999/xlink/namespace /"
   xlink:href    CDATA   #REQUIRED
   xlink:type    (simple|extended|locator|arc)
    #FIXED "simple"
   xlink:role   CDATA   #IMPLIED
   xlink:title   CDATA   #IMPLIED
   xlink:show   (new|embed|replace) "new"
   xlink:title   (onRequest|auto)    "onRequest"
>


<!ELEMENT  Picture #EMPTY >
<!ATTLIST  Picture
```

```
    xmlns:xlink  CDATA  #FIXED " has
          http://www.w3.org/1999/xlink/namespace /"
  xlink:href    CDATA    #REQUIRED
  xlink:type    (simple|extended|locator|arc)
  #FIXED "simple"
  xlink:role    CDATA    #IMPLIED
  xlink:title   CDATA    #IMPLIED
  xlink:show    (new|embed|replace)    "embed"
  xlink:title   (onRequest|auto)       "auto"
>
```

What's going on here? Here's what you need to know:

- ✔ In each case, you must declare xmlns:xlink as a #FIXED attribute with the XLink namespace. This means the parser always considers it to be present even though it's not typed.

- ✔ You must explicitly include any colonized attributes of the <xlink:simple> element that you want to use in your markup. The xlink:href attribute is compulsory. Add whatever others you want.

- ✔ Nothing is stopping you from adding your own attributes, but they shouldn't employ the xlink: prefix.

- ✔ In the Email element, you can expect a conforming browser to open your e-mail client with the correct address already inserted. This behavior varies from client to client because the semantics are not spelled out in XLink. In fact, it would probably be better to use an XHTML <a> link here.

- ✔ In the <Webpage> element, you decide to have any Web page that you access opened in a new window.

- ✔ In the <Picture> element, you decide that you would like the picture to be embedded in the page automatically (just like the <img> element in XHTML). You could use the XHTML <img> element for this.

XHTML versus XLink

Many simple linking tasks can be carried out with XHTML elements instead of XLink elements. XHTML 1.0 mimics the linking behavior of HTML, whereas it's expected that XHTML 2.0 will adopt the linking behavior of XLinks.

It's likely that most XML browsers will support XHTML semantics before they support XLink semantics (because XHTML is a more mature specification), so you might want to adopt XHTML namespaces for your simple linking tasks!

At the time this chapter was written, the XLink working group was still making changes to the specification, so it's far from stable. The broad details of XLink, however, are unlikely to change.

Chapter 16

The XML Path Language

*I*n XML documents, we need something to tell the software where to go in the document. XPath does just that.

In this chapter, you find out what paths are in an XML document. You also discover where paths lead, the language to use to describe them, and how to correctly document them.

Where Do XPaths Lead?

The word *path* has two meanings. It can mean the physical path that you walk along, or it can mean the route you take. When you leave the door of your house and walk to the local coffee bar, you walk along a path — probably a sidewalk. When you end up in a coffee bar, you can say that you've traced a path from your house to that place. The first use of *path* describes the network of sidewalks that makes up the paths in the place where you live. The second use of *path* describes the actual journey from your starting point to your destination.

An XML document also has a set of paths. When you navigate through an XML document using software, you trace a path through the document from one point to another.

Every journey has starting and ending points. In the case of the trip to the coffee bar, the journey starts at your front door and ends at the coffeehouse. Therefore, this path can be described.

Now we're going to throw another scenario your way. Suppose your friend George comes to stay with you and he wants to know how to get to a real bar, not the coffee bar. You might tell him something like this: "Take a left out the front door, go down to Main street, and make a right. The bar is the third building on the right side, and it has a sign that says McGintys."

In this case, you're providing a set of directions that aim to be both clear and concise. (We hope George doesn't have a "software" problem when it comes to navigation, so he can find he way back — unless he spends too much time at the bar, but that's not our concern!)

Note that our sample description includes a starting point (the front door) and a destination (McGintys). We also described three parts, or stages, to the journey. Each stage had not only a starting point and an ending point, but also a direction of travel. The final destination was also described in some detail so the complete description could be written as follows:

```
front door-right-Main St./(Main St.)-left-McGintys[3rd on
          right]
```

When you navigate through an XML document, you navigate along the paths of the XML document and trace a path that can be described. What is needed is a succinct language that not only describes the paths built into a document, but also describes how to follow a route through that document.

Here's how you might describe a path through an XHTML document.

```
"Starting at the top of the document, go to the root element
          <html>, then go to the <body> element, and then
          find the third <p> element."
```

This is quite simple and understandable to a human reader, but what you really want is a common simple language that you can use to describe this path to software. XPath is such a language.

The XPath specification, which you can find at www.w3.org/TR/xpath, is all about naming the XML paths that run through a document and providing a concise language to describe directions for how to get from one place to another in an XML document. The XPath specification is a stable recommendation.

Why do you need directions?

In XML, you need to know how to get from point A to point B only if there's some purpose to your journey. There's no equivalent in XML to the Sunday afternoon drive to see the fall colors. XML gurus navigating XML documents are like stern Puritans who travel only when they have a purpose.

In XML, you need a language to describe how to move about a document for two primary reasons:

- ✔ To find your way to and describe a section of a document that needs to be transformed. (This task involves XSL Transformations, or XLST. See Chapter 13 for more information.)

- ✔ To be able to point to a certain part of the document. (This task involves the use of XPointers. See Chapter 17 for more information on XPointers.)

XPath may be used for other purposes as well, but these two tasks provided the motivation for writing the XPath specification.

The paths and waystations of XML

To understand how XPath describes paths and directions, we're going to use the clients.xml document. This is an example of an XML document we might use to keep track of clients:

```
<?xml version="1.0" ?>
<!-- clients.xml-->
<Clients>
<!--This is the root element of clients.xml-->
  <Client id="c1">
    <Name>Jon Smith</Name>
    <Phone type="home">440-123-3333</Phone>
    <Fax>440-123-3334</Fax>
    <Email>jon@acme.com</Email>
  </Client>

  <Client id="c2">
    <Name>Bill Jones</Name>
    <Phone type="cellphone">330-124-5432</Phone>
    <Fax>440-123-5433</Fax>
    <Email>bjones@someinc.com</Email>
  </Client>

  <Client id="c3">
    <Name>Matt Brown</Name>
    <Phone type="work">220-125-1234</Phone>
    <Phone type="cellphone">233-344-4455</Phone>
    <Phone type="home">234-567-8910</Phone>
    <Fax>2200-125-1235</Fax>
    <Email>matthew@hotstuff.com</Email>
  </Client>
</Clients>
```

This document can be laid out like a tree, as in Figure 16-1.

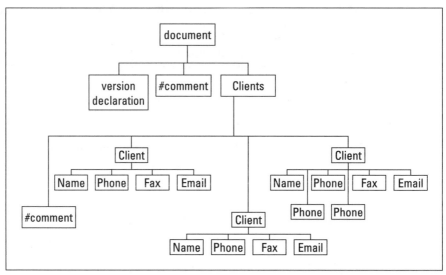

Figure 16-1:
A tree
diagram
shows the
various
parts of an
XML docu-
ment. We
omitted the
text and
attribute
nodes.

In Figure 16-1, all elements and comments in the clients.xml file appear as boxes. In XPath terminology, these are called nodes. *Nodes* in XPath are related to each other using the language of the family tree, which most of us know: child, parent, sibling, descendant, ancestor, and so on. (See Chapter 14 for more information.)

The name *node* is borrowed from biology. Every time a tree or a plant branches, there's said to be a node. Sometimes this comparison is carried even further, so a node that has no children is called a leaf. To clear up a potentially confusing point, various kinds of nodes in XML have different names, for example: text node, element node, comment node, document node, and root element node. For a detailed description of these terms see the "XPath Directions and Destinations" section.

For examples of some text and attribute nodes, see Figure 16-2. The text nodes contain the text content (such as the actual name, phone numbers, fax numbers, and email addresses) for each of the element nodes (Client), and the attribute nodes represent the attributes of these elements, namely the id attributes of client elements and the type attributes of phone elements.

Here are some examples of the XPath relationships among the various nodes in clients.xml:

- ✔ A single node called the document node contains the whole document.

- ✔ The document node contains three children: the version declaration, a comment node, and the root element node (Clients). These three very different nodes are all siblings!

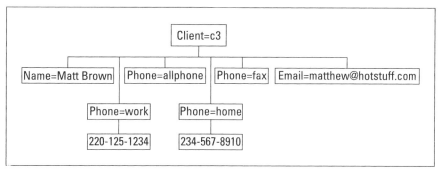

Figure 16-2:
Examples of
the text and
attribute
nodes for
the c3Client.

✔ The Clients node is the root element of the document. It's sometimes called the *document element*.

✔ The Clients node has four child nodes: a comment node and three Client nodes.

✔ The parent of the #comment node is the Clients node. The #comment node has no children (the text of a comment is considered part of the node), but has three siblings in the form of Client nodes.

✔ Each Client node has children of its own. For example, the third Client node has six children, a name node, three phone nodes, a fax node, and an e-mail node. All these nodes are siblings of one another.

✔ Each of these nodes has a text node, which is not shown in Figure 16-1, as a child.

✔ The parent of every phone node is a Client node.

✔ The grandparent of every phone node is the Clients node.

✔ All nodes, including all text nodes and attribute nodes, are descendants of the Clients node.

✔ Every node in the document, including the root element node and all attribute and text nodes, has the document node as its ancestor.

The XPath spec considers the parent of an attribute to be the element that contains it. This is different than the interpretation of the W3C Document Object Model (DOM), in which the attribute is considered to be a property of the element that contains it. So, in the XPath specification, the attribute nodes (not shown in Figure 16-1) have elements as their parents, and attribute nodes are not child nodes of their parents. Got that?

Believe it or not, although the attribute of an element is considered to have the element that contains it as its parent, it's not considered to be the child of its parent (shades of Oedipus, anyone?)! The reason for this contorted reasoning is all nerdy stuff that has to do with namespaces, which (thank goodness) we don't have to concern ourselves with here.

For more information on XML namespaces, see the W3C site at

`www.w3.org/TR/REC-xml-names/`

In addition to the nodes in our document, the XPath specification recognizes namespace nodes and processing instruction nodes — neither of which we need to consider further.

Before moving on and looking at how XPath gives out directions, here's a summary of the various node types recognized by XPath:

- ✔ **Document node:** The document node contains the whole document including all the version declarations and prolog, as well as the root node.

- ✔ **Root nodes:** The root node is the node that contains the whole written content of the document proper that comes after the prolog.

- ✔ **Element nodes:** The name of an element node is the same as its tag name.

- ✔ **Text nodes:** These are the text content of the elements.

- ✔ **Attribute nodes:** The name of an attribute node is the same as its attribute name.

- ✔ **Namespace nodes:** These are beyond the scope of this book. You just need to know they exist.

- ✔ **Processing instruction nodes:** These are also beyond the scope of the book. You just need to know they exist.

- ✔ **Comment nodes:** The comment nodes include the comments. This is not considered a separate text node.

XPath Directions and Destinations

In this section, you look at the language that XPath uses to describe a route through a document. We need to clarify that an XPath is a terse set of directions presented as a string, which is read by suitable software and is said to return a destination node or a set of nodes.

A *string* is a nerdy term for a line of text. Nerds would much rather talk about *a string of characters* than use a regular English expression such as *a phrase* or *a piece of text!* Similarly, when nerds talk about something being *returned,* they're talking about the *answer* a piece of software gives if you ask it a question.

Different implementations can use the set of directions in XPath in various ways. The XPointer specification uses this set of directions in its fragment identifier, and the XSL specification uses it as an attribute. In this chapter, we show you how to form that string using the rules set out in the XPath specification.

We also need to make it clear that XPath says nothing about what to do with a destination after it's been reached. Again, this is left up to the individual implementations that use XPath for their own purposes.

Every trip has three parts:

- ✔ The starting point
- ✔ The journey itself, which can be in various stages
- ✔ The destination

Here is what XPath has to say about each part

- ✔ **The starting point** is usually from the root node of the document. Sometimes, however, it may be another node in a document. Where the journey starts is called the *context node*.
- ✔ **The journey itself** consists of both a direction and a number of steps. XPath describes each of these steps using its syntax. Each step is separated by a forward slash (/). Sometimes a journey consists of one step; other times, many. In the following section, we look at several examples of these steps. Note that XPath calls the most important of its set of directions a LocationPath.
- ✔ **The destination** can be either a single node or a collection of nodes. This concept shouldn't be too difficult. For example, in a real journey, you could say your destination is 27 Palace Court, London, W1, or Europe, or England, or London, UK. All these statements are correct.

XPath says nothing about what to do when you reach your destination: It just describes the destination and how to get there.

LocationPaths: Describing the Journey

XPath uses two types of syntax: an abbreviated form and an unabbreviated form. In this section, you look at both forms. First, you look at the unabbreviated syntax because it's a little more descriptive and easier to follow.

A LocationPath searches for a node depending on the information you give it. The general syntax for a LocationPath is as follows:

```
axisname :: nodetest[expression1] [expression2] ...
```

Each part of this syntax is described as follows:

- ✔ axisname is the type of selection you want to perform. It also tells you the direction in the document that you need to travel. If you select child, descendant, or following-sibling as an axis, you travel forward in the document. If you select parent, ancestor, or previous-sibling, you travel back in the document. If you select self, you don't remain in the same location and don't move anywhere; in other words, you stand still.

- ✔ nodetest tests for the type of node you want to select. This is usually the name of a node.

- ✔ expression appears in square brackets and further refines your selection process for a node or set of nodes. There can be more than one expression (also called a *predicate* in the XPath specification).

Before getting into some of the details of XPath, we'd like to show you a few simple examples of LocationPaths using the clients.xml document. In the examples in the following sections, the starting point, or the context node, is the root element node (Clients) of clients.xml, unless otherwise stated.

Some simple location paths

Here are some simple examples of selection paths. First, we show you the code, and then we give a brief description. Our first example is

```
child::Clients
```

The axis is child and the node test is Clients. This selects all the child nodes of the context node named Clients.

```
child::*
```

The axis is child and the node test is *, which stands for a wildcard selection. This selects all the child nodes of the type element from the context node. Because an XML document can have only one root element, this example also selects all the nodes called Clients.

```
child::node()
```

The axis is child and the node test is node(), which selects all the child nodes of the document root, including the XML version declaration, the comment node, and the element node Clients.

Adding expressions

Here are some simple examples of expressions, which further refine the selection process. As before, first we show you the code, and then we give a brief description. Here's the first example:

```
child::Clients[position()=1]
```

The axis is child and the node test is Clients. We added an expression, [position()=1], which selects the first child node named Clients of the context node.

There's only one Clients node because it's the root element. However, you should still name the position of the specific node you want because software isn't very smart. It can't tell the difference between a list containing just one item and a single item. As far as software is concerned, child::Clients returns a list with a single item, and child::Clients[position()=1] returns a single node.

In this case, you could also use the last() function to return the last node in the list:

```
child::Clients[position()=last()]
```

Because there's only one node, this last node is identical to the first node in the list.

Taking steps

Having taken one step on the path, you can also take another one, and step into the document properly. XPath uses a forward slash to tell you when to take another step. The new context node is the node selected in the preceding step:

```
child::Clients[position()=1]/child::Client
```

Note how after that step, you make a new LocationPath. The previous syntax selects all the Client element children of the root element.

More on adding expressions

The use of the position() function should be obvious:

```
child::Client[position()=last()]
```

The axis is `child` and the node test is `Client`. We added an expression, `[position()=last]`, which selects the last child node of `Clients` named `Client`.

Looking at attributes

You can use the value of attributes to narrow your selection of a destination node. For example:

```
child::Client[attribute::id= "c3"]
```

The axis is `child` and the node test is `Client`. The expression is itself another LocationPath with an axis of `attribute` and a node test of `id= "c3"`. This selects all the child elements of `Clients`, which are not only named *Client* but also have an `id` attribute with a value equal to `"c3"`. In other words, the last Client element is selected.

May I see your ID?

Because an ID attribute is unique in an XML document, we can use a special function, the `id()` function, to select a node in the document. You don't need to describe any steps or trace any paths. If you just write the path

```
id()= "c3"
```

the software will find the correct node!

For this to work, the document must have a DTD so the software can check that the attribute you've called `id` is indeed of type `ID`. See Chapter 17 for more details on IDs.

Going backwards

You can also step backwards. If you start from the document root, you have nowhere to go. It's like the old joke of the man taking a picture of his wife on the edge of the Grand Canyon!

For these next examples, we assume that the context node is the last `<Email>` element of the third `<Client>`, that is, the e-mail element with the content `matthew@hotmail.com`. Here's the first example:

```
preceding-sibling::Fax
```

This returns all the preceding sibling elements called `Fax`, in other words, just one element. The next example:

```
preceding-sibling::Phone
```

returns all the preceding `sibling` elements called `Phone`. In this particular case, it describes three phone elements. Finally:

```
parent::Client
```

returns the parent element provided it's named `Client`. In this particular case, it indeed returns its parent.

Reversing direction

When you start going backwards, you also reverse the direction of counting for the `position()` function. So, if you assumed the same context node as in the preceding section, this example:

```
preceding-sibling::*[position()=1]
```

would return the phone node of `type="home"` and

```
preceding-sibling::*[position()=last()]
```

would return the `name` node.

Null results

Sometimes, we ask for something and nothing is there! For example:

```
parent::MoneyBags
```

returns the preceding parent element provided it's called `MoneyBags`. Alas, there is no parent called `MoneyBags`, so XPath returns a null result.

Null is another one of those nerdy terms that crop up from time to time. It means that not only is nothing there, but also that nothing has ever been there. Null is different from empty, nothing, or zero. As an example of the difference between null and nothing, consider a text box in a form. If you ask (through code) for the contents of that text box before anything has been filled in, you receive a null value. If you fill out the form with your name, you receive a value that is the same as your name. If you erase your name so that the box is empty, you will not receive a null value. You receive an empty string value or, in other words, nothing!

Getting to the root of things

The root of a document is different from the root element. It's one step behind the root element. You can always go back to the root of a document using the forward slash (/). If the context node is still the e-mail node,

```
/child::*
```

would select the root element of the document Clients. The / takes us back to the root of the document, child is an axis that selects the children, and * makes sure that you only select the element children. Because of the rules of XML, there can only be one root element, which means that this construct always selects the root element of the document.

The Axes of XPath

Here are the various axes that XPath provides and a brief description of each:

- ✔ child selects the children of the context node
- ✔ descendant selects from any of the descendants of the context node
- ✔ parent selects the parent node
- ✔ ancestor selects from all the ancestor nodes
- ✔ following-sibling selects from all the following siblings
- ✔ preceding-sibling selects from all the preceding siblings
- ✔ following is any following node other than attribute or namespace nodes
- ✔ preceding is any preceding node other than attribute or namespace nodes
- ✔ attribute contains the attributes of the context node
- ✔ namespace is beyond the scope of this book; you just need to know that it exists
- ✔ self contains just the context node itself
- ✔ descendant-or-self contains the context node or any of its descendants
- ✔ ancestor-or-self contains the context node or any of its ancestors

The Short Version

XPath is designed to be used with XPointers when it will be part of a fragment identifier, or with XSL where it will be part of an attribute. For this reason, it makes sense to provide a less verbose syntax. This is called the abbreviated syntax for XPath.

The most important abbreviation is `child::`. This abbreviates to . . . wait for it . . nothing!

Client axis abbreviations

Here are some of the previous examples from this chapter set out with their abbreviated equivalents:

- ✔ `child::Client` abbreviates to `Client`
- ✔ `child::*` abbreviates to `*`
- ✔ `child::node()` abbreviates to `node()`
- ✔ `child::text()` abbreviates to `text()` and selects all text nodes of the context node

Attribute axis abbreviation

Other important abbreviations are of the `attribute` axis and some of the predicates. The `attribute::` axis abbreviates to the @ symbol. So the example

```
child::Client[attribute::id= "c3"]
```

abbreviates to

```
Client[@id= "c3"]
```

Predicate and expression abbreviations

There are several useful abbreviations for the expressions. The `position` expression abbreviates to nothing; therefore

```
child::Client[position()=1]
```

abbreviates to

```
Client[1]
```

This simply selects the first client element of the context node. The next expression:

```
child::Client[position()=last()]
```

selects the last child of the context node. It must retain the empty parentheses. Therefore, it abbreviates to

```
Client[last()]
```

Here are some other abbreviations:

```
Client[>1]
```

selects all the client nodes other than the first client node. The next one:

```
Client[< last()]
```

selects all the client nodes other than the last client node. And, wait, there's more:

```
Client[last()-1]
```

This selects the client node immediately before the last client node. Finally:

```
child::Client[position()=1]/child::phone
```

abbreviates to

```
Client[1]/phone
```

Some more abbreviations

Here are a few more abbreviations. The context node abbreviates to a dot (.). The descendant axis abbreviates to a forward slash, so the following:

```
descendants::Phone
```

which select all the phone elements in the document, abbreviates to

```
/Phone
```

Several more XPath abbreviations and functions are possible, but the previous examples are the ones you'll use in all but the most esoteric cases. To see the other examples, consult the specification at www.w3c.org/TR/xpath.

Using XPath with XPointer and XSL

By themselves XPath expressions are not much good. They're just language that describes how to select a set of nodes or a single node from a document. To be of use, you must combine them with some other application.

In XPointers, the expressions of XPath are used to point software to a particular spot in the document. See Chapter 17 for more information.

In XSL, XPath expressions are used to select a node or a whole series of nodes so they can either be transformed from one XML tag set to another tag set or have styles applied to them.

There are other potential uses for XPath expressions, such as a simple XML query language for retrieving hunks of data from an XML document.

Where Now?

XPath is a bit abstract because it's really a tool designed to be used with XML documents. You can look at one of its uses in Chapter 17, and you can see how you could use XPath with XSL in Chapter 13.

Another fun application of XPath is foiund in a language called Schematron, which uses XPath (and some XSL) to describe document structures. (To find out more about Schematron, visit `www.ascc.net/xml/resource/ schematron/schematron.html`.) To you, all this XPath stuff might not seem like fun, but in the drab lives that document nerds live, it looks like Mardi Gras!

Chapter 17

The XML Pointer Language

In This Chapter

▶ Examining the purpose of XPointers

▶ Figuring out what XPointers do

▶ Discussing how XPointers work

*I*n this chapter, you find out about the XML XPointer specification. In addition, you find out how to use XPointers to pinpoint locations inside a
document.

Anchors (and Fragments) Away

A *pointer* takes you to a specific spot inside a document. You're probably
familiar with the concept of pointers from surfing the Web; when you click a
hyperlink, you're taken to a location in a Web document. This location can be
at the head of a new page, in the middle of a page, or at a specific heading in
a page.

A similar event happens if you click a hyperlinked table of contents — you're
taken down the page to a specific heading. In classic HTML, this trick is
accomplished using the name attribute in an anchor (<a>) element. You're
not so much pointed to a spot as you are led there.

Consider the following HTML document:

```
<html>
<title>Origins of the Great Depression</title>
<p>Lots of markup and content goes here</p>
<a name= "h3hoover"></a>
<h3>Hoover's role in the economy</h3>
<p> President Hoover was a most unlikely villain. Rarely has
          a public figure been so unjustly blamed. . .</p>
<p>lots more markup and content goes here</p>
</html>
```

To get to the "Hoover's role in the economy" section, you'd probably click a link somewhere with something similar to the following syntax:

```
It's important to understand <a href=
        "depression.htm#h3hoover"> Hoover's role</a> in
        the economy. . .
```

The part of the URL after the hash mark (#), is known as a *fragment identifier* (see Figure 17-1). It associates the document fragment, "Hoover's role," with the <a> element named h3hoover.

Figure 17-1:
The
fragment
identifier of
the URL.

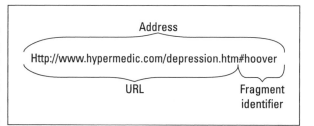

Using the anchor element and the fragment identifier works fairly well, but this method has one major drawback: To point into a resource, you must have not only access the document containing the link but also access to the destination document and the ability to edit it. Remember that this method doesn't really point into the document; it leads you by the nose to the spot where it wants you to be!

Why Do We Need XPointers?

We need a method for getting to places inside a document even though we don't have editing privileges for that document. This is where XML Pointers (XPointers) come into play. XPointers provide several mechanisms to create links into specific document locations. The XPointer syntax can take you to a place inside a document and also select a large chunk of that document.

You saw the beginnings of this syntax in the HTML markup in the preceding section. Reconsider that HTML markup; this time assume, for the sake of argument, that the h3 heading included an id attribute:

```
<h3 id="hoover_role">Hoover's role in the economy</h3>
<p> President Hoover was a most unlikely villain. Rarely has
        a public figure been so unjustly blamed. . .</p>
```

Now you can point inside the destination document even though you don't have access to it. The link in the URL looks like this:

```
It's important to understand<a href=
           "depression.htm#hoover_role"> Hoover's role</a> in
           the economy. . .
```

Now the fragment identifier appears as the value of an id attribute in the destination document. The URL depression.htm#hoover_role would also take you to the correct spot in the destination document! Of course, you'd have to be using a browser that supports XPointers — because it's up to your software to implement this method. To paraphrase how Winston Churchill might have addressed browser makers, "We can give you the tools, but you will have to finish the job yourself."

The term URL, which stands for Uniform Resource Locator, is hallowed by tradition, but more and more the more generic term Uniform Resource Identifier (URI) is used.

The Promise of XPointers

HTML pointers have proven their worth, but XPointers promise much, much more! A future XPointer-based application will be able to not only point into any part of a document (even if its elements aren't labeled with id attributes), but also select an entire section of a document. Okay, so you're asking what exactly do you mean by "select an entire section of the document?" Here's a little further explanation.

Presently, an HTML browser that supports HTML pointers can take you to the section that you want as long as the right anchor element is defined. For example, suppose that you access a large document with 30 subsections, and you're interested in section 25 of that document. Current HTML-based browsers download and display the whole document and move the cursor to the beginning of section 25. This is useful, but the drawback is that even though you're not interested in the other 29 sections, you must still download and display them!

A browser based on the new XML-based XPointers would give you the option of selecting only section 25 for download and display. To do this, the browser needs a mechanism to identify not only the start point for the display but also its end point. XPointer syntax makes this possible because it allows you to select a range in the document. In other words, XPointer syntax allows you to isolate a complete section of the document.

How Do XPointers Work?

As of this writing, the XPointer language is a candidate recommendation of the W3C.

Check out the XPointer specification at

```
www.w3.org/TR/xptr
```

XPointer provides three methods to point into a document as follows:

- ✔ The first is a shorthand method that employs IDs.

- ✔ The second is a shorthand method that uses a simple syntax to step you through a document.

- ✔ The third method uses full-blown XPath syntax. With this method, XPointer also provides a mechanism to select a section or a range within a document.

See Chapter 16 for more information on XPath.

Now you need to understand how each of these XPointer methods works with an XML document. We'll use the same Clients.xml document that's in Chapter 16. (The id attribute of the client element has been declared to be of type ID. See the "What if I don't have my ID?" section later in this chapter for more details.)

```
<?xml version="1.0"?>
<!DOCTYPE clients SYSTEM "clients.dtd">
<Clients>
<!--This is clients.xml-->
  <Client id="c1">
    <Name>Jon Smith</Name>
    <Phone type="home">440-123-3333</Phone>
    <Fax>440-123-3334</Fax>
    <Email>jon@acme.com</Email>
  </Client>
  <Client id="c2">
    <Name>Bill Jones</Name>
    <Phone type="cellphone">330-124-5432</Phone>
    <Fax>440-123-5433</Fax>
    <Email>bjones@someinc.com</Email>
  </Client>
  <Client id="c3">
    <Name>Matt Brown</Name>
    <Phone type="work">220-125-1234</Phone>
    <Phone type="cellphone">233-344-4455</Phone>
```

```
    <Phone type="home">234-567-8910</Phone>
    <Fax>2200-125-1235</Fax>
    <Email>matthew@hotstuff.com</Email>
  </Client>
</Clients>
```

Show me your ID

You assign the ID in XPointer in the same way you do in HTML. The fragment identifier is simply the name of the ID attribute, so the URI (User Resource Identifier, a reference mechanism that works much like a URL):

```
Clients.xml#c3
```

points the *user agent* (known to ordinary mortals as a *browser*) to the client element with id c3, which is the element with all the information on Matt Brown.

If there's no c3 id, the pointer-enabled browser acts as if the fragment identifier is not present and points to the top of the document.

Please step me through this!

The second shorthand method to point into a document involves a set of integers separated by forward slashes. Each slash represents a level of nesting, and each integer represents the position of some element in that nesting level.

The first forward slash (/) represents the root of the document and, because there can be only one root element, is always followed by 1. Thus:

```
Clients.xml#/1
```

points you to the Clients element.

Adding a step, such as

```
Clients.xml#/1/2
```

points you to the second child element of the Clients element, namely the second Client element. Finally:

```
Clients.xml#/1/2/4
```

points you to the fourth child of the second child of the Clients element, namely, the Email element of the second Client's element.

See whether you can figure out where

```
Clients.xml#/1/3/1
```

takes you! (Hint: It's the first child of the third child of the Clients element, namely the Name element of the Matt Brown record.)

Show me the path

The third method for XPointers is very powerful! It uses XPath to describe a document location. To use this method, we use the xptr() function in our fragment identifier. Here's the general syntax for a fragment identifier:

```
#xptr( XPath expression )
```

xptr, which must be all lowercase, tells the browser that we're about to use an XPath as a locating device.

Now all we have to do is insert an XPath expression. (Note that XPath is used by both XSLT and XPointer.) Because this is covered in detail in Chapter 16, we show only one example here.

The following URL points to the second client element in our document:

```
Clients.xml#xptr( child::Clients[1]/child::Client[posi-
         tion()=2]) )
```

Here's an abbreviated version:

```
Clients.xml#xptr(Clients[1]/ Client[2]) )
```

Here's an even more abbreviated version:

```
Clients.xml#xptr(// Client[2]) )
```

Note that all these abbreviations are explained in Chapter 16.

The context node of an XPointer is the document node, not the root element, so we have to step to the first element.

The *root node* of a document is a node that contains the whole document, including the version declaration and the document element.

Where do I start?

When you write an XPath expression, you start tracing the path from a start position, which XPath calls the *context node* for the path. In XPointer, this start position is always the root node of the document, so

```
Clients.xml#xptr(child::*[position()=1])
```

which can be abbreviated to

```
Clients.xml#xptr(*[1])
```

always selects the document node of a well-formed XML document. In the Clients.xml document, it selects the root element `Clients`. (See Chapter 16 for more information on abbreviations.)

However, what happens in the common situation in which a link in a document refers to some other place in the same document? Is the `context` node of XPath still the root node of the document? The answer is "Yes!"

In a way, this is a good thing, because it means you can use the same syntax for every single pointer reference, no matter where it appears in a document.

Sometimes, you might like to make a reference using the place where the reference occurs as the context node, or starting point. XPointer gives you a way to start from where such a link appears in your document by using the `here()` method.

Check out the following section of code:

```
<Section>
    <Para>In the Middle Ages the Church appeared to be. .
            .</Para>
    <Para>As in any monopoly, the temptation for abuse of
            power was always present. . .</Para>
    <Para>In the
        <Mylink
            xlink:href="#xptr(here()/parent/parent[1])">first
            paragraph<Mylink> we saw that. . .</Para>
</Section>
```

The XPointer is

```
#xptr(here()/parent/parent[1])
```

We used the abbreviated XPath syntax. Here's how things work:

- ✔ The `here()` function puts the context node at the node that contains it, which happens to be the `mylink` element.

- ✔ The first step, `/parent`, selects the parent node of `mylink`, which is the `para` element containing the `mylink` element.

- ✔ The second step, `/parent[1]`, selects the parent node of the `para` element, which is the `section` element. The `[1]` selects the first child of this node, in other words, the first child element.

What if I don't have my ID?

In the United States, if you have a baby face and want to buy beer, chances are you'll be asked to show an ID to prove that you're of legal drinking age. If you don't have your ID, the rule is "No ID, no beer!" (Some of us are long past the age where anyone asks for our ID, though.)

A similar thing happens with XPointers. When an XPointer-enabled browser comes across a fragment identifier that claims to point at an ID, it demands to see some proof that the attribute is indeed of the type ID. The only way it can do this is to look at the document type declaration. If a Document Type Definition (DTD) isn't present or can't be found, a similar rule applies: "No ID, no can point!" See Chapter 5 for more information on DTDs.

However, the Lords of XML are not as hard-hearted as our enlightened legislators. They have provided you with an alternative should you fail to find your ID! They allow you to string two pointers together, so if the first pointer fails, the browser can move on to a second pointing method! (Sort of like going to another store in the hopes that the clerk thinks you actually look your age.)

Here's how this works. Following is the fragment identifier that can find an ID:

```
#xptr( id()= "c3")
```

Now, this works just fine if your browser can find the DTD for Clients.xml. But, what if it can't? In that case, it returns an error and shows you the whole document starting from the top. Note that the DTD may very well be there, but for some reason the browser just can't access it — an all-too-common occurrence!

However, if you use this markup instead

```
#xptr( id()= "c3")xptr(//*[@id= "c3"/parent::node()])
```

your browser goes on to evaluate the second XPointer expression if the first fails. Because the second expression doesn't rely on the fact that the id attribute is of type ID, it succeeds.

You provided yourself with an insurance policy. You can run together as many xptr() expressions as you want, and they are evaluated from left to right. The second is evaluated only if the first returns an error, and the third is evaluated only if both the first and second return an error, and so on. Just another case of persistence paying off.

How much can I get you?

As mentioned, one of the cool things about XPointers is that they can identify not only a start point but also a whole section of a document. None of the current browsers supports XPointers yet, but when they do, they'll have the option of displaying the entire document or just a portion of it.

XPointers allow us to display just a portion of the document because they can specify a range by using the to keyword with an XPath expression on either side. For example:

```
Xptr(id("c2") to id("c3"))
```

selects the following part of the Clients.xml document:

```
<Client id="c2">
    <Name>Bill Jones</Name>
    <Phone type="cellphone">330-124-5432</Phone>
    <Fax>440-123-5433</Fax>
    <Email>bjones@someinc.com</Email>
</Client>
```

Ranges can get quite complicated. The only rule you need to know is that the start of the range must occur before the end of the range, and that the range must occur in the same document.

Other XPointer methods and functions

XPointer provides several other functions that you may use in esoteric situations, but what has been described in this chapter describes 99 percent of the functionality of XPointers.

If you want to involve yourself in the minutia of XPointers, read the W3C specification at

```
www.w3.org/TR/WD-xptr
```

Happy pointing!

Part VI
Sampling XML Applications

The 5th Wave   By Rich Tennant

"Just how accurately should my Web site reflect my place of business?"

In this part. . .

The real power of XML comes from its capability to capture, organize, and represent data of many different kinds. Part VI helps give some substance to this claim, as you explore three of the most popular XML applications in broad use today.

Chapter 18 covers the Channel Definition Format (CDF), used to create so-called push channels for automatic delivery of information across the Web. Next, Chapter 19 waxes mathematical, as it covers the Mathematical Markup Language (MathML). Chapter 20 examines the markup required to create book-length projects using XML by tackling the industry-standard DocBook initiative, originally developed for software documentation.

Chapter 18

XML Can Channel from Many Sources

*C*hannel is one of the many Internet buzzwords used today. This chapter introduces you to the concept of channels and where and how they're being used. The XML vocabulary behind active channels is the Channel Definition Format (CDF). In the next few pages, you find out how this XML-based format is defined and how you can use it to create your own channels. As channel technology has developed, its uses have been expanded to provide more than just delivery of Web data. With CDF, you can add channels to your Web pages and find out how to use an XML vocabulary at the same time.

What Is a Channel?

The word *channel* can appear in many different contexts, some of which seem to have little in common. The best-known use of the word *channel* is in reference to television programming. Although we might use the term daily, we rarely think about what a channel really is and how it's defined.

If you're interested in sports, you tune into your favorite sports channel on TV; if the latest news is what you want, you find a 24-hour news station. In other words, a *channel* — in the television world anyway — provides you with an established resource for a particular kind of information. These days, every subject — from animals, to cartoons, to soap operas — has its own TV channel. When you want the latest and greatest of a particular kind of information, you simply tune into an appropriate channel.

Now take the concept of a channel one step further and apply it to newspapers and periodicals. When you choose a newspaper or a magazine, your motivations are similar to those when selecting a TV channel. You might choose a newspaper with a focus on business or finance, such as *The Wall Street Journal*, or one with a focus on local events, such as the *Austin American-Statesman* (if you live in Austin, that is).

Even magazines and newspapers are subdivided into information channels. If you're interested in sports, local news, or the comics, you can turn directly to the corresponding section that is a part of a larger newspaper channel.

Are you starting to see a pattern here? TV channels, newspapers, and magazines all classify information by type and present it to you in a way that makes it easier for you to find the particular bits of information that interest you. Channels on the Web use the same concept to deliver specific, focused information.

Web channels allow you to categorize and describe Web site content and to make that data available to users on demand. When you sort and categorize information, it's easier for your users to access and utilize your offerings. In addition to making it easier for users to locate information as they surf, Web channels also make it possible for you to send updated content directly to your users' browsers or desktops without requiring them to request that content explicitly, using a standard Web address. This automatic delivery of information is called *push publishing,* or *push technology*.

Smart pull and push

When you surf the Internet, your browser retrieves pages from a Web browser. This type of retrieval is usually known as *pulling* because your browser pulls pages from a server at your command and displays them on your desktop.

Channels allow you to go much further. Assume — for the time being anyway — that you can browse information in your Web browser (which you can with Internet Explorer 4.0 and 5.0). Your browser uses channels to gather information in one of two ways:

  ✔ **Smart pull** is similar to a regular pull — the browser pulls Web pages from Web servers — but with two important differences

> **The pull is directed**: You use a file that tells the browser where to find relevant information, so it can return to that same location posthaste to get you the latest and greatest content.

> **You can automate the pull**: You can set up the browser so it automatically checks for new information on any server you specify. Channels are more than bookmarks because they not only mark a great site but also revisit that site on a regular basis — without any action on your part — to gather the latest information posted to that site.

✔ **Push** reverses the idea of traditional Web browsing. Instead of you, the user, directing the browser to get information from a site, a process on the server sends all the latest information from a site directly to your Web browser. In a nutshell, the browser no longer has to go out to the Web — the Web comes to the browser.

Automated smart pull and push work only if your computer is on and connected to the Internet through a modem or a network. If you plan to use smart pull or to sign up for a channel that uses push technology, remember that you need to turn your computer on and hook it up to the Internet before you can receive new data. Conversely, if you plan to use channels on your Web site to provide information to your users, make sure the users know how important it is that their computers be powered up and connected to the Internet before they can take full advantage of channel updates.

Technically, smart pull can cause a browser to have a computer dial out and make a connection to the Internet automatically. A browser has this power over the computer and the phone line only if users give it that power in their browser preferences.

Don't panic and worry that push publishing and channels mean that any content provider can send any content they want to your Web browser — sort of like junk mail or commercials. You can receive information from a channel through push only if you subscribe to that channel and set your preferences to indicate that you want to receive regular push publishing updates from that channel.

Where does XML fit in?

The concept of channels is a cool one, but you may be wondering exactly where XML fits into the big picture. It's fairly simple really: The instructions that create a channel are described using CDF, which is an XML application.

CDF tags and attributes provide channel developers with a set of tools to define their channels, to identify logos representing their channels, to schedule channel updates, and more. We examine CDF in depth in just a few pages (see the "Building Channels with Basic CDF" section later in this chapter) and show you how to describe your own channel. First, however, we thought you might like to see some results and maybe even subscribe to a channel or two yourself.

Subscribing to channels

Before you think about creating your own channels, you might want to spend some time looking at other channels to see how other developers use them to describe and deliver content.

Remember that a channel is just a different way to receive Web content. XML describes a channel, but the actual channel content is plain ol' Web content consisting of HTML documents, graphics, scripting, and maybe some multimedia.

Before you can subscribe to a channel, you need a Web browser that supports CDF and channels. Because CDF is a Microsoft initiative, Internet Explorer is your best bet for subscribing to and taking full advantage of channels. If you don't have Internet Explorer 4.0 or 5.0, you won't be able to see channels in all their glory.

All the instructions and screen shots in this chapter use Internet Explorer 5.0 for Windows. If you have Internet Explorer 4.0 for Windows or Macintosh, the steps for creating a channel are slightly different. Check your help system for specific instructions.

To subscribe to a channel, you have to visit a Web site that offers channel services. If you don't know where to start, choose Channels from the Internet Explorer Favorites menu, as shown in Figure 18-1, for some suggestions.

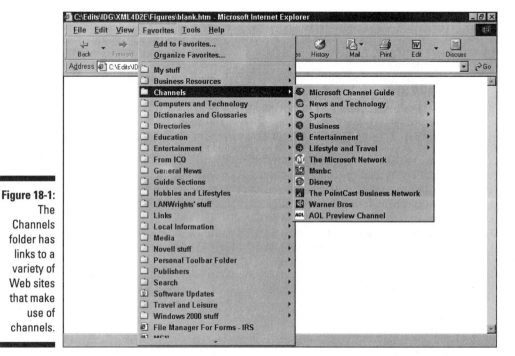

Figure 18-1:
The Channels folder has links to a variety of Web sites that make use of channels.

If you're interested in news and the latest goings-on in the world, *The New York Times* has a great channel. To subscribe to *The New York Times* channel, point your browser to www.nytimes.com/channel/home.html and simply click the Add Channel link, as shown in Figure 18-2.

Internet Explorer grabs the channel information from *The New York Times* Web server, and then a dialog box appears letting you know that the channel has been added to your Favorites menu. In addition, you have an opportunity to specify a folder for the channel link to live in, as shown in Figure 18-3.

After you click OK in the Add Channel dialog box, the channel becomes a fixture in your Favorites menu until you delete it. *The New York Times* listing in the Favorites menu actually includes five different links to various information, including quick news and special features, shown in Figure 18-4.

Figure 18-2:
Click Add Channel to subscribe to *The New York Times* Web channel.

Figure 18-3:
A channel is
being added
to your
Favorites
menu.

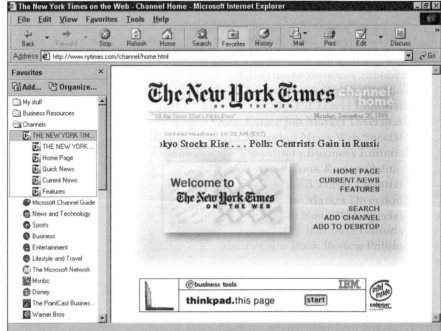

Figure 18-4:
When you
subscribe to
a channel,
you often
have access
to multiple
channel
pages on
one Web
site.

Setting a schedule to download content

So you've subscribed to a channel, but so far, it's really no different than any other site you've added to your favorites. How do you take the channel one step further and set up schedules to download the latest content? It's fairly simple:

1. **Right-click on the channel name — not any of the pages listed under the channel — and choose Properties from the drop-down menu.**

   The channel's Properties dialog box appears.

2. **Click to add a check mark to the Make This Page Available Offline option.**

   This adds two more tabs to the dialog box and gives you the options you need to schedule downloads, as shown in Figure 18-5.

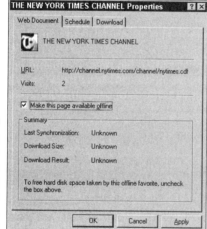

Figure 18-5:
This is where you can schedule downloads.

3. **To schedule specific times for your browser to check a site for new content, select the Schedule tab.**

4. **Click the Use the Following Schedule(s) option and then click the Add button.**

   The New Schedule dialog box appears, as shown in Figure 18-6.

5. **Enter your desired schedule.**

   If your online time or disk space is limited, you can control what and how much content is downloaded each time your browser checks a channel for an update from the Download tab. You can also tell your browser to send you email automatically when there's new content to view, as shown in Figure 18-7.

6. **When you've finished making your selections, click OK.**

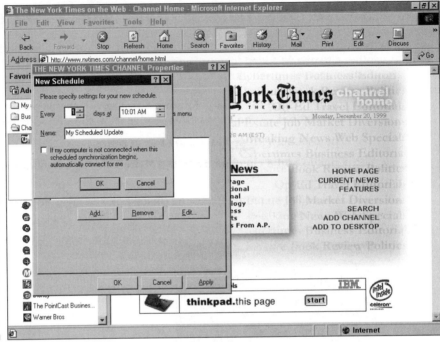

Figure 18-6:
Create your own schedule for checking a channel for new information.

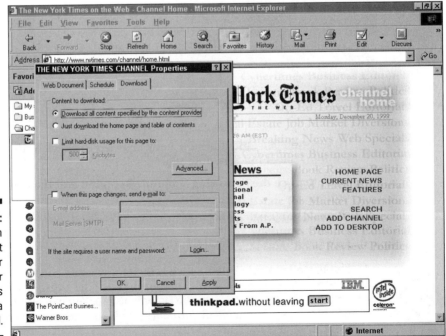

Figure 18-7:
You can control what content your browser receives from a channel.

And that's all there is to subscribing to a channel. Now that you know how to subscribe to a channel, it's time to find out how to build them for your users.

Building Channels with Basic CDF

The Channel Definition Format (CDF) is an XML application designed to describe channel information. Microsoft is not the only vendor that supports CDF; other vendors, including DataChannel and PointCast, use this delivery mechanism as part of their specialized intranet solutions.

In this section, you encounter the basic elements of CDF, find out what type of data the elements describe, and discover what it takes to add a channel to a Web page.

In the following example, we show you a simple but good example of a CDF file that can live on a Web server and direct the day-to-day functions of a Web channel:

```
<?xml version="1.0" ?>
<CHANNEL HREF="http://www.myxml.net">
    <TITLE>MyXML - XML for Everyone</TITLE>
    <ABSTRACT>
        MyXML is a non-profit organization that wants to
        foster the adoption of XML technology. MyXML members
        are drawn from different industries and countries all
        over the world. Here you will find all relevant
        information about using XML in your information
        delivery solutions.
    </ABSTRACT>
</CHANNEL>
```

MyXML is a fictitious non-profit organization whose goal is to promote the use and adoption of XML technology. The site isn't real — not yet, anyway.

The preceding code represents the most basic of CDF files; its elements are found in just about every real CDF file in use. Because you'll see these elements over and over again, here's a line-by-line analysis:

✔ `<?xml version= "1.0" ?>` is a processing instruction. It states that the document is a version 1 XML application, which makes sure there isn't any confusion on the subject.

✔ `<CHANNEL>. . .</CHANNEL>` is the document element for any CDF file. All the information about a channel, as well as the other channel elements, is nested within this element. The `<CHANNEL>. . .</CHANNEL>` element takes one important attribute — `HREF` — which you probably recognize from HTML.

- ✔ HREF= "http://www.myxml.net" points to the top level of the fictitious www.myxml.net site. In the *New York Times* channel you subscribed to, the value for this attribute would be http://www.nytimes.com/channel/home.html because that's the URL for the site's channel-related information. The HREF attribute can point to just about any site you want it to, but it usually points to a top-level HTML page that is the starting point for a collection of channel resources.

- ✔ <TITLE>. . .</TITLE> allows you to describe the content of a channel in a few concise words.

- ✔ <ABSTRACT>. . .</ABSTRACT> allows you to provide a more wordy and detailed description of the information in your channel.

The title and abstract for your channel can be crucial to its success because they're the first things users see when they investigate any channel. Titles and abstracts often help users decide whether they want to venture into your channel content and become subscribers. Make your title short and concise. Naming your channel "My Channel" may be a bit too concise and is certainly too vague. We titled our channel "MyXML — XML for Everyone" for our example. Your abstract should provide a succinct description of the type of information users can expect to get from your channel. (The code earlier in this section shows our abstract.)

CDF Unleashed

In this section, we tell you all about CDF and provide you with the information you need to get started building channels. When you're finished with this section, you'll be a channel master. Just try not to let it go to your head, grasshoppa.

Scheduling channel updates

Remember, when you subscribe to a channel, you can schedule how often you want your browser to check the channel for new information. On the channel side, you can specify how often you're going to update your channel information — after all, it's your channel and you control it. It's not surprising that the CDF element for a schedule is <SCHEDULE>. . .</SCHEDULE>. To specify that the MyXML channel updates information every four hours, add this bit of code to the CDF document that describes the channel:

```
<SCHEDULE>
    <INTERVALTIME HOUR="4" />
</SCHEDULE>
```

To specify that the channel is updated only once every four days, use this bit of code:

```
<SCHEDULE>
    <INTERVALTIME DAY="4" />
</SCHEDULE>
```

You can also assign a start and end date to your schedule using the START and END attributes with the <SCHEDULE>. . .</SCHEDULE> tags, like this:

```
<SCHEDULE START="2000-01-01" END="2001-01-10">
    <INTERVALTIME HOUR="4" />
</SCHEDULE>
```

When you specify start and end dates, the only format you can use is YYYY-MM-DD.

What if you're a content provider with thousands of clients accessing your system? If each and every client is set to download updates from your site — even if it's every hour or every other day — your servers are going to get hit hard every time the scheduled update time comes around. This is not a good thing. Recognizing this dilemma, the developers of CDF created a way for you to specify a time during which clients can get updates, instead of one specific time. Here's how you do that:

```
<SCHEDULE>
    <INTERVALTIME HOUR="12" />
    <EARLIESTTIME HOUR="1" />
    <LATESTTIME HOUR="2" />
</SCHEDULE>
```

This bit of code uses the <INTERVALTIME> element to specify how many hours (12 in this example) should elapse between update windows. The <EARLIESTTIME> element specifies when the update window opens, and the <LATESTTIME> element specifies when the window closes. Therefore, our bit of code creates two update windows each day: the first between 1 a.m. and 2 a.m. and the second between 1 p.m. and 2 p.m.

Controlling Web page retrieval

Remember that HTML pages represent the content that makes up your channels. You can use CDF to control how different Web pages that make up a channel get downloaded. A variety of attributes appended to the <CHANNEL> . . . </CHANNEL> element help describe how channel pages should be handled, including the following:

✓ LASTMOD specifies when the channel content was last updated. A browser can check this attribute and download only those pages that have been updated after the date specified by this attribute. You can specify both date and time using this format: YYYY-MM-DDTHour:Minute.

✓ PRECACHE specifies whether your content should be stored in a Web browser's temporary memory after download. The default value for this attribute is YES, although you can set it to NO. If you turn pre-caching off (make the value of the attribute NO), users aren't able to download channel content and read it off line.

✓ LEVEL specifies how many levels of pages of your channel's content will be downloaded during an update. A value of LEVEL="1" causes all pages that can be reached with one hyperlink jump to download to a browser; LEVEL="2" causes all pages within two hyperlink jumps to be downloaded; and so on. Before you set the value of this attribute to 50, remember that many users have limited connection time. The more content you try to make them download, the less likely you are to keep them as subscribers. Keep your updates short and simple, with only one or two levels of pages downloading at a time, and your users will appreciate your site even more.

This next snippet of code directs browsers to download pages modified after 3 p.m. on January 1, 2000. It also fetches all pages that are two hyperlink jumps away or less and allows the downloaded pages to be stored in the user's cache:

```
<CHANNEL HREF="http://www.myxml.net"
    LASTMOD="2000-01-01T15:00"
    LEVEL="2"
    PRECACHE="YES">
</CHANNEL>
```

Defining sections within your channel

The New York Times channel has several different sections in it, each relating to a specific topic, including:

✓ Home Page

✓ Quick News

✓ Current News

✓ Features

Each of these topics is an individual item within a CDF document. As you might expect, the ⟨ITEM⟩. . .⟨/ITEM⟩ element describes each specific section of a channel. You can create individual titles for each item and describe each item with an abstract as well.

For fun, suppose you want to break the MyXML site down into three different sections:

- ✔ Online Resources
- ✔ XML News
- ✔ Tools and Techniques

To do so, you expand the original CDF document so it looks like this:

```
<?xml version="1.0" ?>
<CHANNEL HREF="http://www.myxml.net">
   <TITLE>MyXML - XML for Everyone</TITLE>
   <ABSTRACT>
      MyXML is a non-profit organization that wants to
      foster the adoption of XML technology. MyXML members
      are drawn from different industries and countries all
      over the world. Here you will find all relevant
      information about using XML in your information
      delivery solutions.
   </ABSTRACT>

   <ITEM HREF= "http://www.myxml.net/online/">
      <TITLE>MyXML - Online Resources</TITLE>
      <ABSTRACT>
         The MyXML Online Resources provides links to a
         variety of XML and related resources online.
      </ABSTRACT>
   </ITEM>

   <ITEM HREF= "http://www.myxml.net/news/">
      <TITLE>MyXML - XML News</TITLE>
      <ABSTRACT>
         The MyXML News section includes the most recent
         news articles and press releases related to XML.
      </ABSTRACT>
   </ITEM>

<ITEM HREF= "http://www.myxml.net/tools /">
      <TITLE>MyXML - Tools and Techniques</TITLE>
      <ABSTRACT>
         The MyXML Tools and Techniques section provides
         downloads of the best tools for developing XML
         solutions as well as tips from XML developers.
      </ABSTRACT>
   </ITEM>
</CHANNEL>
```

A section described using an `<ITEM>. . .</ITEM>` tag is like a channel within a channel. If you use items wisely, you can help your users navigate through the variety of resources on your site to find the information that is of the most immediate interest to them.

Identify your channels with logos

CDF allows you to specify an image as a logo for a channel. A logo may be displayed with its channel information as an icon, an image, or a larger image. Internet Explorer has specific size constraints for each different logo display:

- **Icon**: 16 x 16 pixels
- **Image**: 32 x 80 pixels
- **Larger image**: 23 x 194

Other clients may not have these same requirements, but if you want your channel to work with Internet Explorer, you must stick to these requirements. Use the `<LOGO>. . .</LOGO>` tags to add a logo to a CDF file. Then use the `HREF` attribute to specify where the graphic for your logo resides. The `STYLE` attribute specifies how a logo should be displayed; your options are

- `ICON`
- `IMAGE`
- `IMAGE-WIDE`

This bit of code describes a logo used as an icon for the MyXML channel:

```
<LOGO HREF="http://www.myxml.net/images/channel_icon.gif"
      STYLE= "ICON" />
```

Logging channel user activities

Web developers and managers alike want to know who hit their Web site and when as well as how frequently users hit their sites. To support the bean counting that seems to be a requirement in today's Web world, CDF includes a way to specify page-hit logging. The `<LOGTARGET>. . .</LOGTARGET>` element indicates that channel activities should be logged and saved to a file on the server. The element uses these attributes to control logging:

✔ HREF specifies where the logging information should be saved.

✔ METHOD specifies how information should be saved to the Web server. The value for this element can be either POST or PUT. Just about any Web server supports the POST method. Only those running the Hypertext Transfer Protocol (HTTP) 1.1 support PUT. To be on the safe side, use POST.

✔ SCOPE specifies which channel activities to log. The possible values for this attribute are

- ONLINE: Only pages that are read online are reported.

- OFF-LINE: Only pages that are read off-line, from cache, are reported.

- ALL: All pages read either online or offline are reported.

This chunk of code specifies that logs should be sent to the MyXML server using the POST method and that information about all channel activities should be included in the logs:

```
<LOGTARGET HREF="http://www.myxml.net/logging/"
    METHOD="POST"
    SCOPE="ALL">
</LOGTARGET>
```

The CDF vocabulary provides you with all the elements you need to set up and manage a channel. The beautiful thing about CDF is that it's easy to use and even easier to implement.

In the following, we combine all the examples from this section into one CDF document, so you can see how the elements work together to describe a channel:

```
<?xml version="1.0" ?>
<CHANNEL HREF="http://www.myxml.net"
    LASTMOD="2000-01-01T15:00"
    LEVEL="2"
    PRECACHE="YES">

<LOGO HREF="http://www.myxml.net/images/channel_icon.gif"
     STYLE= "ICON" />

    <TITLE>MyXML - XML for Everyone</TITLE>
    <ABSTRACT>
       MyXML is a non-profit organization that wants to
       foster the adoption of XML technology. MyXML members
       are drawn from different industries and countries all
       over the world. Here you will find all relevant
       information about using XML in your information
       delivery solutions.
    </ABSTRACT>
```

```
<SCHEDULE START="2000-01-01" END="2001-01-10">
    <INTERVALTIME HOUR="4" />
</SCHEDULE>
<LOGTARGET HREF="http://www.myxml.net/logging/"
    METHOD="POST"
    SCOPE="ALL">
</LOGTARGET>

<ITEM HREF= "http://www.myxml.net/online/">
    <TITLE>MyXML - Online Resources</TITLE>
    <ABSTRACT>
        The MyXML Online Resources provides links to a
        variety of XML and related resources online.
    </ABSTRACT>
</ITEM>

<ITEM HREF= "http://www.myxml.net/news/">
    <TITLE>MyXML - XML News</TITLE>
    <ABSTRACT>
        The MyXML News section includes the most recent
        news articles and press releases related to XML.
    </ABSTRACT>
</ITEM>

<ITEM HREF= "http://www.myxml.net/tools /">
    <TITLE>MyXML - Tools and Techniques</TITLE>
    <ABSTRACT>
        The MyXML Tools and Techniques section provides
        downloads of the best tools for developing XML
        solutions as well as tips from XML developers.
    </ABSTRACT>
</ITEM>
</CHANNEL>
```

Adding a Channel to Your Home Page Step by Step

If you've read the previous sections, you know how CDF elements work together to build a channel. If you want to actually add a channel to your site and make that channel active, you have to do a bit more than simply write a CDF document. This section shows you how to move from writing a CDF file to publishing a channel on your Web server.

First things first — the right server setup

Before you can serve up Web pages and sites that include channels, you must use a server that knows what to do with CDF files and browser requests for channels. Currently, such server options are limited to Microsoft products. Both Internet Information Server (IIS) and *Personal Web Server* (PWS) support CDF and active channels.

You can add support for CDF files to most Web servers by adding the MIME type `application/x-netcdf`. However, just because the server recognizes CDF files and can send them to browsers doesn't mean that the server supports active channels. Read through your server's documentation before you attempt to serve channels to your users.

If you're posting your Web pages on someone else's Web server — as is often the case if you use a hosting service rather than run your own Web server — you must find out whether your service supports active channels. The easiest way to find out whether your hosting service supports active channels is to call its customer service department and ask the obvious question ("Do you support active channels?"). You could even read through the FAQs on the hosting service's Web site and look for mention of such support.

To find out more about the Microsoft Web server options that support active channels, visit `www.microsoft.com/iis/`.

Deploying your channel

When you're sure that your server setup supports channels, you're ready to post your channel and open it to subscribers, using these steps:

1. **Open your favorite text editor and create a new file.**

2. **Use CDF to define your channel.**

   You can start with our template and modify it or build your own from scratch.

3. **Copy the CDF file to the root directory of your Web site.**

4. **Create an HTML page with a pointer to the CDF file.**

   This step is similar to the Add Channel link on *The New York Times* channel page we discussed in the "Subscribing to channels" section.

5. **Point your Web browser to the HTML page you just created and click the Add Channel link.**

   Let Internet Explorer do the rest.

That's really all there is to it. Five simple steps and you can add your own channel to your Web site.

Microsoft's plethora of CDF resources and tools

Because Microsoft is the creator of CDF and its support for channels is an important aspect of Internet Explorer, the Microsoft Developer Network (MSDN) workshop area includes a variety of resources and tools to help you build and deploy CDF files. Some of the best CDF and channel resources on the MSDN workshop are

- Active Channel Technology Overview
  `http://msdn.microsoft.com/workshop/delivery/channel/`
  `overview/ overview.asp`

- Active Channel Technology Tutorials
  `http://msdn.microsoft.com/workshop/delivery/channel/`
  `tutorials/tutorials.asp`

- The CDF reference
  `http://msdn.microsoft.com/workshop/delivery/cdf/`
  `reference/CDF.asp`

- The CDF generator (a tool for building CDF files)
  `http://msdn.microsoft.com/workshop/delivery/cdf/cdfgen.asp`

Chapter 19

The Mathematical Markup Language

*T*he Mathematical Markup Language (MathML) provides a way to represent mathematical and scientific content on the Web. MathML is a
double-whammy implementation: It can display mathematical and scientific
notation in a highly readable form, and it can also capture the meaning of
such formulas. This allows MathML to support usable text-to-speech data
delivery for people with visual impairments and to export or import formulas
from mathematical or scientific software that "understands" math.

If you don't like math or aren't interested in adding partial differential equations or integrals to your Web pages, skip this chapter. It has the highest
"geek quotient" in the book. It's okay with us if you don't want to read it!

As its inclusion in this book suggests, MathML is an XML application. Soon,
ordinary Web browsers should be able to render mathematics using MathML
and an appropriate style sheet. Today, however, you must use a browser or
an editor that understands MathML. For this reason, we end the chapter with
a set of pointers to software so you can take advantage of MathML's power
and capabilities — and see the results of your work.

MathML Explored

MathML defines a collection of XML elements to mark up equations or formulas so you can determine how they appear on-screen (their presentation) and accurately capture what they mean (their semantics).

Thus, MathML solves one of the problems that derailed the HTML 3.0 specification, which was supposed to — but never did — include support for complex mathematical markup.

MathML is closely related to HTML and looks familiar if you already know HTML. MathML provides low-level format controls for mathematics in a way that makes sense to computers. The W3C Math Home Page (which you can visit at www.w3.org/Math) states "MathML is not intended for editing by hand, but is for handling by specialized authoring tools such as equation editors, or for export to and from other math packages." Nevertheless, we feel it's important to understand how this markup looks and works; that's why we cover basic elements of the MathML specification in this chapter.

The MathML specification is a W3C recommendation (an official, approved standard) that governs this markup. The current version of this standard as of this writing is 1.01, dated July 7, 1999. However, you can always find the most current version of the MathML specification at the W3C Web site at www.w3.org/Math/.

As of October 1999, an XML namespace for MathML is available. (See Chapter 7 for more on namespaces.) If you reference the MathML namespace in an XML document, you can use math markup without including a pointer to the MathML DTD. To use this special capability, include the following XML markup in the DOCTYPE code (or in an external DTD) in your XML documents:

```
<math xmlns="http://www.w3.org/1998/Math/MathML">
```

On the other hand, if your XML processor doesn't support namespaces, you can include an explicit reference to the MathML DTD in your documents instead. In that case, this code provides a good example of what's required:

```
<?xml version="1.0" standalone="no"?>
<!DOCTYPE MathML SYSTEM "MathML.dtd">
```

The SYSTEM keyword invokes the DTD locally, so you must visit the W3C and download the DTD from its Web site. Referencing a local copy of a DTD significantly speeds parsing and validation when you use a validating XML processor. You can download a zipped version of the MathML DTD from www.w3.org/1999/07/REC-MathML-19990707/appendixA.html.

More modern XML applications — and we hope that includes your own — should be able to use the MathML namespace reference shown at the beginning of this section. If you can use the namespace to invoke MathML, we strongly suggest that you do so!

For more on MathML

 Because we can deliver only limited coverage of MathML in a single chapter (it's worth a book of its own to get into all the nitty-gritty details), here are some useful chapters from the MathML specification (which is over 300 pages long) that supply more details. The table of contents for this document is found at www.w3.org/1999/07/REC-MathML-19990707/toc.html.

- ✔ Chapter 3 provides complete details on MathML Presentation Markup. If you want to understand how to create readable equations on screen, this is a must-read chapter.

- ✔ Chapter 4 provides complete details on MathML Content Markup. If you want to understand how to capture the semantics of equations and formulas using MathML, this, too, is a must-read chapter.

- ✔ Chapter 5 explains more than we can cover about why you might want to mix both kinds of markup — that is, presentation and content markup. This chapter helps you understand what's involved in using MathML.

- ✔ Chapter 6 provides a comprehensive list of all the MathML Character Entities you can use to represent mathematical notation within MathML markup. Although we provide numerous tables that summarize the most common mathematical operators and functions, an alphabetized version of the complete list is available at www.w3.org/1999/07/REC-MathML-19990707/chap6/byalpha.html.

- ✔ Chapter 7 explains how to include MathML markup within HTML documents. Because this is currently the easiest way to use MathML on your Web pages, we highly recommend this approach!

MathML markup

Now that we've covered the location of important MathML files and documentation, you can dive into some details. In this section, you find out more about descriptive and content MathML markup, as well as how to represent formulas and equations. To begin, here's an example.

This code gives you a quick look at MathML markup for the expression

```
x² + x - 4
```

Here's is a simple way to create MathML code for any given mathematical expression:

1. **Represent the expression using a binary tree structure (see Figure 19-1).**

2. **Apply the appropriate MathML tag to each node in the tree and group nodes together appropriately, as follows:**

```
<mrow>
    <mrow>
        <msup>
            <mi>x</mi>
            <mn>2</mn>
        </msup>
    </mrow>
    <mo>+</mo>
    <mi>x</mi>
    <mo>-</mo>
    <mn>4</mn>
</mrow>
```

See Figure 19-2 for an illustration of how the previous code looks in a properly equipped Web browser.

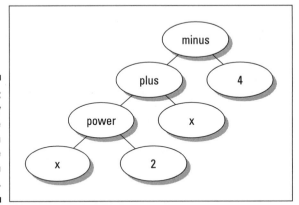

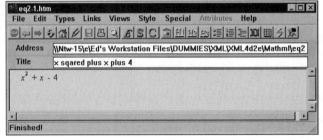

In the following sections, you discover more about this markup (which is purely presentation MathML markup) and how to understand what you see.

MathML Presentation Markup

Presentation elements match the basic kinds of symbols and expressions that support any kind of mathematical notation. Presentation elements are designed to be independent of their medium, so they can be delivered using audio and Braille in addition to more traditional visual representations.

MathML's presentation elements express mathematical structure in notation in much the same way that titles, sections, and paragraphs capture structure in a text document. Many mathematical expressions consist of multiple component expressions, called *subexpressions*. For example, the expression x + a/b actually consists of x + e, where e is the subexpression a/b.

In MathML, individual rows of identifiers and arguments do not typically appear in a single `<mrow>` element that produces a single, horizontal row of mathematical notation. This is a simple, straightforward approach, but one that takes no account of an expression's structure. Rather, a complete expression in MathML usually consists of multiple nested `<mrow>` elements to capture the relationships between and among those elements. The example x + a/b is pretty simple, so we expressed it in the following form to improve its looks. (We wrapped the fraction in a set of parentheses using the `<mfenced>` . . . `<mfenced>` tags. We also used the `<mfrac>`. . . `</mfrac>` tags to give the resulting output an "over and under" representation (see Figure 19-3) because the default is to use a side-by-side presentation, as in a/b.)

```
<mrow>
  <mi>x</mi>
  <mo>+</mo>
  <mrow>
    <mfenced>
      <mfrac>
        <mi>a</mi>
        <mi>b</mi>
      </mfrac>
    </mfenced>
  </mrow>
</mrow>
```

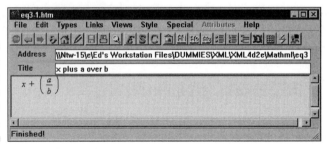

Figure 19-3:
A screen
shot of the
expression x
+ a/b.

This approach to markup — namely, breaking out subexpressions within `<mrow>. . .</mrow>` pairs — makes it easy to add subscripts or superscripts to complete expressions. The idea is to match the way that markup appears on a computer display as closely as possible to the way a mathematician would write it on a piece of paper.

In MathML markup, presentational elements belong to one or two classes:

- **Token elements** are individual symbols, names, numbers, labels, and so forth. Those symbols, names, numbers, labels, and so on, can only consist of characters, numbers, and entity references or a vertical alignment element, `<malignmark/>`.

- **Layout schemata** build expressions out of symbols or other MathML elements, and take primarily token elements as content. A handful of empty elements are also used with specific layout schemata. These layout schemata control how expressions are arranged and how they're positioned when they're displayed.

A token form of presentation

All symbols in a mathematical expression should take the form of MathML token elements. Here's a list of those elements:

- `<mi>. . .</mi>` labels a math identifier or symbol.

- `<mn>. . .</mn>` labels a constant or a number.

- `<mo>. . .</mo>` labels a math operator (such as +, -, or *), a fence (such as opening and closing parentheses and other grouping constructs), or a separator of some kind.

- `<mtext>. . .</mtext>` labels text to be included in a mathematical expression.

✔ `<mspace/>` is an empty tag that allows you to include white space in a math expression (white space is otherwise ignored in MathML); it takes `width` and `height` attributes to control how much space is inserted.

✔ `<ms>. . .</ms>` is a string literal or text expression used as an argument in a math expression.

MathML's layout schemata

MathML layout schemata control how expressions are arranged and positioned. They also identify specific components or types of expressions, such as tables and matrices. These layout schemata fall into four categories, each with its own markup tags:

✔ **General layout schemata:** Markup to manage expressions and subexpressions, fractions, roots, style changes, and bracketing of expressions. See Table 19-1 for a list of general layout schemata tags.

✔ **Script and limit schemata:** Markup to assign superscripts, subscripts, underscripts, overscripts, and even prescripts or tensor indices to base expressions. See Table 19-2 for a list of script and limit schemata tags.

✔ **Tables and matrices:** Markup to identify tables or matrices and the rows and entries of which they consist. This is the category to which the empty alignment tags `<maligngroup/>` and `<malignmark/>` belong (because alignment matters most when tables and matrices are in use). See Table 19-3 for a list of table and matrix tags.

✔ **Enlivening expressions:** Markup to bind actions (such as animation, calculation, or other programmed behavior) to a MathML subexpression. The only such tag is `<maction>. . .</maction>`, which is why we don't present a table. The number of arguments depends on the value of the `actiontype` attribute for this tag.

Table 19-1	General Layout Schemata
Tag Pair	***What It Does***
`<mrow>. . .</mrow>`	Groups any number of subexpressions on a single horizontal line.
`<mfrac>. . .</mfrac>`	Forms a fraction from two subexpressions. Takes two arguments: the numerator and the denominator.
`<msqrt>. . .</msqrt>`	Forms a square root sign (radical without root index). Takes a single argument, the radicand.

(continued)

Table 19-1 *(continued)*

Tag Pair	What It Does
`<mroot>. . .</mroot>`	Forms a radical with a specified root index. Takes two arguments: the radicand and the root index.
`<mstyle>. . .</mstyle>`	Applies a style change to the enclosed elements. Style attributes applied to the first `<mstyle>` tag persist until the closing `</mstyle>` tag.
`<merror>. . .</merror>`	Encloses an error message, usually a syntax error from a preprocessor or a math application.
`<mpadded>. . .</mpadded>`	Adjusts the space around content.
`<mphantom>. . .</mphantom>`	Makes content invisible; preserves size.
`<mfenced>. . .</mfenced>`	Surrounds content with a pair of fences (such as parentheses or brackets) to help readers understand expression structure and precedence requirements.

Table 19-2   **Script and Limit Schemata**

Tag Pair	What It Does
`<msub>. . .</msub>`	Attaches a subscript to a base expression. Takes two arguments: the base expression or value and the subscript.
`<msup>. . .</msup>`	Attaches a superscript to a base expression. Takes two arguments: the base expression or value and the superscript.
`<msubsup>. . .</msubsup>`	Attaches a subscript, superscript pair to a base expression. Takes three arguments: the base expression or value and the superscript, followed by the subscript.
`<munder>. . .</munder>`	Attaches an underscript to a base expression. Takes two arguments: the base expression and the underscript.

Tag Pair	What It Does
`<mover>. . .</mover>`	Attaches an overscript to a base expression. Takes two arguments: the base expression and the overscript.
`<munderover>. . . </munderover>`	Attaches an overscript, underscript pair to a base expression. Takes three arguments: the base expression, the overscript, and the underscript.
`<mmultiscripts>. . . </mmultiscripts>`	Attaches prescripts and tensor indices to a base expression. Takes at least three arguments: a base expression, followed by a subscript and a superscript in parentheses, optionally followed by one or more `<mprescripts/>`, each of which is followed by values for the `presubscript` and `presuperscript` in parentheses. Note that all markup described fits between the opening and closing tags.

Table 19-3	Tables and Matrices Schemata
Tag Pair	**What It Does**
`<mtable>. . .</mtable>`	Brackets an entire table or a matrix.
`<mtr>. . .</mtr>`	Brackets a row in a table or a matrix.
`<mtd>. . .</mtd>`	Brackets a single entry in a table or a matrix.
`<maligngroup/>`	Controls the placement of a group of entries. It's an alignment marker.
`<malignmark/>`	Controls placement of a single entry. It's an alignment marker.

For examples of this markup, please consult the MathML specification. The specification includes examples of nearly every tag it defines, plus tips, tricks, and warnings galore. The *XML For Dummies* CD also mentions most of the tags covered in this chapter, in some form or fashion.

MathML Content Markup

By using MathML content markup, you can encode a mathematical expression's meaning. Remember that MathML presentation markup is for rendering and controls how formulas and equations appear on the screen. MathML content markup encodes formulas and equations so mathematical programs or applications can understand them.

The MathML specification includes the following important but cryptic utterance in Chapter 4: "MathML predefined functions and operators are all canonically empty elements." This means empty tags, followed by their arguments, represent most common math functions in MathML. Common examples include arithmetic operators such as `<plus/>` and `<minus/>` and trigonometric functions such as `<sin/>` and `<cos/>`. You'll find plenty of such operators in the sections that follow. But first, a word about containers and the identifiers that go in them.

Because so many predefined functions that MathML's content markup provides are empty tags, MathML also includes a specific set of tags to manage how those functions are applied to their arguments. This tag pair consists of the `<apply>. . .</apply>` tags and is used to enclose an empty tag function and all its relevant arguments.

Furthermore, content markup includes two tags very much like the presentation tags to label individual arguments to these functions (except they start with the letter *c* for content instead of *m* for MathML):

- ✔ `<ci>. . .</ci>` labels a content identifier
- ✔ `<cn>. . .</cn>` labels numbers or constants

To apply the `<power/>` tag to raise a number to some power — for example, x squared (x^2), or raised to the second power — the proper MathML content syntax is

```
<apply>
   <power/>
   <ci>x</ci>
   <cn>2</cn>
</apply>
```

The equivalent presentation markup, shown in Figure 19-4, is

```
<mrow>
   <msup>
     <mi>x</mi>
     <mn>2</mn>
   </msup>
</mrow>
```

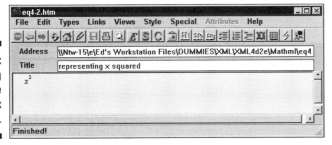

Figure 19-4:
Representing
the
quantity x
squared.

Arithmetic and algebraic elements

Table 19-4 lists arithmetic and algebraic elements and their MathML tags.

Table 19-4	Arithmetic and Algebra Elements
Operation	*MathML Tag*
Addition	`<plus/>`
Subtraction	`<minus/>`
Division	`<divide/>`
Multiplication	`<times/>`
To the power of	`<power/>`
Exponentiation	`<exp/>`
Remainder	`<rem/>`
Factorial	`<factorial/>`
Maximum	`<max/>`
Minimum	`<min/>`

Here's how you use basic arithmetic and algebraic elements to create a poly-nomial fraction in MathML (shown in Figure 19-5). The expression is

```
(x² - x -6)/(x + 2)
```

Here goes:

```
<apply>
    <divide>
        <apply>
            <minus/>
            <apply>
                <minus/>
                <apply>
                    <power/>
                        <ci>x</ci>
                        <cn>2</cn>
                </apply>
                <ci>x</ci>
            </apply>
            <cn>6</cn>
        </apply>
        <apply>
            <plus/>
            <ci>x</ci>
            <cn>2</cn>
        </apply>
</apply>
```

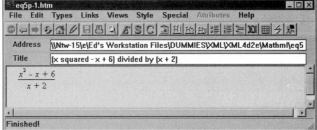

Figure 19-5:
Presenting a
polynomial
fraction!

From now on, we won't bother showing you presentation markup. Instead, we concentrate on content markup (you can find both forms on the CD).

The first `<apply>` is followed by `<divide>` to separate the numerator and denominator of the fraction. The second `<apply>` subtracts 6 from the value of the third `<apply>`, which is $x^2 - x$, and calculates the numerator by incorporating the value of the fourth `<apply>` x^2. The fifth `<apply>` adds the terms of the denominator. In general, this example shows why indenting code is a good idea and also why writing MathML code is best automated through an editor! That's a LOT of markup for a basically simple equation.

Basic content elements

Table 19-5 lists the basic content elements and their MathML tags.

Table 19-5	Basic Content Elements
Element	*MathML Tag*
User-defined function	`<fn>. . .</fn>`
Generic separator	`<sep/>`
Generic inverse function	`<inverse/>`
Applies an operation or function to its arguments	`<apply>. . .</apply>`
Interval constructor	`<interval>. . .</interval>`

Linear algebra

Table 19-6 lists linear algebra functions and their MathML tags.

Table 19-6	Linear Algebra Functions and Their MathML Tags
Function	*MathML Tag*
Vector	`<vector>. . .</vector>`
Matrix	`<matrix>. . .</matrix>`
Matrix row	`<matrixrow>. . .</matrixrow>`
Transpose matrix	`<transpose/>`
Determinant	`<determinant/>`

Relations

Table 19-7 lists mathematical relations and their MathML tags.

Table 19-7	Mathematical Relations and Their MathML Tags
Relation	*MathML Tag*
Equal to	`<eq/>`
Not equal to	`<neq/>`
Greater than	`<gt/>`
Less than	`<lt/>`
Greater than or equal to	`<geq/>`
Less than or equal to	`<leq/>`

Sequences and series

Table 19-8 lists sequences and series elements and MathML tags. (`<tendsto/>` shows a function's behavior as a value approaches a limit.)

Table 19-8	Sequences and Series Elements
Element	*MathML Tag*
Sum	`<sum/>`
Product	`<product/>`
Limit	`<limit/>`
Tends-to	`<tendsto/>`

Set theory

Table 19-8 lists set relations and their MathML tags.

Table 19-8	Set Relations and Their MathML Tags
Relation	*MathML Tag*
Set	`<set>. . .</set>`
Union	`<union/>`
Intersection	`<intersect/>`

Relation	MathML Tag
Is in	`<in/>`
Is not in	`<notin/>`
Is a subset	`<subset/>`
Is a proper subset	`<prsubset/>`
Is not a proper subset	`<notprsubset/>`

Statistics

Table 19-10 lists statistical functions and their MathML tags

Table 19-10	Statistical Functions and Their MathML Tags
Function	**MathML Tag**
Average	`<mean/>`
Median	`<median/>`
Standard deviation	`<sdev/>`
Variance	`<variance/>`
Mode	`<mode/>`
Moment	`<moment/>`

Trigonometry

Table 19-11 lists trigonometric functions and their MathML tags.

Table 19-11	Trigonometric Functions and Their MathML Tags
Function	**MathML Tag**
Sine	`<sin/>`
Cosine	`<cos/>`
Tangent	`<tan/>`

(continued)

Table 19-11 *(continued)*

Function	MathML Tag
Arcsine	`<arcsin/>`
Arccosine	`<arccos/>`
Arctangent	`<arctan/>`
Hyperbolic sine	`<sinh/>`
Hyperbolic cosine	`<cosh/>`
Hyperbolic tangent	`<tanh/>`
Secant	`<sec/>`
Cosecant	`<cosec/>`
Cotangent	`<cotan/>`
Hyperbolic secant	`<sech/>`
Hyperbolic cosecant	`<cosech/>`
Hyperbolic tangent	`<cotanh/>`

Logarithms and calculus

Table 19-12 lists logarithmic and calculus functions and their MathML tags.

Table 19-12   **Calculus Functions and Their MathML Tags**

Function	MathML Tag
Logarithm	`<log/>`
Natural logarithm	`<ln/>`
Derivative	`<diff/>`
Partial derivative	`<partialdiff/>`
Definite integral	`<int/>`
Lower limit of integral	`<lowlimit>. . .</lowlimit>`
Upper limit of integral	`<uplimit>. . .</uplimit>`
Bound variable	`<bvar>. . .</bvar>`
Degree within nth derivative	`<degree>. . .</degree>`

Mixing Markup: Presentation and Content

The basic difference between presentation markup and content markup in MathML is that presentation markup captures the order of math notation and content markup captures the mathematical structure of formulas and equations. What kind of markup you must use depends not only on how the information is to be presented (which leans to the presentation side), but also on how (and if) that mathematical information needs to be used.

Using only presentation tags limits your ability to reuse MathML markup in other applications, particularly when formulas or equations are needed to drive calculations, analysis, or further editing. On the other hand, using only content markup makes it difficult to present the mathematical information, without access to a sophisticated renderer driven by a style sheet mechanism to manage display of content elements. That's why we use presentation markup for the screen shots in this chapter. That's also why we include presentation markup to complement content markup for materials on the CD (so you can have something "nice" to look at in your Web browser).

Unless you have access to a mathematical package that understands math notation and MathML, such as Mathematica or LiveMath Maker (both are covered briefly at the end of this chapter), you probably won't be able to reuse MathML markup, anyway. But as MathML becomes more widely used and content markup becomes more important, this might turn into a more critical issue than it is today. Just don't say we didn't warn you!

Basic MathML Design Guidelines

When using MathML, you must play by its rules and follow certain design guidelines when representing a given mathematical expression:

- ✔ **Every element must be well formed.** This means all tag pairs must include a starting tag (`<mi>` or `<ci>`) and an ending tag (`</mi>` or `</ci>`). Likewise, empty MathML tags such as `<plus/>` and `<minus/>` must terminate properly with `/>`. Using a MathML editor automates this process, but if you edit anything by hand, double-check your work (just like real math). And remember, you can count on most XML parsers to scream if a document is not well formed!

- ✔ **Indent your MathML code properly.** Indentation improves code readability and maintenance and helps you keep track of what's going on in the code. Here again, an editor can do this for you.

✓ **To generate a MathML representation from any given expression, follow that expression from left to right and write equivalent MathML content or presentation markup.** Make sure you follow rule number 1; that is, use proper tags for each MathML element.

✓ **To generate a MathML representation from any given expression, represent the expression as a binary tree.** "Walk" down the tree and identify the MathML tags you can use to represent each node in that tree.

✓ **To verify whether a MathML representation you generate is correct, regenerate the expression from your MathML markup.** If you recreate the same expression you started from, your MathML is correct.

If you follow these guidelines, you'll be doing the same thing that most editors do when constructing MathML. You'll also be reproducing the process that any XML parser uses to validate the markup it sees.

Using MathML in HTML Documents

Although incorporating MathML markup in HTML documents might sound scary, it's pretty easy — as long as your users bring the right browsers (or plug-ins) to bear. In fact, this exercise requires two simple steps in addition to making sure that users approach MathML content with the right tools:

1. **In the `<head>. . .</head>` section of any HTML document that will include MathML markup, you must add the following declaration:**

   ```
   <META Content-math-Type="text/mathml">
   ```

   This instructs the browser to watch for MathML markup and names the MIME (Multipurpose Internet Mail Extension) type to associate with that markup. This tells the browser to invoke its own built-in knowledge of MathML or to invoke an associated plug-in if one is needed.

2. **Begin all MathML markup in a document with `<math>` and end with `</math>`. It's okay to include multiple sections of such code in an HTML document, as long as each section of MathML opens and closes with those elements.**

If you check the HTML documents associated with this chapter on the *XML For Dummies* CD, you'll see they all follow this strategy (and all include only a single MathML section because each one shows a single example).

Here's short but complete HTML document that displays the term x^2 (x squared) using MathML presentation markup, to show you what's involved:

```
<html>
<head>
<title>representing x squared</title>
<META Content-math-Type="text/mathml">
</head>
<body>
<math>
<!-- x**2  -->
<mrow>
  <msup>
    <mi>x</mi>
    <mn>2</mn>
  </msup>
</mrow>
</math>
</body>
</html>
```

This markup produces the screen shot shown in Figure 19-4 earlier in this chapter, in case you need to refresh your memory about what it looks like.

MathML Tools and More

One big difference between the first and second editions of this book is that when we wrote the first edition, MathML tools were scarce. Even though the big browsers — namely, Internet Explorer and Netscape Navigator — still don't support MathML natively, lots of alternatives support MathML on Web pages.

We used the W3C's Amaya Web browser/editor to make screen shots for this chapter. Amaya is free, relatively compact, and allows you to edit MathML visually. On the other hand, you do get what you pay for — Amaya supports only MathML presentation markup and includes no support for content markup. Worse, Amaya doesn't support the formatting controls that MathML presentation markup can specify. It's a bare-bones tool. Even so, Amaya is a great way to investigate MathML (and a natural tool for viewing MathML on the Web). You can download it from `www.w3.org/amaya/`.

Dave Raggett is a long-time member of the W3C's professional staff. He helped spearhead the original work for HTML 3.0 that culminated in MathML. He and Davy Batsalle have created a freeware tool that's available through the generous support of Hewlett-Packard, called HP EZMath. As with Amaya, the price is right but complete MathML support is lacking. HP EZMath does offer great support for a wide range of equations and formulas. HP EZMath also includes a math editor and a separate browser plug-in (that works with both of the big browsers), along with documentation. All are available through the following Web page (the download link is partway down the page, so look for it): `www.w3.org/People/Raggett/EzMath/`.

The folks at Geometry Technologies put together a comprehensive library of Java programs, called WebEQ, to create and display interactive scientific documents. As a teaser to promote this technology, they offer a freeware Web browser plug-in called WebEQ Math Viewer, which adds MathML display capability to the big browsers. You can download this excellent Web extension from `www.webeq.com/`.

Donald Knuth, the eminent computer scientist from Stanford, took a hiatus from his famous series of texts called The Art of Computer Programming to create a computer-based typesetting program called TEX (pronounced "tech"). To make a long story short, part of what TEX delivers is a sophisticated set of mathematical typesetting instructions and capabilities, endorsed by the American Mathematical Society, no less. For those with a background in mathematical or scientific typesetting, there's a natural bridge between TEX and MathML. That's why you'll find numerous tools to convert TEX to MathML and vice versa. For more information, check the W3C's list of MathML software under the heading of "MathML Implementations" at `www.w3.org/Math/`.

You can find lots of expensive options to convert between mathematical software packages and MathML notation. (This should be useful for those who want to use MathML notation to capture and manipulate the semantics of equations and formulas.) Some players who support MathML follow:

- ✔ Design Science, Inc., creators of MathType (`www.mathtype.com/`), $129

- ✔ Wolfram Research, Inc., creators of Mathematica (`www.mathematica.com/`), $1495 (single user)

- ✔ IceSoft, AS, creators of Ice Browser 5 (`www.icesoft.no/`), $1,000 to $5,000

- ✔ Theorist Interactive, LLC, creators of LiveMath Maker 3.0 (`www.livemath.com/`), $99 but a free plug-in is available

Of these offerings, the best known are Wolfram's Mathematica (long a favorite tool of academics and professional researchers) and LiveMath (formerly known as Theorist and MathView). Because MathML has so much to offer by way of presentation and content capture, we think it's just a matter of time before everyone does math with MathML markup. In the meantime, these tools should give you a great place to start!

Chapter 20

DocBook for XML

*T*his chapter gives you a first brush with a heavy-duty, industrial-strength, Document Type Definition (DTD). DocBook is a document type whose primary mission was to promote the interchange of UNIX documentation based on the *troff* markup tool. What happened since then is a typical case of a good idea attracting even more adherents — and uses — along the way to broad adoption and use.

In addition to its primary role in organizing and capturing software documentation, DocBook is also used in numerous other applications, such as authoring, publishing, and cataloging. DocBook is large! It contains more than 350 different element types, and many people have devoted their careers to understanding and refining DocBook. This chapter not only sets out to show you the incredible power of XML within the context of a well-developed document type, but also, we hope, leads some of you to graduate to the full DocBook document! When that happens, you might not be a "Lord of XML" but you will certainly be a "Squire!"

What Is DocBook?

DocBook is a popular document type mainly used for authoring books, articles, and manuals, particularly those of a technical nature. DocBook is especially popular for marking up computer documentation — the motivation behind DocBook was to produce a common markup language that different computer companies could share.

The current, official DocBook, Version 4, is a Standard Generalized Markup Language (SGML) document type. Currently, there's no official XML version of DocBook. You'll have to wait for Version 5.0 of DocBook before an official XML version is released. However, Norman Walsh, one of the authors of *DocBook: The Definitive Guide* (published by O'Reilly & Associates), has written an XML version of DocBook. Please visit www.nwalsh.com to obtain the latest scoop on this project.

DocBook: The Definitive Guide by Norman Walsh and Leonard Muellner is also the official documentation for DocBook.

Booking it

DocBook is a so-called Book DTD. In plain English, this means it's a DTD designed for writing books and articles, especially technical books. As such, its markup is chiefly structural and semantic.

To say that markup is *structural* means that the markup is designed to enforce order and structure on a document by dividing it into various divisions, such as books, chapters, sections, and paragraphs. To say that it is *semantic* means that the markup describes the content in such a document. In other words, DocBook helps manage the form and function of technical documents!

Get in line!

To apply style information to DocBook, you must use a style sheet — that does not mean, however, that DocBook says nothing about rudimentary style! DocBook elements are clearly designed as either inline elements or block elements. The official documentation spells out which is which.

The history of DocBook

DocBook began as collaboration between O'Reilly & Associates and HaL Computer Systems, who formed the Davenport group in 1990. Their idea was to produce a system whereby software manuals could be exchanged between software companies. Sometime in 1998, the original Davenport group reorganized as the non-profit Organization for the Advancement of Structured Information Standards (OASIS) consortium.

When the history of XML is written, it might be stated that DocBook is where the Lords of XML cut their teeth. Most of the original authors of DocBook went on to play a major role in the development of XML. In fact, the original group that designed XML drew heavily on the Davenport technical committee's work on DocBook.

Although the original design goal of DocBook was to enable the exchange of computer documentation, it soon became one of the most popular book-authoring systems because of its powerful descriptive capabilities.

How Is DocBook Organized?

DocBook has an incredibly rich assortment of element types. These element types are grouped into classes. Parameter entities are used to represent each class of element.

Getting classy

The name of a class entity takes the general name of `*.class`, where `*` stands for a descriptive term of the elements in that class. In other words, `para.class` in the following example contains references to the different types of paragraph elements. For example, here's the declaration for one of the smaller classes — the `para.class` class:

```
<!ENTITY % para.class
        "FormalPara|Para|SimPara %local.para.class;">
```

We cover parameter entities in some detail later in this chapter (see the "Parameter entities" section).

Classes of elements are all of the same type. However, most elements require content from several different classes. In other words, they need a mix of various classes to do their jobs properly.

Mixing it up

When an element requires content elements from different classes (and most of them do), this content is described by another entity with the general name of *.mix, where * is a descriptive term. Here's the declaration for para.mix, which, as you can see, contains several different classes:

```
<!ENTITY % para.mix
    "%list.class; |%admon.class;
    |%linespecific.class; |%informal.class;
    |%formal.class; %local.para.mix;">
```

This group of classes can now be assigned as content to the Para element just by referencing para.mix.

Modularizing DocBook

When modularizing DocBook, all the different elements are essentially put into two different modules contained in separate files. The top-level elements are put into a hierarchy module called dbhier.mod, and the other elements are put into an information pool module called dbpool.mod. You then include these modules in DocBook.dtd by referencing them as external entities. (See Chapter 6 for more information on external entities.)

Don't worry if you don't understand this right now. Just make a note that all the elements in DocBook are organized into logical classes that can be mixed and matched as needed.

The Structure of DocBook

Before we can talk about DocBook in anything more than the most general terms, you must understand the general structure for DocBook and what it contains. Essentially, DocBook has three rich layers of structure:

- ✔ The **top layer** sets out all the main divisions in the document.
- ✔ The **middle layer** supports various sections and titles. DocBook enforces a logical sequence for the sections in this layer.
- ✔ The **bottom layer** contains numerous markup elements that describe almost any kind of content.

The following sections cover these layers in detail.

What's on top?

Although DocBook does not formally use elements to divide its topmost structure into a head section, a body section (like `<html>`, for example), and a footer section, such a de facto division, does in fact exist. In this section, you look at what can be considered the body of a DocBook document — in other words, the elements you must include.

The body of DocBook

Figure 20-1 shows obligatory elements for DocBook. Every Book must contain at least one of the following four elements: `Chapter`, `Part`, `Reference`, or `Article`. A DocBook can have more than one of these elements, and they can be mixed up; however, at least one of these element types must appear.

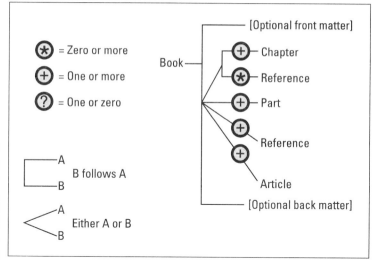

Figure 20-1: The top-level, compulsory elements of DocBook.

The following shows a minimal DocBook document. (Chapters must contain at least a title and a paragraph element.)

```
<Book>
  <Chapter>
    <Title>A minimal DocBook document</Title>
    <Para>This is a Valid DocBook document</Para>
  </Chapter>
</Book>
```

The front end of DocBook

Front matter usually contains information pertinent to a document as a whole. This data can include such material as a title, a summary, author and contributor information, lists of illustrations, and tables of contents. Front matter in DocBook does not have its own little compartment, but it's front matter nonetheless. All front matter in DocBook is optional. Look at Figure 20-2.

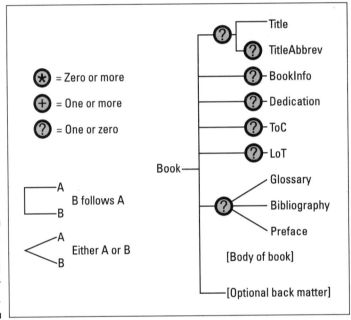

Figure 20-2:
The allowed top-level front matter in DocBook.

The front matter can include numerous elements. You can omit any of these elements, but those you include must appear in this order: `Title`, `BookInfo`, `Dedication`, `ToC`, `LoT` (**List of Tables**), `Glossary`, `Bibliography`, and `Preface`.

The back of DocBook

Just as with the front matter for DocBook, no formal element contains the back matter for DocBook but it's there nonetheless (see Figure 20-3).

As you can see in Figure 20-3, the optional back matter for DocBook contains all the elements you would normally expect. This material can include `Appendices`, `Glossaries` or `Bibliographies`, `Indexes` or `SetIndexes`, `LoT` (Lists of Tables), and a `ToC` (Table of Contents). All this top-level material lies on a middle layer that includes titles and sections.

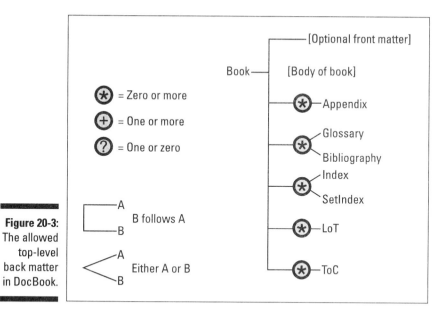

Figure 20-3:
The allowed top-level back matter in DocBook.

What's in the middle?

In the interest of brevity, we examine only the Chapter element from the middle layer (see Figure 20-4). Note that the Part, Reference, and Article elements all have similar organizations that are equally rich.

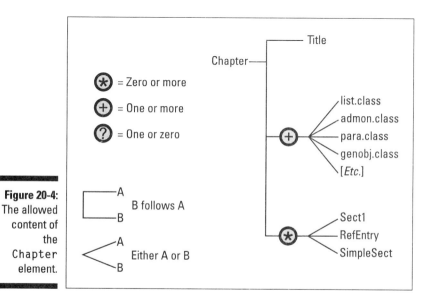

Figure 20-4:
The allowed content of the Chapter element.

Each Chapter element must take an obligatory title. (In fact, nearly every top- and middle-level element in DocBook requires a title.) After the title comes content for the chapter, which can include different types of paragraphs, lists, general objects, tables, and other elements too numerous to mention.

If you want, you can also enforce more formal structure in your chapter using DocBook's section elements (Sect1 through Sect5). These elements impose a rigid, structural hierarchy on your content. Sect5 must be contained by a Sect4, and Sect4 must be contained by a Sect3, and so on — all the way back to Sect1.

Each section must contain a title and can then include the gamut of lower-level content. As you can see in Figure 20-5, each section must contain its own title, can have its own content (it must have at least some minimal content other than a title and another section), and can optionally include a text-section level as well as several simple sections. (A *simple section* is a section without any implied hierarchy.) Sect5 cannot contain a Sect6 because there is no Sect6!

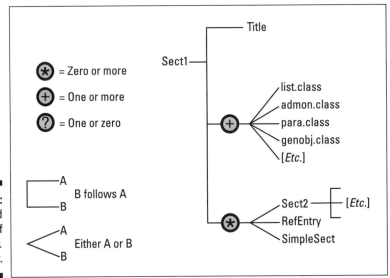

Figure 20-5:
The allowed content of the Sect1 element.

What's down below?

The lower-level structure of DocBook is what makes it so great! There's a semantic tag to meet your every need. Most users of DocBook probably don't use more than 15 to 20 percent of its low-level elements, but if you do need an element to describe the content of what you write, you can usually find it. In the unlikely circumstance that you can't, you can simply add your own markup.

Lists

DocBook contains a list for nearly every conceivable need. The following code is taken directly from the DocBook DTD and shows the content of the entity declaration for all the recognized lists:

```
"CalloutList|GlossList|ItemizedList|OrderedList|SegmentedList
         |SimpleList|VariableList %local.list.class;"
```

If you can't find a list type to suit your needs, the `"%local.list.class;"` code allows you to declare your own.

Paragraphs? We got paragraphs!

Up to now, we bet you just thought that a paragraph was a paragraph was a paragraph. Wrong! DocBook supports formal, regular, and simple paragraphs. Here's the entity from `dbpool.mod`. (See the "Modularizing DocBook" section, shown previously, if you forget what `dbpool.mod` is.)

```
"FormalPara|Para|SimPara %local.para.class;"
```

A formal paragraph (`FormalPara`) is like a miniature chapter. A regular paragraph (`Para`) can contain a whole bunch of different markup, including lists, figures, and tables. A simple paragraph (`SimPara`) is restricted to much simpler content.

Can you table that?

DocBook uses tables from a different DTD: the so-called CALS table model, which supports almost any table permutations that you can imagine. Many authors take out this module and substitute their own table modules instead. The XHTML table module is a popular one to use in its place.

DocBook goes into details

Down at the lowest of levels of DocBook is a detailed structure that can meet almost every need. We can mention only a few of the classes of elements here.

✔ **Address:** Here's an example of DocBook's element declaration for an Address:

```
<!ELEMENT Address
      (#PCDATA|Street|POB|Postcode|City|State|
      Country|Phone|Fax|Email|OtherAddr)*>
```

As you can see, you can mark up an address in as simple or as complex a way as you might wish.

✔ **Phrase:** Here again, DocBook has a rich choice of elements to describe the phrases and terms in your article or chapter. Here are just a few of them:

```
"Abbrev|Acronym|Citation|CiteRefEntry|CiteTitle|
Emphasis | FirstTerm| ForeignPhrase| GlossTerm|
Footnote| Phrase| Quote| Trademark| WordAsWord
   %local.gen.char.class;"
```

And if none of these elements suits your needs, use the `%local.gen.char.class;` entity to declare your own!

A DocBook Example

You might be wondering what possible use you could have for such a complicated document type as DocBook. Well, most users of DocBook use — and are familiar with — only a small subset of the DTD. For example, we wrote this chapter using a simple subset of DocBook containing about 20 elements.

The original chapter marked up in DocBook is on the *XML For Dummies* CD.

What's So Great about DocBook?

Now it's time for us to brag about DocBook's outstanding capabilities. Although a DTD as popular as DocBook needs no extolling — its popularity speaks for itself — in this section, we cover some of the reasons why this is so.

DocBook is a living DTD

DocBook is a living document type — it's overseen by a highly experienced and competent (no, we weren't paid to say that) technical committee. This committee listens to the needs of authors and is always looking for ways to make DocBook better. A new revision to DocBook comes out about every year, and it's structured to be backward compatible with the other versions of DocBook.

DocBook is stable

DocBook has a rule that permits only backward-compatible versions for minor, or *point,* releases. So, if you use DocBook, you can be sure that your current tools can read legacy documents. To produce a DTD that's not backward compatible, the change must be advertised for at least one full version of the DTD. For example, here's a notice from the Version 3.0 DTD about the BookBiblio element:

```
<!ENTITY % bookinfo.module "INCLUDE">
<![ %bookinfo.module; [
<!--FUTURE USE (V4.0):
.....................
BookBiblio will be discarded.
.....................
-->
```

DocBook is versatile

DocBook has more than 350 different elements to choose from. This means that the out-of-the-box DocBook meets the needs of all but the most demanding or specialized authors. Although DocBook might not be ideal for marking up medical records, for example, it's ideal for most general-purpose projects, particularly those that deal with technical subjects (like this book).

DocBook is extensible

If you can't find the markup you need, you can always add it because DocBook is extensible. Medical records are a good example. When one of our authors was faced with the problem of writing a DTD for patients' medical records, it proved easier for him to use DocBook as the base and to add a medical markup module to it, rather than start from scratch. It was also possible to prune a lot of markup that wasn't needed for medical documentation. This is possible because of the unique way that DocBook handles parameters.

Because of the modular nature of DocBook and because of the use of conditional sections, it's relatively easy to remove large parts of the DocBook DTD without editing the DTD itself.

When Not to Use DocBook

DocBook might be the greatest thing since sliced bread, but there are times when you won't want to use it. For example:

- ✔ If you're authoring exclusively for the Web and aren't interested in archiving or searching your content. In that case, use XHTML.
- ✔ If you have no interest in describing the content of your documents. In that case, use a word processor.

✔ If you have a small set of fixed items, such as a record set, that you want to reference. In that case, create your own specialized markup.

✔ If the 600-pound gorilla rule applies — that is, if you're working with a large organization such as the military that uses another SGML document type. In that case, jump to your feet and yell "Yes SIR! We would be more than happy to use your DTD, SIR!"

Reading DocBook's DTD

Your first look at the DocBook DTD can be a daunting experience. When one of our authors, Frank Boumphrey, first opened it and realized the scope of what he was going to have to understand, he was forced to imbibe a large number of amber brews (purely for their restorative effects).

The DocBook DTD can look daunting for a number of reasons:

✔ It's very large: 362 element types last time we counted (compared to 77 for HTML).

✔ It uses parameter entities (covered in detail in Chapter 9) extensively.

✔ It uses conditional sections extensively (covered later in this section).

✔ It uses modules.

All these reasons make DocBook seem complex and forbidding but they are also what make it versatile and easy to modify for your own needs.

Parameter entities

In this section, we provide you with a brief description of parameter entities. (For more in-depth coverage, check out Chapter 9.) Parameter entities are similar to entities, except they can appear only in a DTD. For example, you can declare the following parameter entity:

```
<!ENTITY % headings "h1|h2|h3|h4|h5|h6"
```

Note the use of the percent sign (%), which declares this to be a parameter entity and not a general entity.

Now, if you have the following element declaration:

```
<!ELEMENT section (#PCDATA|%headings;)*>
```

this expands to take the form:

```
<!ELEMENT section (#PCDATA|h1|h2|h3|h4|h5|h6)*>
```

If you take a look at the DTD, you'll see that empty strings are declared as entities in many places. Here's a typical example from the `list.class`:

```
<!ENTITY % local.list.class "">

<!ENTITY % list.class

    "CalloutList|GlossList|ItemizedList|OrderedList|
    SegmentedList | SimpleList |VariableList
    %local.list.class;">
```

This arrangement, in fact, allows you to include your own type of list if you want. To add a list called bulleted list, for example, you could re-declare the `local.list.class` entity somewhere before the empty `local.list.class` declaration. (Remember that in SGML/XML, the first entity declaration is always used.) Here is what you would declare:

```
<!ENTITY % local.list.class "|BulletedList">
```

You've included a `BulletedList` element at the end of the `list.class` entity. (You see how to add a module to a DTD later in this chapter.)

Although parameter entities make this DTD a little harder to read, using them means that if you decide to change any of the content for any of a DTD's classes, you need do so only in one place. As you'll see later, this ability to modify content in the parameter entity is also of tremendous importance when it comes to modifying the DTD in any way.

Are you ignoring me?

If you look at all the ELEMENT declarations in DocBook, you'll see that they all follow the same general pattern. Here's the entity declaration for the Para element, for example:

```
<!ENTITY % para.module "INCLUDE">
<![ %para.module; [
<!ENTITY % local.para.attrib "">
<!ENTITY % para.role.attrib "%role.attrib;">
<!ELEMENT Para - O ((%para.char.mix; | %para.mix;)+)>
<!ATTLIST Para
    %common.attrib;
    %para.role.attrib;
    %local.para.attrib;
>
```

So, what exactly is going on here? Both SGML and XML allow you to insert material conditionally in a DTD by using the keywords INCLUDE or IGNORE. For example, suppose you want the Widget element in some but not all of your documents. However, you don't want to write two separate DTDs. You could put the Widget element declaration in a conditional construct, as follows:

```
<![INCLUDE[ <!ELEMENT Widget (#PCDATA)>]]>
```

The Widget element declaration would then be read by your parser as if it were run through the DTD. In the documents where you don't want Widget elements, change the INCLUDE to IGNORE, as follows:

```
<![IGNORE[ <!ELEMENT Widget (#PCDATA)>]]>
```

The parser ignores this declaration, and if your document contains a Widget element, the parser signals an error.

DocBook does this for every element, but it reads INCLUDE into a parameter entity. Therefore, in the previous example from DocBook, the Para element declaration

```
<!ENTITY % para.module "INCLUDE">
<![ %para.module; [ . . .
```

is the same as

```
<![ INCLUDE [ . . .
```

This approach makes it easy to edit and customize the DocBook DTD.

Modularization

The DocBook 3.0 DTD is a collection of five different files:

- ✔ dbhier.mod: The DocBook document hierarchy module that contains all top-level elements for DocBook. It depends on the pool module.
- ✔ dbpool.mod: The DocBook information pool module.
- ✔ cals-tbl.dtd: Contains the CALS table model, which is the table form that DocBook uses.
- ✔ dbgenent.mod: A convenience module where you can declare all your own general entities.
- ✔ docbook.dtd: The actual DTD that pulls together all the modules by using entity references.

Beginners need concentrate on only the hierarchy and pool modules. It's important to remember that the hierarchy module makes several references to entities declared in the pool module.

SGML versus XML

DocBook is an SGML DTD. The versions of DocBook included on the *XML For Dummies* CD are Versions 3.0 and 3.1. By the time Version 5.0 comes around, DocBook will be fully converted to XML. Before then, you should understand the differences between an SGML and an XML DTD and how to convert one to the other.

In this section, we present a brief summary of the major differences between XML and SGML.

Differences in documents

The differences between an XML document and an SGML document are legion. For the purposes of this discussion, these are the differences that matter the most:

- SGML allows the complete omission of some tags, such as the ⟨HEAD⟩ tag in HTML, and allows the omission of some closing tags, such as the ⟨P⟩ tag in HTML. In XML, every element must have a complete set of tags.

- In SGML, empty element tags do not have to take a special form, as with the ⟨IMG⟩ tag in HTML. In XML, they must take the form ⟨Empty /⟩, so that in XHTML, for example, the ⟨IMG⟩ tag becomes ⟨img /⟩.

- In SGML, tag names are not case sensitive; for example, ⟨Atag⟩, ⟨ATAG⟩, and ⟨atag⟩ all represent the same tag. XML is case sensitive, so these three strings represent three different tags.

- In HTML, only certain attribute values need to be quoted. In XML, all attribute values must be quoted.

Some noteworthy differences exist also between SGML and XML DTDs, but far fewer than you might expect!

Differences in DTDs

At first glance, an SGML DTD such as DocBook 3.0 or HTML 4.01 looks just like an XML DTD. Subtle differences are at work, however. Thus, to get an SGML DTD to parse properly in an XML parser, you must make some key alterations. In this section, we show you the primary alterations you must look for. The other necessary changes are quite rare, so you're unlikely to encounter them.

Minimization

Look at the following Element declaration for Chapter:

```
<!ELEMENT Chapter - O ((%bookcomponent.title.content;),
        ToCchap?,
    (%bookcomponent.content;),
        (Index|Glossary|Bibliography)*)
    +(%ubiq.mix;)>
```

Immediately after the element name is a hyphen followed by an O (- O). This tells you — and an SGML parser — that the opening tag is compulsory but that the closing tag is optional. This markup causes errors in an XML parser and must be removed.

Comments

Comments in SGML can appear inline between `--` and `--`. These are illegal in XML. The following

```
<!ATTLIST Sect1
    --
    Renderas: Indicates the format in which a heading
    should appear
    --
```

must change as follows to become valid XML:

```
<!--
    Renderas: Indicates the format in which a heading
    should appear
-->
```

Exclusions and inclusions

Here again, take a look at the Chapter declaration:

```
<!ELEMENT Chapter - O ((%bookcomponent.title.content;),
    ToCchap?,
    (%bookcomponent.content;),
    (Index|Glossary|Bibliography)*)
    +(%ubiq.mix;)>
```

The plus at the beginning of the final line means that the elements in the parameter entity `ubiq.mix` can also appear in content. This is called an *inclusion* and is illegal in XML DTDs. If that markup started with a minus sign, it would be an *exclusion,* for example:

```
-(%another.mix;)
```

This means that the elements contained in the entity `another.mix` could not appear as `Chapter` content. Inclusions and exclusions are the biggest headache when converting an SGML DTD to an XML DTD. Quite often, the best thing to do is simply to ignore them!

Mixed data

Mixed content must take the form `(#PCDATA| Elname)*` in XML. Whenever mixed data occurs in an SGML DTD, it's important to convert it to the XML format.

Element data

Element data can be declared to be of type CDATA in SGML (both the `<STYLE>` and `<SCRIPT>` element types are so declared in HTML. These must be converted to `#PCDATA` in an XML DTD.

You must use `<![CDATA[... ]]>` markup if you want to include markup in XML.

Also, a declaration such as the following, where the same content is declared for the A, B, and C elements, is allowed in SGML:

```
<!ELEMENT (A|B|C) - - (PARA+) >
```

In an XML DTD, each element must be declared individually.

Attribute types

Several attribute types, such as the `NAME`, `NUMBER`, and `NUTOKEN` types, are allowed in SGML but not in XML. You must convert these to `CDATA` types. With these changes in mind, let's take another look at the DocBook DTD.

The DocBook DTD

The DocBook Version 3.0 DTD is included on the *XML For Dummies* CD. It's called `docbook.dtd`. If you open it, you'll see at the beginning a lot of comments and copyright notices followed by a list of notation declarations. Towards the end of the DTD is the following:

```
<!-- DTD modules........ -->
```

The next few lines represent the business end of this DTD. We copied the relevant lines here and added numbers for ease of reference:

```
1. <!-- Information pool ............. -->
2. <!ENTITY % dbpool PUBLIC
"-//Davenport//ELEMENTS DocBook Information Pool V3.0//EN">
3. %dbpool;
4. <!-- Document hierarchy ........... -->
5. <!ENTITY % dbhier PUBLIC
"-//Davenport//ELEMENTS DocBook Document Hierarchy V3.0//EN">
6. %dbhier;                           •
```

This is really the entire DocBook DTD. The preceding code declares the two main modules containing all the markup of DocBook as parameter entities, and then references them. Here's the breakdown of what each line does:

- ✓ **Line 1**: A comment that identifies the information pool module declaration.

- ✓ **Line 2**: The public declaration of dbpool.mod as a parameter entity named dbpool.

- ✓ **Line 3**: The reference to the entity in Line 2.

- ✓ **Line 4**: A comment that identifies the document hierarchy module declaration.

- ✓ **Line 5**: The public declaration of dbhier.mod as a parameter entity named dbhier.

- ✓ **Line 6**: The entity reference to the entity in Line 5.

In this section, you find out how to modify DocBook. If we used the entire DocBook DTD, things would get pretty overwhelming. Therefore, we created a simple subset of DocBook and converted it to XML. The name of this simple subset is DocBook_ultralite.

DocBook lite

The files for DocBook Ultralite are on the *XML For Dummies,* 2nd Edition CD. The DTD files are DocBook_lite.dtd, DocBook_lite2.dtd, table_lite.mod, dbpool_lite.mod, and dbhier_lite.mod. The test files are dbsamp1.xml and dbsamp2.xml. Also included on the CD is a simple parser, parser.htm, which you can use if you have Internet Explorer 5 or better on your system.

DocBook_ultralite follows the same structure as DocBook but we've stripped the majority of the elements, leaving just 21 intact.

Here is the meat of docbook_lite.dtd:

```
<!ENTITY % dbpoollite SYSTEM "dbpool_lite.mod">
<!ENTITY % dbhierlite SYSTEM "dbhier_lite.mod">
%dbpoollite;
%dbhierlite;
```

Both `dbpool_lite` and `dbhier_lite` must be in the same folder as the `docbook_lite` DTD. We declared both module files as parameter entities, and then simply referenced them. That's all there is to it!

Adding to DocBook

Next, we show you how to add a module to DocBook. Well, we used DocBook Ultralite, but you can add a module to DocBook in the same way.

As you can see, DocBook Ultralite lacks a table type. You might therefore decide to add a simple table system to the DocBook Ultralite DTD. Something like the following, perhaps:

```
<Table>
    <Title></Title>
    <Row><Cell></Cell></Row>
</Table>
```

You can reuse the `<Title>...</Title>` element from the Information pool module of DocBook. You can use the same type of structure for your table module that DocBook uses.

If you want to follow along with this example, open `table_lite.mod` on the *XML For Dummies* CD.

Because we want to keep this as close as possible to the DocBook architecture, the first thing to do is declare a table class as an entity:

```
<!ENTITY % local.table.class "">
<!ENTITY % table.class
    "Table %local.table.class;">
```

Now, you must write element declarations for your table elements. If you open `table_lite.mod`, you can see that we've included these in conditional sections just as DocBook does. For clarity, we omitted the markup you find on the CD:

```
<!ELEMENT Table (Title,Row+)>
<!ELEMENT Row (Cell+)>
<!ELEMENT Cell (#PCDATA)>
```

Your table must contain a `Title` element and at least one `Row` element. Each `Row` must include at least one `Cell`. A `Cell` can contain `PCDATA`. It doesn't get any more basic than this.

Suppose that you also decide that you would like to be able to put a table anywhere that you can put a `Para` element. The question is: "How can you add this to your DTD?" Read on.

Here's the DTD for DocBook Ultralite Version 1.0:

```
<!ENTITY % dbpoollite SYSTEM "dbpool_lite.mod">
<!ENTITY % dbhierlite SYSTEM "dbhier_lite.mod">

%dbpoollite;
%dbhierlite;
```

What happens if you add your module, as shown next?

```
<!ENTITY % dbtablelite SYSTEM "table_lite.mod">
<!ENTITY % dbpoollite SYSTEM "dbpool_lite.mod">
<!ENTITY % dbhierlite SYSTEM "dbhier_lite.mod">
%dbtablelite;
%dbpoollite;
%dbhierlite;
```

Unfortunately, the answer is "not much." You've included <Table> in the element declarations in all the places in the pool and hierarchy modules where Para is allowed, a daunting and tedious task even in a small DTD such as this one. (It's an almost overwhelming task in a large DTD such as the full DocBook.)

This is where parameter entities and the way DocBook is set up come to your rescue.

If you look at the DBpool document, you can see that, it doesn't declare Para as content. Instead, it declares the entity reference %para.class; as content. When it sets up the entity para.class, as follows:

```
<!ENTITY % local.para.class "">
<!ENTITY % para.class
    "Para %local.para.class;">
```

The authors of DocBook had the foresight to include an empty string as a placeholder. So all you must do to show Table wherever you want Para to occur is to fill that placeholder with your table.class. To do so, redeclare local.para.class as follows:

```
<!ENTITY % local.para.class "|%table.class;"
```

To get this revised declaration to work, you must place it after your declaration of the table.class entity and before the declaration of the local.para.class entity. By doing so, you ensure that this redeclaration overrides the empty entity declaration.

Thus, here's what your final DTD looks like:

```
<!ENTITY % dbtablelite SYSTEM "table_lite.mod">
<!ENTITY % dbpoollite SYSTEM "dbpool_lite.mod">
<!ENTITY % dbhierlite SYSTEM "dbhier_lite.mod">
%dbtablelite;
<!ENTITY % local.para.class "|%table.class;">
%dbpoollite;
%dbhierlite;
```

One other thing before you finish: This is now a different DTD, so rename it! If you're the owner of the original document, you can simply change the version number, as we show here. If you're not the owner of the original document, give it a new name. Also, add the original DocBook copyright information to stay on the right side of the law.

Taking away from DocBook

Some day you might want to remove an element from DocBook. Here is how you do it. Removing material from DocBook can be simple or complex. We're sure you'll be pleased to know that we describe only the simple way in this section.

Suppose you want to remove the Sect3 element from DocBook Ultralite. This is what the original declaration looks like:

```
<!ENTITY % sect3.module "INCLUDE">
<![ %sect3.module; [
<!ENTITY % sect3.role.attrib "%role.attrib;">
<!ENTITY % local.sect3.attrib "">
<!ELEMENT Sect3 ((%sect.title.content;),
    (((%divcomponent.mix;)+,
    ( SimpleSect*))
    |   SimpleSect+))
    >
<!ATTLIST Sect3
    %common.attrib;
    %sect3.role.attrib;
    %local.sect3.attrib;
    >
<!--end of sect3.module-->]]>
```

We just override the sect3.module entity as follows and change INCLUDE to IGNORE:

```
<!ENTITY % sect3.module "IGNORE">
<!ENTITY % dbpoollite SYSTEM "dbpool_lite.mod">
<!ENTITY % dbhierlite SYSTEM "dbhier_lite.mod">

%dbpoollite;
%dbhierlite;
```

That's all there is to it! We don't even have to bother removing the references to Sect3 in the Sect2 element declaration because XML allows us to refer to undeclared content. Note that this would be different if Sect3 was obligatory content in the Sect2 element. But because it's not, we can cheerfully ignore it.

When you start working your way through DocBook, you might find yourself on a journey that leads you to the giddy title of "Lord of XML." Even if you do not aspire to such heights, you will still find DocBook useful for nearly all your publishing needs.

Part VII

Cool XML
Technologies Rule!

The 5th Wave   By Rich Tennant

TARZAN — LORD of the WEB

Maybe you write memos too long — last one make server traffic move like hippo through mud pit.

What your problem? No can swing link to link? Try going "ahAHahAHahAHah!" real loud next time you click — ahhahahaha

This guy real interesting. Wonder how long it take to call in elephant stampede?

Why you say this not elegant interface? Tarzan work hard to design warthog icons!

In this part. . .

A short but useful collection of information about XML tools and resources makes up this part. Chapter 21 covers a dynamite collection of some favorite freeware, shareware, and commercial XML editors, authoring systems, parsers, and validators. Somewhere in this toolbox, you might find just the thing you're looking for! Chapter 22 provides a list of the very best XML resources available online, including specifications, tutorials, information, and mailing lists. This chapter may not slice and dice vegetables, but it can help you slice and dice your data. Look out, RonCo!

Chapter 21

Cool Tools

In This Chapter

▶ Discovering the tricks of the trade

▶ Creating XML documents with your favorite tools

▶ Validating is a breeze with a parser

▶ Viewing XML documents gets easier

*A*s you can imagine, nobody but nobody tackles a lot of XML authoring without the help of some authoring tool, nor should anyone try to manage a collection of XML documents without using some software tools along the way. For that reason, we've collected a list of some of our favorite tools for authoring, checking, and viewing XML documents. If your resources or your time are limited, these are the tools you absolutely must check out!

To the Point

In the rest of the chapter, we take a moment to tell you a bit about each tool. Table 21-1 provides you with a quick reference that outlines each product.

Table 21-1		Summary of Cool XML Tools		
Product Name	*Tool Type*	*URL*	*Price*	*Free Demonstration Copy*
Adept Editor	Authoring v9.0	www.arbortext.com	$1495	N/A
Clip! XML Editor v1.5	Authoring	www.t2000-usa.com	$99	Yes
XMetaL	Authoring	www.softquad.com	Less than $199	Yes

(continued)

Table 21-1 *(continued)*

Product Name	Tool Type	URL	Price	Free Demonstration Copy
XML Authority	Authoring DTDs	www. extensibility. com	Less than $99	Yes
XML Pro v2.0	Authoring	www.vervet.com	Less than $199	Yes
Ælfred v1.2a	Nonvalidating parser	www.opentext. com/microstar	Free	N/A
expat v1.1	Nonvalidating parser	www.jclark.com	Free	N/A
SP v1.3	Validating parser	www.jclark.com	Free	N/A
LARK	Nonvalidating parser	www.texuality. com/Lark/	Free	N/A
XML4J Parser	Validating parser	www.alphaworks. ibm.com/tech/xml4j	Free	N/A
Amaya	Browser	www.w3.org/ Amaya/	Free	N/A
Jumbo	Browser	www.xml-cml. org/jumbo/	Free	N/A
Mozilla	Browser	www.mozilla.org	Free	N/A

If You Build It, They Will Come

Well, we don't know exactly who *they* are, but we do know you have to build your XML documents whether anyone visits them or not. To help you get them under construction, we have compiled a list of some of the best XML authoring tools available.

It's common knowledge that the first step in working with XML is to create it! If you're familiar with the Hypertext Markup Language (HTML) and you're anything like us, you probably used your trusty old text editor to create your first XML documents. Well, don't get too attached to going it alone, because we've found a few editors that might change your habits.

Keep in mind that as long as XML continues to create a buzz, more tools will emerge on the scene. To keep up to date on the latest technology, be sure to read Chapter 22.

Adept Editor v9.0

ArborText has built Standard Generalized Markup Language (SGML) editors for years and helped pave the way for XML tools. Adept Editor comes from that SGML background and has been adapted for XML. It's best described as a powerful tool for SGML that provides editing capabilities for HTML, XML, and other simpler document types.

Adept Editor is best used when you need to handle large document collections or documents with multiple authors. This product is definitely designed for advanced XML creation. Although Adept Editor is expensive, it's complete and worth every pretty penny if you're building complex documents with XML or SGML. Visit ArborText's site at www.arbortext.com to learn more about this groovy tool.

Clip! XML Editor v1.5

Techno 2000's new editor, Clip!, supports many easy-to-use features, such as multiple authoring environment support, subdocument editing, Document Type Definition (DTD) structure view, guided editing, real-time validation, and DTD creation. Clip!'s capability to generate DTDs from the XML documents you create makes this editor one of the most helpful tools available today. If you decide to exercise this outstanding feature in Clip!, however, be sure to double-check the resulting DTD to make sure it won't affect future document edits adversely.

At a pocketbook-friendly price of $99 (in the U.S.), Techno 2000's editor is definitely worth trying out. You may also download an evaluation copy. Check out Clip! at www.t2000-usa.com. Figure 21-1 shows an XML document and a DTD generated using the Clip! program.

XMetaL

SoftQuad Software Inc. — best known as the makers of the popular HTML editor, HoTMetaL PRO — developed XMetaL. Its low price ($199 in the U.S.) is one of the reasons you'll find it attractive for authoring XML.

Like many XML editors, XMetaL offers users a familiar word processing environment that's easy to use. XMetaL also anticipates the next generation of browsers by offering Cascading Style Sheets (CSS) editing capabilities as well. XMetaL conforms to numerous standards including SGML, XML, CALS tables, Document Object Model (DOM), CSS, and HTML. Find out more at www.softquad.com.

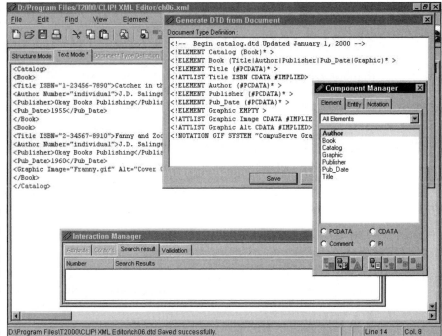

Figure 21-1:
An XML
document
and a DTD
generated in
the Clip!
program.

XML Authority v1.1

Extensibility's XML Authority 1.1 is a wonderful upgrade from its initial release. New documentation, syntax checking, and import/export features make XML Authority 1.1 well worth the money (only $99). XML Authority is not designed for the beginner; a working knowledge of XML and an under-standing of schema design basics are assumed.

XML Authority is a graphical design tool that accelerates the creation and enhances the management of schemas for XML. It includes a toolset to help convert existing application and document structures to schemas, defining the basis for well-formed and valid XML documents. In addition, it has import and output support for XML-schema, XDR, BizTalk, DCD, SOX, and DTDs. XML Authority fully supports and extends the XML 1.0 specification for schema. Read more about XML Authority at www.extensibility.com.

XML Pro v2.0

A more basic product — and a more inexpensive alternative to XMetaL — is XML Pro, developed at Vervet Logic. XML Pro sure can edit, but doesn't claim to do much more.

You can create and edit XML documents while using a clean and easy interface (see Figure 21-2). The newest release claims to be fully W3C XML 1.0 compliant and features IBM's XML4J parser. Currently, there's no support for document conversion, DTD creation, or style sheet design. You can read more at www.vervet.com.

Because many of the editors listed come at a hefty price, we recommend that you test drive demo versions when they're available. Demos should be accessible on the product pages.

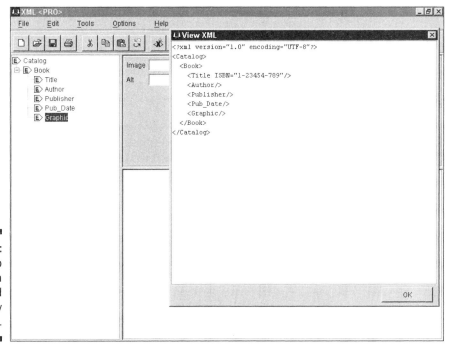

Figure 21-2: XML Pro v2.0 sports a clean and easy interface.

Valid and Well-Formed Documents Always Get Along

Your XML document is a carefully crafted work of art and adheres to strict XML 1.0 compliance. You believe you've followed the rules, and now you're ready to check your work. Luckily, you don't have to check each element by hand — parsers do that for you!

It's a parser's job to ensure that XML documents are well formed and, if linked to a DTD, valid as well. (See Chapter 4 for more information on valid and well-formed XML documents.)

Parsing is a basic but important step in XML publishing. Errors can be the death knell to any XML document. Forget those old HTML days when browsers picked up your slack. An XML document must be well formed, and it must be valid as well if it uses a DTD. Parsers help enforce these requirements.

Some parsers check only that a document is well formed; others check for validity as well. Make sure you examine the parser's capabilities when you're selecting one that's right for your needs.

Ælfred v1.2a

The folks at Microstar, which was recently acquired by Open Text, created a Java-based parser and offer it to the public for free. Ælfred is a nonvalidating parser, which means that it checks documents only for well formedness. According to its designers, Ælfred concentrates on optimizing speed and size rather than error reporting, so it's most useful for deployment over the Internet. Read more at `www.opentext.com/microstar`.

SP v1.3 and expat v1.1

James Clark is a legend in the SGML community because of his amazing collection of tools that support all kinds of cool functionality — most of it in the form of freeware that works like the dickens. His state-of-the-art SP parser, SP v1.3, can be configured to parse and validate XML as well as SGML and makes a dandy tool for that very reason. Likewise, Clark's Jade tool implements support for an SGML view of document style as defined in the Document Style Semantics and Specification Language (DSSSL, pronounced *distle,* to rhyme with *whistle*). Download this free parser at `www.jclark.com`.

You might want to give another James Clark contribution a try. This time, he presents expat v1.1, a nonvalidating XML parser written in C. Here again, Clark's offering is free and quite useful. Check out this parser at `www.jclark.com/xml/expat.html`.

IBM's XML4J

IBM created an XML parser written in Java that's available to users for free. This parser is the subject of a lot of buzz and seems to lead the pack in online reviews. Tools like this help to explain IBM's stellar reputation in the tool development department. "Big Blue" seems to be creating many XML tools, technologies, and resources as it expands its technology arsenal. Find more information about XML4J and other tools at `www.alphaworks.ibm.com/tech/xml4j`.

Tim Bray's Lark

Tim Bray has been a member of the W3C's XML Working Group since long before it operated under that name. (It all started as a special interest group within the SGML cadre at the W3C.) His work on XML is widely recognized and deservedly renowned. Among other things, Tim was the coeditor of the XML specification.

Mr. Bray also created a Java-based XML processor called Lark, which he built as a way to sanity-check the XML design requirement that "it shall be easy to write programs that process XML documents." Lark could be useful for other programmers who seek to follow in his footsteps, but it's also a pretty great tool in its own right. The fruits of Tim's labor are available for download at `www.textuality.com/Lark/`.

Much of the software listed in this chapter is free for the downloading. The only payment you will be asked to give is feedback. XML tools are still pretty green; this means you must watch out for bugs. Make sure you report any bugs you find to the responsible parties. They'll thank you for it!

View It with a Browser

According to most Web designers, XML can revolutionize the way people look at — and transfer — information across the Web. However, before XML can start that revolution, browsers must provide their support. Microsoft Internet Explorer and Netscape Navigator do not currently support XML fully. A few other browsers, however, do provide such support. We found the browsers covered in this section to be noteworthy.

Amaya

Amaya is the W3C's browser and authoring tool and may be used to demonstrate and test many new developments in Web protocols and data formats. See Figure 21-3 for an example of Amaya in action.

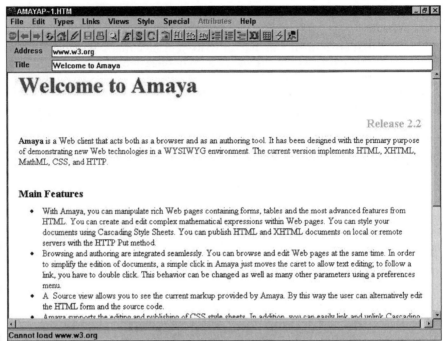

Figure 21-3:
A sample
view of
Amaya in
action.

Amaya is versatile and extensible, which makes it easy to add new features. Along with support for XML, Amaya supports HTML and the Extensible Hypertext Markup Language (XHTML) as well. (See Chapter 2 for more information on XHTML.) If it's good enough for the W3C, it may be good enough for you! Read more at `www.w3.org/Amaya/` and then download the software.

Internet Explorer 5

Microsoft's king of browsers can't be left in the cold. Internet Explorer also offers XML support. In XE "browsers:recommended" addition to supporting XML+CSS and XML+XSL display, Internet Explorer 5 introduces support for namespaces. You can't beat the price — it's free! — and if you're using one of the current flavors of Windows you probably already have it.

Jumbo

As the first browser to pop onto the XML scene, Jumbo knows its XML. It was created by The Virtual School of Molecular Sciences at the University of Nottingham. Jumbo is an XML viewer created specifically to view Chemical Markup Language (CML) documents. Jumbo can render not only simple XML documents but also complex molecule models — and it can also show extensive chemical formulas. Although aimed at a particular XML application, Jumbo can be a useful tool for those interested in XML in general. Take a look at www.xml-cml.org/jumbo/.

Mozilla

Like many free XML tools, Mozilla is built around publicly available source code. Mozilla is fully compliant with standards for HTML 4.0, XML, CSS, and DOM. It includes expat (see the "SP v1.3 and expat v1.1" section previously in this chapter) for XML parsing, supports CSS display for XML, and provides partial support for namespaces and simple XLinks.

The folks at Mozilla.org are dedicated to debugging and updating this software, and you should be too. Mozilla.org provides users with an open forum to report bugs. To download this software or keep up with changes, visit www.mozilla.org.

The Ultimate XML grab bag and goodie box

We've outlined some individual software packages, and now we want to identify some companies that do it all.

POET Software

POET Software offers all kinds of XML resources: white papers, an XML repository, and an XML resource library. POET makes a powerful, object-oriented database that embodies the Common Object Request Broker Association's (CORBA) model to provide shared access to data across many database engines and applications. Apparently, they've also taken the cross-platform, open-ended capabilities of XML seriously, because they promote this technology relentlessly and enthusiastically. For access to POET's treasure trove of goodies, which includes an ever-changing set of pointers to interesting XML software, visit www.poet.com.

Microsoft Does XML Too!

In its search to extend the reach and capability of its Internet software, particularly the Internet Explorer browser, Microsoft is an unexpected and ardent XML supporter, particularly for the Channel Definition Format (CDF)

Resource Definition Framework (RDF) — among other XML applications. As it begins to add additional XML support to the next release of Internet Explorer, Microsoft offers numerous other XML tools as well. To read more about Microsoft's view of XML, visit `http://msdn.microsoft.com/xml`.

Automating XML excellence

webMethods has constructed the core of its web automation toolkit (called webMethods B2B) around XML and Java technology. They market it heavily for use in electronic commerce and related applications and to automate access to a variety of Web-based data and services, both in HTML and XML. webMethods B2B has been well received in the marketplace and is worth investigating for those who seek to improve data access, data handling, and data security on their Web sites.

To obtain an evaluation copy of webMethods B2B, or for more information about the company and its products, please visit `www.webmethods.com`.

There's no way we can cover all the wonderful XML tools available. To find a complete guide on XML software, check out `www.xmlsoftware.com`.

This ends our tour of some of our favorite XML tools. Don't forget to consult the "About the CD" appendix to help you explore the CD's contents. Also don't overlook this book's glossary. When it comes to decoding the sometimes-mysterious terminology you're likely to encounter when canvassing the wild and wooly intellectual landscape of XML, a glossary can be invaluable!

Chapter 22

Ultimate XML Resources Online

* * *

In This Chapter

▶ Saying it all with specifications

▶ Admiring how well the W3C knows its XML

▶ Abounding XML information all over the Web

▶ Covering the basics with tutorials

▶ Mailing it to yourself

* * *

*A*s the XML buzz continues to grow, so will the number of online resources. As with ice cream, some flavors are just plain better than others. We've documented a list of our favorite online resources, so get your keyboards ready because we're about to share the results of our extensive research with you!

In this chapter, we discuss online resources that fall into the following categories:

✔ Specifications

✔ General information

✔ Best tutorials

✔ Mailing lists

Specifications

Get your information straight from the horse's mouth. The World Wide Web Consortium (W3C) creates official specifications for Web technologies and has done so since 1994. From the Hypertext Markup Language (HTML), to Cascading Style Sheets (CSS1 and CSS2), to the Extensible Markup Language (XML), the W3C rules this particular markup roost!

You can find the complete XML 1.0 specification on the *XML For Dummies* CD.

We would also like to point you to Tim Bray's annotated XML 1.0 specification, in which he breaks down the technical lingo and explains that specification in plain English. Here are the URLs for these and other XML-related specifications. We put them in most useful order rather than, say, alphabetical order:

- ✔ **Extensible Markup Language (XML) 1.0 — Recommendation:** `www.w3.org/TR/REC-xml`

- ✔ **Tim Bray's Annotated XML 1.0 Specification:** `www.xml.com/axml/axml.html`

- ✔ **The Extensible HyperText Markup Language (XHTML) 1.0 — Recommendation:** `www.w3.org/TR/xhtml1/`

- ✔ **XML Linking Language (XLink) — Working Draft:** `www.w3.org/TR/xlink/`

- ✔ **XML Path Language (XPath) — Recommendation:** `www.w3.org/TR/xpath`

- ✔ **XML Pointer Language (XPointer) — Working Draft:** `www.w3.org/TR/WD-xptr`

- ✔ **Extensible Stylesheet Language (XSL) — Working Draft:** `www.w3.org/TR/WD-xsl/`

- ✔ **Associating Style Sheets with XML documents, Version 1.0 — Recommendation:** `www.w3.org/TR/xml-stylesheet/`

General Information

The following sites provide a little of everything. They're the so-called "Jack or Jill of all XML-related trades" sites. If you need a specific article on XPath or XSL, or even if you just want to read about the newest XML tools, the following sites are where you should begin your search:

- ✔ **World Wide Web Consortium (W3C):** `www.w3.org/xml/`. You probably know that the ultimate source of Web wisdom resides at the W3C's Web site. And where XML is concerned, this site is no exception to the rule. You get one heck of a list of pointers to XML information on the Web. It's a must for anyone who wants to keep current on XML.

- ✔ **Robin Cover's SGML/XML Web page:** `www.oasis-open.org/cover/`. Robin Cover is a well-known expert on matters related to SGML and XML. This might be the most exhaustive XML site on the Web — and the most exhausting site on the topic, too. If you have the time to wade through his many articles and pointers, you're likely to find the answer to just about any XML question. Beginners beware: This is an advanced site.

✔ **XML.com:** www.xml.com. If you want to find an article on XML, this site might become your favorite library. You can find a wealth of information here. By far, XML.com is one of the easiest sites to navigate your way through. It's definitely worth a visit (or two)!

✔ **xmlhack:** www.xmlhack.com. This site is updated frequently — almost daily — so it's a great place to look for the latest breaking XML news. You'll also find a wonderful list of XML-related resources, including many mailing list resources. This is the place to go to find up-to-date information and tips from other XML developers.

✔ **The XML Working Group FAQ:** www.ucc.ie/xml/. On the Internet, creating and maintaining a list of frequently asked questions (FAQs) — and more importantly, the answers that go with them — is part of the standard method to help newcomers find their way around any subject area. Here again, the best FAQ comes to you on behalf of the folks at the W3C.

Remember that whenever you consider asking for help on any topic in the Internet world, your first step should be to read the FAQ before asking your question in public. Follow this advice and you'll never get embarrassed by rehashing old, timeworn topics.

✔ **ZDNet Developer Site:** www.zdnet.com/devhead/. Select XML from the list of options and this site and you're on your way. The ZDNet site is not XML specific. Rather, it's a Web developer site that provides users with information on a number of Web-related technologies. So while you're there, you might want to brush up on CSS or HTML too!

✔ **Developer Exchange (a.k.a DEV-X):** www.xml-zone.com/. The DEV-X site not only gives you articles, conference information, and a good beginner's guide to XML, but also hosts the first XML-only magazine. As this book goes to print, XML Magazine consists of only one issue, but it promises good things. We don't now how XML Magazine will fare, but our bets are that it will be worth checking out.

✔ **IBM's XML Web Site:** www.ibm.com/developer/xml. IBM hosts one of the younger XML sites. It keeps adding information, and from what we have seen, it's all good! This site contains info about IBM's XML-related products, plus a short XML tutorial and many articles on the subject.

✔ **Graphics Communication Association (GCA):** www.gca.org/whats_xml/default.htm. Despite its somewhat nondescript name, GCA has long been active as a purveyor of conferences, training, and publications for the SGML community. Now it's taken that expertise into the XML world, with predictably excellent results. Whether you're looking to mingle with other XML-ites, take a class, or survey a list of available publications, you can find good stuff on GCA's XML pages.

- **MSDN Online, XML Developer Center:** `http://msdn.microsoft.com.workshop/xml/default.asp`. Despite its reputation as a "dog in the manger" when it comes to standards versus proprietary technologies, Microsoft offers plenty of information about XML to go along with its software offerings that support this technology.
- **Café con Leche:** `http://sunsite.unc.edu/xml/`. Elliotte Rusty Harold created this site, and it provides readers with mailing lists, a list of XML books, and links to other XML resources and XML news updates. There are no tutorials, but he does list several good XML examples.

Tutorials

The following sites could easily be listed with the URLs in the preceding section. We set them apart because we want to call attention to their tutorials, which we think are pretty darn good:

- **Web Developer's Virtual Library:** `http://wdvl.com/Authoring/Languages/XML/`. If you need a helping hand in understanding just what a DTD is and how to use it, this is the place to go. Web Developer's Virtual Library offers tutorials on almost any XML topic. This site also provides links to other resource sites, updated XML news, and guides to XML-related software.
- **Project Cool:** `www.projectcool.com/developer/xmlz/`. As with the Web Developer's Virtual Library, this site brims with wonderful tutorials. You will not be able to walk away from this site and create large complex XML documents, but the basics are covered — and covered well. If you need a quick refresher or a fast introduction, this is the place to start.

Mailing Lists

Mailing lists can help you stay on top of any debate — but they can also flood your inbox! If you decide to sign up for a mailing list, select carefully. In the beginning, you don't *have* to participate; you can just sit back, prop your feet up, and read. But remember, these are ongoing conversations — feel free to jump in at any time. Visit the following sites for current XML mailing lists:

- `www.w3.org/XML/#discussion`
- `www.oasis-open.org/cover/lists.html#discussionLists`

When signing up for a mailing list, it's always smart to find out whether they offer a digest version. Digest versions, which are sent out daily or weekly, compile all messages into one. That way, you won't be bombarded with e-mail all day long.

Part VIII
The Part of Tens

In this part. . .

*H*ere is the revered and traditional closing in all ...*For Dummies* books. With tongue planted firmly in cheek, this part of the book summarizes, epitomizes, and concentrates the most important content that appears in this book. Thus, Chapter 23 describes ten meaningful ways to make legitimate use of XML technology. Chapter 24 lists the top ten ways to use style sheets (or style descriptions) with XML content. Chapter 25 closes out this fiesta with a description of the ten most widely used XML applications on today's Web sites. We can't help it: We give this section a solid 10 rating! We hope you will, too.

Chapter 23

Ten Reasons to Enjoy XML — Really!

*Y*ou can realize many benefits using XML. In this chapter, you're introduced to just ten of them. Before we take you there, however, we define two major areas where XML is helpful.

First, XML can be used as a representational mechanism, allowing XML to

✔ Create shortcuts using character entities

✔ Use single links to perform multiple actions simultaneously

✔ Apply built-in document quality control through syntax checking and automated validation

The items in this list are covered in the first three sections of this chapter.

Second, XML can represent all kinds of arbitrary and complex data, making it suitable for everything from abstruse mathematical notation to defining graphical interfaces or even printing mailing labels. The reason why this is so special is covered in the remaining sections of this chapter.

Save Time — Use ENTITY

Among its many capabilities, the XML — and Standard Generalized Markup Language (SGML) — `ENTITY` DTD declaration makes it possible to substitute properly formatted strings of characters that take the form `&name;`, where `name` is an easy-to-write — and remember — shortened version of a long name. For example, you could replace "The AA ACME Merchandising Company" with `&acme;` in the text of any document where the proper `ENTITY` declaration occurs, namely:

```
<!ENTITY acme "The AA ACME Merchandising Company">
```

Every time you use `&acme;` in the document body, the full company title — The AA ACME Merchandising Company — is called up.

Create Your Own Rules

Finally, this stuff makes sense! With XML, you can create — and therefore structure — your own markup. For those of us who have been struggling with random tags and browser capability problems when using HTML, XML is a welcome change. Understanding your data is key to providing useful information.

What helps make XML so powerful is its capability to give form and structure to any type of data — no matter how abstract. Your document is self-describing and if coded correctly, anyone can understand it! (For more information on creating your own markup, visit Part II of this book.)

Add Style the Easy Way

Web designers have learned the hard way that formatting is not always an easy task with HTML. Until Cascading Style Sheets (CSS), formatting was downright scary.

XML differs from HTML in that it gives you the power to create your own markup tags so you can describe your content in the best possible way; the XML tag set is literally unlimited. Style sheets are a necessary — and welcome — approach to adding style.

Although the idea of adding style with anything other than CSS is still under construction at the W3C, you should become familiar with both the Extensible Stylesheet Language (XSL) and XSL Transformations (XSLT). For more information on adding style, visit these sites:

✔ **XSLT specification site,** www.w3.org/TR/xslt

✔ **XSL specification site,** www.w3.org/TR/WD-xsl/

✔ **Robin Cover's site on XSL,** www.oasis-open.org/cover/xsl.html

XML Complements HTML

You might have heard about the Extensible Hypertext Markup Language (XHTML) — or you might have read about it in Chapter 2. The W3C defines XHTML 1.0 as a reformulation of HTML 4.0 as an XML 1.0 application. This will bring the structure of XML to HTML and allow for cleaner, easier HTML code.

XHTML is modular, which means it will be easy to create markup tags for multimedia, math, electronic commerce, and more. Content providers — that's us — will find it easier to produce content for a wide range of platforms and will no longer have to worry about how that content is rendered. Anyone ready for the power of the Web to be found in the increasing number of browser platforms, including cell phones, televisions, cars, wallet-sized wireless communicators, kiosks, or desktops?

Read more about the XHTML recommendation on the W3C site at www.w3.org/TR/xhtml1/.

Searching for Something?

XML markup contains contextual information; therefore, queries are more likely to retrieve relevant information or files. Search engines can even find a portion of a document that contains the relevant information. Say goodbye to the <meta> tag and hello to smart searches. XML not only increases the relevance of searches (because it can eliminate irrelevant matches) but also produces search results faster!

Again, you're hearing the rallying cry for creating structured XML documents from well-organized data. If you haven't noticed, this is what XML is all about: information. Take advantage and start mapping out your data today. You never know when you might want to share it.

Rich Links Enrich Functionality

With XML Linking Language (XLink), you can add the wonders of hyperlinks to your XML documents. XLink gives you the ability to define more structure for complex links, providing easier control and maintenance. Not only does

XLink allow hyperlinking in the same ways that HTML delivers, but it also allows all kinds of wonderful new types of links. For more information, check out Chapter 15.

For more information about this topic and the underlying technologies, visit the W3C Web site (www.w3.org) and look for link information under the XML home page. Also check out these pages:

- ✔ www.xml.com/pub/Guide/Linking_Technologies, XML.com's resource site on linking technologies

- ✔ www.oasis-open.org/cover/xll.html, Robin Cover's excellent set of pointers, including a discussion of the emerging XLink language

Well-Formed XML Guarantees Readability

Part of the mechanism inherent in parsing any XML document for rendering involves checking that the related Document Type Definition (DTD) is in agreement with the document contents that follow the DTD, whether that DTD is implied, as in the case of a well-formed XML document, or is present by inclusion or by references, as in the case of a valid XML document. Unlike HTML, every XML document that does not exhibit such agreement between DTD and content is flagged with error messages and might not be displayed by some viewers.

The possibility of display errors puts considerable pressure on content developers to publish XML documents that do not provoke such error messages. It also helps guarantee viewing experiences that are substantially the same for document readers, no matter which operating system or software they use to view the documents. The requirements of XML should help to overcome the Tower of Babel effect that plagues so many complex HTML-based sites nowadays, where Webmasters must create multiple versions of the same pages to ensure that their content can reach the broadest possible audience. XML should help consolidate this fragmented audience and bring them all together under a single standard and software umbrella.

MathML Captures Mathematical Requirements

MathML (discussed in Chapter 19) is not likely to be of interest to you if your document content does not require representing things mathematical. But for those with complex notation or formulas to dispense, nothing else will do the trick. That's why MathML is perceived as a boon to mathematicians everywhere and offers long-sought closure to early proponents of HTML 3.0, who tried to introduce mathematical support in that version of the language.

For more information on MathML, start your research by reading the W3C recommendation on the topic, which can be found at `www.w3.org/TR/ REC-MathML/`.

CDF Brings Channels to the Web

The Channel Definition Format (CDF), covered in Chapter 18, has been endorsed by all types of Internet industry players, including DataChannel and Microsoft. CDF defines a mechanism whereby collections of data, called channels, are defined and delivered from a *push server* to lists of subscribing clients. This permits a single server to deliver (or push) an almost arbitrary number of different information feeds, software updates, and other regularly changing types of data to clients. This technology supports, among other applications, the channels that Internet Explorer can now open on any desktop.

Robin Cover's overview page provides a great starting point for finding out more about CDF. Visit the site at `www.oasis-open.org/cover/gen- apps.html#cdf`.

But Wait, There's More. . .

Take some time to do your own research and discover how XML might benefit you. You might just stumble on yet another reason to tackle an XML project.

Unlike the old Ronco ads, you won't get a free set of Ginsu knives with each XML purchase, but the list of potential benefits covered in this chapter by no means exhausts all the capabilities in the works for XML. And while we don't plan to slice a beer can in half, and then do the same to some poor tomato, we would like to point out that lots of new functionality and new markup dialects may be coming soon to a Web site near you! These include the Extensible Stylesheet Language (XSL), an attempt to bring dynamic behavior to style data for XML, all kinds of electronic commerce initiatives based on XML, and further developments to enrich XML's multitalented linking mechanisms. (XSL is covered in detail in Chapter 12.)

A good way to keep up with the latest XML developments is to visit the resource sites recommended in Chapter 22 regularly.

You can also track what's new with XML at the W3C's XML home page, which you might call the "mother of all XML resources." It's located at www.w3.org/XML/.

We hope that we've shown you not only that XML makes custom markup easy, but also that the markup it makes has nearly limitless representational capabilities. Although it's unlikely that you'll ever need to use all these capabilities in a single document or that you'll draw on multiple XML dialects at the same time, it's nice to know they're there.

Chapter 24

Ten Stylish XML Extensions

*W*e assume that many of you who read this book aspire to use XML on the Web. If that is indeed what you want to do, you'll want to read this chapter. Without style sheets, your pages will look just like that text you spend weeks coding — nothing more. Add a little style, however, and you're on your way to beautiful — and manageable — Web pages.

The truly exciting thing about XML is that it does not begin or end at the Web. You can take one XML document and present it in countless formats. A single document can appear to the board of directors in slide format, to the online community through a Web page, and to co-workers as plain text. You can even use it to create personalized customer information. The list goes on and on. Simply add a style sheet and the presentation changes before your very eyes. We like that — a lot. So will you!

In this chapter, we examine a few ways you can add some pizzazz to your pages. If this chapter piques your interest, you might want to visit Part IV for an in-depth overview of the wonderful world of XML style.

Add Tables with HTML

In this section, we show you a quick way to add tables with HTML. Wait, HTML? Yes, that's right — with a little HTML, you can add a table to an XML document. Using HTML is not the only way to add tables; you can use also the Extensible Stylesheet Language (XSL). However, we assume that many of you already know HTML, so we thought you might like to put your knowledge to work.

We don't have time to get into the issues of namespaces and their semantics, but take a look at what you can do with this the following bit of information:

1. **First, declare an HTML namespace:**

```
<Table xmlns:html="uri:html">
. . .
</Table>
```

2. **In the document body, use <Table> as a basic XML element; the remainder of the code is produced by the use of the HTML namespace. After you declare an HTML namespace, you can construct a table in much the same way you do in HTML, Here's an example:**

```
<Table xmlns:html="uri:html">
  <html:table border="0">
    <html:tr>
      <html:td>Cell 1</html:td>
      <html:td>Cell 2</html:td>
    </html:tr>
  </html:table>
</table>
```

The preceding code produces a table with two adjacent cells. Best of all, it works enough like HTML to be easy to use.

Use CSS for Easy Formatting

One motto that seems to echo throughout the style sheet pages at the World Wide Web Consortium is "Use CSS when you can, and use XSL when you must." This is sound advice that we recommend you follow.

For adding simple styles, CSS (Cascading Style Sheets) has many advantages. CSS is easy to use, easy on the pocketbook, and easy to learn. In fact, you might wonder why XSL exists, given what CSS can do. Well, although CSS has many undeniable advantages over XSL, its ease of use also imposes limitations.

When you find that you must transform your data from one Document Type Definition (DTD) to another — not just add a little style — you must use XSL (or its derivative, XSLT). As XSL-related specifications mature and related tools become more widely available, other powerful reasons to use XSL will no doubt emerge as well. You'll find more details on these subjects in Part IV, particularly in Chapter 14.

Combine Those Sheets

In XML, just as in HTML, sometimes one style sheet isn't enough. For example, you might want your Web site to deliver a consistent look and feel, but you also realize that some pages require individual styles.

When this is the case, you can define an overall style sheet to control the look and feel for the entire Web site. Then you can supply additional style information on a case-by-case basis.

You can combine style sheet information in several ways:

✔ Importing one style sheet into another

✔ Including one style sheet within another

✔ Embedding style sheets directly in XML documents

We discuss these three methods in Chapter 14. Take some time to visit or revisit these materials.

Combine XSL and CSS

Think about how XSL works. First, XSL enables you to extract data from an XML document. Second, it enables you to format that data. Sometimes it makes sense to use XSL to extract data, but use your good ol' buddy (HTML) to add a little simple style, particularly when the data is destined for display on the Web.

For instance, if you create an XML document to keep track of home run leaders in the major leagues over the past 100 years, you might include an XML element called `team` (coded `<team>...</team>`) wherein the name of each player's team appears.

If you want that team name to appear in bold italics in the final HTML document, you can tell XSL to find all instances of the `<team>` element and output them in bold italics after applying the HTML `<b>...</b>` and `<i>...</i>` containers.

Display It Again, Sam!

One of our favorite features of XML is its capability to display the same data in multiple formats. Think about it: Creating multiple presentation targets can easily save you time — and money.

After you map your data and create your XML documents, you're ready to think about presentation(s). If you want to create a detailed customer list to appear in a browser window, you can use simple CSS.

If you decide to generate a more detailed customer list for your marketing team, you can do that, too. Just create another style sheet, apply it, and you're back in the game!

This can make the world of difference when you work with large XML documents that contain lots and lots of data. You don't want to have to recreate entire XML documents — and the folks at the W3C thought you might not want to do that, either.

Add Variables with XSL

Much like entities, xsl:variable can save time and aid in the fight to create cleaner code. The xsl:variable element defines a named value that you can use throughout a style sheet by inserting an attribute value template.

An xsl:variable has a single attribute, name, that you use to refer to the variable elsewhere in a style sheet. The replacement text appears in the contents of the xsl:variable element. Here's an example:

```
<xsl:variable name="lanw">
LANWrights, Inc.
</xsl:variable>
```

This code defines a variable with the name lanw and defines the replacement text as LANWrights, Inc. Now you're probably wondering how to use this little gem.

To access the replacement text — or value — you use the value of the attribute's name and prefix a dollar sign ($). To insert this in an attribute, use an attribute value template, such as

```
<block company_name="($lanw)">
</block>
```

To insert a variable's replacement text — or value — into the output document, you can use xsl:value-of as follows:

```
<xsl:value-of select="$lanw"/>
```

You can use xsl:variable to manipulate style sheets in many fun ways. For example, you can add markup to xsl:variable and even include other XSL instructions. Properly applied, the xsl:variable offers tremendous flexibility and power.

Attribute Value Templates

Attribute value templates copy data from element content in the input — such as a document — to attribute values in the style sheet. From that point forward, the data appears as output. Take a look at this table of values:

```
<Person_Name="Sam"
   Person_Age="22"
   Person_Weight="140"
   Person_Height="5.9"
/>
```

What if you want to convert the previous information into empty elements using the above attribute-based form? To do this, you need to extract the contents of the elements in the input document and place those into attribute values in an output document. You might think the next step should look like this:

```
<xsl:template match="Person">
   <Person_Name="<xsl:value-of select='Name'/>"
     Person_Age="<xsl:value-of select='Person_Age'/>"
     Person_Weight="<xsl:value-of select='Person_Weight'/>"
   />
</xsl:template>
```

But this isn't correct because you can't use the less-than and greater-than — < and > — characters inside an attribute value. Instead, you must use curly braces { and } to enclose that data, like this:

```
<xsl:template match="Person">
   <Person_Name="{Name}/>"
     Person_Age="{Person_Age}"
     Person_Weight="{Person_Weight}"
   />
</xsl:template>
```

Here, {Name} is replaced by the value of the Name child element, {Person_Age} is replaced by the value of the Person_Age child element, and so on. Pretty neat, huh?

Find Style with XHTML

The W3C has created an easy way to use HTML as an application of XML — and devoted HTML users are ready to jump into the fray. The Extensible Hypertext Markup Language (XHTML) allows you to work with tags that you're already familiar with — remember `<p>` and `<br>`? — but still work within the framework of XML.

What that means for you is that all those pages you created and thought were passé aren't quite dead. With a little tweaking — remember, XML is case sensitive — your code can be up with the latest style. In minutes, your pages will be hip again!

Create Style the Easy Way

If you want to create basic style sheets using XSL but you're a little crunched for time, check out all the wonderful software that can help you with this task at `www.xmlsoftware.com/xsl/`. No one ever said you had to whip up all your creations from scratch. Even the best chef sometimes needs an Emeril Lagasse video for some inspiration.

Because XSL is fairly new, it will be more difficult to locate a software product of your dreams, but we've found a few that we really like and included them on the *XML For Dummies* CD.

Let Companies Talk to Each Other

The Extensible Stylesheet Language Transformations (XSLT) 1.0 specification, a recent addition to the XML family, defines a standard way to convert XML documents from one form — or schema — into another, changing XML tag names and tree structures as needed.

XSLT's strength comes in its useful server-to-server communications, but it has not yet been widely adapted for use in document publishing. Be on the lookout because after most companies catch the XML bug, they — or at least their information — will want to talk to each other. And XSLT is what will allow them to do it!

Chapter 25

Ten Top XML Applications

*B*y itself, XML is nothing but plain, simple text. When you enrich XML with XML-based technologies, however, its benefits can't be overstated. XML applications provide powerful tools to display and work with the data in your XML documents.

Remember, industry requirements drive a lot of XML development. Thus, it makes sense that many XML applications represent industry initiatives. Many such applications are already available — for free! In this chapter, we highlight a few of the most interesting XML applications designed for specific uses.

Channel Definition Format (CDF)

Brought to you by Microsoft and DataChannel, the Channel Definition Format (CDF) is a DTD that describes push channels. CDF is no newcomer — CDF files first appeared in Microsoft Internet Explorer 4.0.

CDF defines ways for Web publishers to provide frequent updates to collections of information, or *channels*. These updates are automatically delivered to users — from any Web server. If you serve a large audience, CDF might be the application for you. One of the benefits of CDF is the way it allows Web authors to optimize the broadcast of their content to millions of Internet users. For more information on CDF, see Chapter 18, which is devoted to CDF.

Read more about CDF on the W3C Web site at `www.w3.org/TR/NOTE-CDFsubmit.html`. Robin Cover's site also provides useful CDF coverage, at `www.oasis-open.org/cover/gen-apps.html#cdf`.

DocBook, Anyone?

DocBook is a standard SGML DTD designed to capture computer documentation and other types of lengthy, complex documents. In addition, DocBook's emerging XML implementation makes it interesting to XML authors. DocBook already enjoys worldwide use in hundreds of organizations that manage millions of pages of documentation, in a variety of print and online formats. Chapter 20 covers DocBook in detail.

Visit Robin Cover's site at `www.oasis-open.org/docbook/` for more information on this subject.

Mathematical Markup Language (MathML)

Based on years of hard labor, the most recent version of the MathML 1.01 specification appeared on July 7, 1999. Before MathML came along, it was tricky to express mathematical equations in Web pages. As an XML application, MathML supports mathematical and scientific markup for use on the Web. But, it doesn't end there: You can also use MathML for computer algebra systems, mathematical typesetting, and voice synthesis. Chapter 19 covers MathML in detail.

Read more about MathML at its W3C home at `www.w3.org/Math/`. Robin Cover's site also offers a wealth of information on this application. Visit `www.oasis-open.org/cover/xml.html#xml-mml` for more information.

Scalable Vector Graphics (SVG)

Scalable Vector Graphics (SVG) is a language for describing two-dimensional graphics in XML. SVG is currently a working draft at the W3C, which means that it's still in the development stages. However, its potential is promising.

SVG allows for three basic types of objects: vector graphic shapes (paths consisting of straight lines and curves), images, and text. The drive behind SVG is to develop a standard for the Web-based display of such objects.

Graphical objects can be grouped, styled, and added to previously rendered objects. What's more exciting is that these objects can be dynamic and interactive! The Document Object Model (DOM) for SVG, which includes the full XML DOM, allows authors to use scripting to create straightforward and efficient vector graphics animation for any SVG graphical object.

We wish we could outline all the fun ways to create graphics using SVG, but that would require its own book. To read more about SVG, visit the W3C at `www.w3.org/TR/SVG/`.

Resource Description Framework (RDF)

The Resource Description Framework (RDF) is a framework for *metadata* — the stuff that machines sometimes exchange when they talk to each other. RDF assures interoperability between applications that exchange application- or platform-specific information — you know, metadata — across the Web.

Why might this concern you? Because RDF helps increase the relevance of your searches. That alone gets us excited and might be a boon to you, too. Anything to keep from wading through countless documents only to find irrelevant information on a two-headed reptile from New Guinea is okay in our book! Briefly put, RDF provides a basis for generic tools for authoring, manipulating, and searching machine-readable data on the Web.

The RDF specification resides at `www.w3.org/TR/REC-rdf-syntax/`. To read more about RDF, visit Dave Beckett's excellent site on this subject at `www.cs.ukc.ac.uk/people/staff/djb1/research/metadata/rdf.shtml`.

Synchronized Multimedia Integration Language (SMIL)

We talked a little about graphics, so now we turn your attention to multimedia. Ever since desktop systems started to include loudspeakers, multimedia has played a significant role on some Web sites. If this kind of thing interests you, you might want to keep up with the Synchronized Multimedia Integration Language (SMIL, pronounced "smile").

SMIL enables you to integrate a set of independent multimedia objects into a synchronized multimedia presentation. As stated by the W3C, using SMIL, an author can

✔ Describe the temporal behavior of the presentation

✔ Describe the layout of the presentation on a screen

✔ Associate hyperlinks with media objects.

This means that SMIL enables authors to create television-like content for the Web, yet avoid the limitations of traditional television while lowering the bandwidth requirements to transmit such content across the Internet. What, movies on the Web? In theory, producing audio-visual content is easy with SMIL. The best part is that using SMIL doesn't require that you learn a programming language; you can create it with a simple text editor.

To keep track of SMIL progress, stay tuned to `www.w3.org/TR/REC-smil/`.

Web Interface Definition Language (WIDL)

Business plays a key role in XML development, as it has from the get-go. In this discussion of industry-driven applications, we can't omit the one whose focus is to make e-commerce easier. The Web Interface Definition Language (WIDL) uses XML to enable direct access to Web data from e-commerce or business applications. WIDL enables a practical and cost-effective way for diverse systems to integrate readily across corporate intranets and the Internet.

As always, Robin Cover's site pulls through with plenty of information. You can find that information at `www.oasis-open.org/cover/xml.html#widl`. You should also visit the W3C site at `www.w3.org/TR/NOTE-widl`.

XML-Data

A highly collaborative effort produced the XML-Data specification, which provides a mechanism to reference binary data within XML documents. We include XML-Data in our application list because of its unique implications for XML. The XML-Data specification proposes that XML document types be described using an XML document itself, rather than through SGML-based DTD syntax.

XML-Data represents an XML tag set that allows you to precisely describe text structures, relational schemas, and more. Simply put, at the center of XML-Data is a DTD for describing DTDs. But, wait, we don't want to confuse anyone here. XML-Data does not replace a DTD; it's just an alternative expression for that DTD. Its beauty is that it can specify so much more than an ordinary DTD.

To read more about XML-Data, and understand its powers, visit `www.w3.org/ TR/1998/NOTE-XML-data/`. To be fair, you should also read the W3C's XML Schema work. Part one of a two-part discussion is found at `www.w3.org/TR/xmlschema-1`.

Extensible HyperText Markup Language (XHTML)

If you're a regular on the Web, you're already familiar with the Hypertext Markup Language (HTML). Now with XML on the stage and grabbing all the attention — deservedly so — the W3C went back to the drawing tables and designed a way combine both HTML and XML. XHTML is HTML as an application of XML. In other words, you get the extensibility that XML offers while using the same ol' HTML tags you're used to.

To read more — and we think you should — visit the W3C's XHTML specification at `www.w3.org/TR/xhtml1/`. You might want to also read the W3C's HTML Compatibility Guidelines found at `www.w3.org/TR/xhtml1/ #guidelines`.

Create XML Applications with Zope

We want to switch gears for a second. Although this chapter focuses on applications used with XML, we'd like to also point you to software that allows you to create your own XML application. Zope 2.1.1 is a free, open-source application server that enables you to create your own XML applications. Created by Digital Creations, Zope runs on both Windows and UNIX platforms.

Zope works in an object-oriented environment. More plainly, Zope views a Web application in terms of objects, which define not only types of data, but the kinds of operations (called *methods* in object-oriented programming lingo) that may be performed on those objects.

Thus, Zope enables you to combine objects to create powerful and flexible ways to acquire, manage, and manipulate all kinds of data. As you'd expect, these object collections can respond to Web requests dynamically, making it easy to build interactive Web-based applications. The result is dynamic content and a happy content creator. Therefore, if you can't find the right XML application for your needs, you might want to create one yourself using Zope. Read more about this open-source treasure at `www.zope.org`.

This is the end of our chapter on XML applications, but that doesn't mean these are the only applications worth investigating. To see a fairly exhaustive list, visit `www.oasis-open.org/cover/xml.html#applications` or `www.xml.com`. If you do a little research on your own, you might find an application that's perfect for your needs!

Appendix

About the CD

. . . .

*Y*ou'll find the following goodies — and more — on the CD:

- ✔ The W3C's own XML-aware Amaya Web browser
- ✔ Microsoft's IE 5.0 Web browser
- ✔ Vervet Logic's XML Pro v2.0 XML Editor
- ✔ Techno2000 USA's cool (and cheap) Clip! XML Editor

The CD does not have a customized user interface. Instead, we built the contents around HTML files that you can open with any Web browser. Look for a file named readme.txt and use its index to search most of the content of the CD. The only stuff not accessible through the HTML interface is a collection of folders containing software for your evaluation and use. This material is documented in this appendix in the section entitled "What You'll Find."

System Requirements

Make sure your computer meets the minimum system requirements listed next. Otherwise, you might have problems using the contents of the CD.

- ✔ A PC with a 486 or faster processor or a Mac OS computer with a 68030 or faster processor.
- ✔ Microsoft Windows 95 or later or Mac OS system software 7.5 or later.
- ✔ At least 8MB of total RAM installed on your computer. For best performance, we recommend that Windows 95-equipped PCs (or newer) and Mac OS computers with PowerPC processors have at least 16MB of RAM installed.
- ✔ At least 150MB of hard drive space available to install all the software from the CD. (You need less space if you don't install every program.)
- ✔ A CD-ROM drive — quad speed (4x) or faster.
- ✔ A sound card for PCs. (Mac OS computers have built-in sound support.)

✔ A monitor capable of displaying at least 256 colors or grayscale.

✔ A modem with a speed of at least 14,400 bps.

If you need more information on the basics, check out *PCs For Dummies,* 7th Edition, by Dan Gookin; *Macs For Dummies,* 6th Edition, by David Pogue; *Windows 98 For Dummies, Windows 95 For Dummies, Windows NT Workstation For Dummies,* or *Windows 2000 Professional for Dummies,* all by Andy Rathbone (the last two titles include contributions from Sharon Crawford and Microsoft Corporation) and all published by IDG Books Worldwide, Inc.

Using the CD with Microsoft Windows

If you're running Windows 95, 98, NT, or 2000, follow these steps to get to the items on the CD:

1. **Insert the CD into your computer's CD-ROM drive.**

   Give your computer a moment to take a look at the CD.

2. **When the light on your CD-ROM drive goes out, double-click the My Computer icon. (It's probably in the top-left corner of your desktop.)**

   This action opens the My Computer window, which shows you all the drives attached to your computer as well as the Control Panel and a few other handy things.

3. **Double-click the icon for your CD-ROM drive.**

   Another window opens, showing you all the folders and files on the CD.

4. **Double-click the file called License.txt.**

   This file contains the end-user license that you agree to by using the CD. When you've finished reading the license, close the program (most likely NotePad) that displayed the file.

5. **Double-click the file called Readme.txt.**

   This file contains instructions about installing the software from this CD. It might be helpful to leave this text file open while you're using the CD.

6. **Double-click the folder for the software you are interested in.**

   Be sure to read the descriptions of the programs in the next section of this appendix (much of this information also shows up in the Readme file). These descriptions give you more precise information about the programs' folder names and about finding and running the installer program.

7. **Find the file called Setup.exe, Install.exe, or something similar (it varies depending on the software), and double-click that file.**

   The program's installer walks you through the process of setting up your new software.

Using the CD with the Mac OS

To install the items from the CD to your hard drive, follow these steps:

1. **Insert the CD into your computer's CD-ROM drive.**

   In a moment, an icon representing the CD you just inserted appears on your Mac desktop. Chances are, the icon looks like a CD-ROM.

2. **Double-click the CD icon to show the CD's contents.**

3. **Double-click the Read Me First icon.**

   This text file contains information about the CD's programs and any last-minute instructions not covered here.

4. **To install most programs, just drag the program's folder from the CD window and drop it on your hard drive icon.**

5. **Some programs come with installer programs; with those, you simply open the program's folder on the CD and double-click the Install or Installer icon.**

   After you've installed the programs you want, you can eject the CD. Carefully place it back in the plastic jacket of the book for safekeeping.

What You'll Find

The following sections provide a summary of the software on the CD arranged in alphabetical order by package name. The product names correspond to the folders that appear on the CD, so they should be easy to find!

Adept Editor LE

www.arbortext.com/Products/products.html

ArborText has long been one of the leading lights in SGML technology, so it's not surprising that they've taken to XML in the past two years. The company's Adept Editor LE is a entry-level text editor that can handle both XML and SGML DTDs and offers basic editing and validation services. A 30-day evaluation version is included on the CD for Windows desktops only. The company also offers a full-blown XML and SGML editor called Adept Editor, which supports more advanced editing and user interface customization features. ***Note:*** You'll need a key to access this program. Please review the ReadMe.txt file within the Adept file for more details.

Ælfred v1.2a

www.microstar.com/aelfred.html

Ælfred is a small, fast, DTD-aware Java-based XML parser from Microstar Software, Ltd. It's designed especially for Java programmers who want to include XML support in applets without incurring major performance overhead. The freeware version included on the CD is Windows-only and operates within several demonstration applets included with the software distribution on the CD. This is more of a developer's tool than an end-user tool, so consider yourself warned!

Amaya

`www.w3.org/amaya/`

Amaya is a freeware, XML-aware Web browser developed under the aegis of the World Wide Web Consortium (W3C), mostly so they could have a tool that would let them view XML documents online. You might find this tool handy for the same reason. Versions of Amaya have been built for Linux, Solaris, and Windows; the source code for this tool is available, so it can be compiled for other platforms as well. The CD includes only the Windows version of Amaya.

Clip! XML Editor v1.52

`www.t2000-usa.com/product/clip_index.html`

Clip! from Techno2000 USA, Inc is another $99.95 XML package that offers surprisingly sophisticated features and functions. We used its capability to auto-generate DTDs from XML markup to build many of the DTDs that appear on the CD. A limited-functionality, Windows-only version of the program appears on the CD.

Expat

`www.jclark.com/xml/expat.html`

Expat is a powerful XML parser toolkit that can not only parse XML files, but can also be reused when building XML-based applications. Expat also offers validation services, which makes it pretty valuable. The version included on the CD is freeware and has been compiled for use on Windows desktops. The author, James Clark, makes source code for this tool available on his Web site, so it's possible to compile this code for use on other platforms as well.

HP EzMath v1.1

`www.w3.org/People/Raggett/EzMath/`

Dave Raggett is an employee of the W3C who has worked on Web-based mathematical notation for years and is the W3C's liaison to the MathML working group. In his copious spare time, he developed a simple MathML-based mathematics editor with Davy Batsalle for use on the Web. It's called HP EzMath (the work was funded in part by Hewlett-Packard; hence their initials appear in the software's name). The program is freeware and is currently available only for Windows desktops (but support for other platforms is under development).

Internet Explorer 5.0

www.microsoft.com/ie/

Yes, folks, we have the world's most popular and widely used Web browser on the CD, courtesy of Microsoft Corporation. Although IE 5.0 doesn't support XML completely or directly, it does as well as any of the major browsers do nowadays. Translation: You need plug-ins to enable IE 5.0 to display the fruits of your XML labors — that's why we've included several such plug-ins in this collection of software!

Jumbo

www.vsms.nottingham.ac.uk/vsms/java/jumbo/

Peter Murray-Rust is one of the originators of the Chemical Markup Language (CML). He developed Jumbo — a freeware, Java-based XML browser — primarily to display his CML markup. This tool works either as an applet within a Web browser (on any platform with a Java 1.0.2 Java Virtual Machine or newer) or as a standalone application (Windows only). It's a good place to start looking at XML documents in their native form.

Lark v1.0

www.textuality.com/Lark/

Tim Bray is a charter member of the XML working group at the W3C. He's also the author of Lark, a simple, nonvalidating XML processor. This package is freeware, and is available only for Windows desktops. It's a compact, handy tool for working with XML files.

LiveMath Maker (and plug-in v3.0)

www.livemath.com/

LiveMath, from Theorist Interactive, LLC, is a well-known mathematical modeling and analysis package, with strong general support for a wide variety of functions and applications. The current version just happens to support MathML, which is why we include a trial version of the commercial package on the CD along with a freeware plug-in that can read and display the contents of LiveMath Notebooks directly.

Mozilla

www.mozilla.org/

Mozilla, from the Mozilla Organization, is an open source implementation of the Netscape Navigator Web browser. This version includes some capabilities to read and render XML markup, which is why we include it on the CD. Use it to view XML markup, especially when the markup has a CSS style sheet to help control its online appearance.

SP

www.jclark.com/sp/index.html

SP is a powerful SGML (and XML) parser that the redoubtable James Clark created for public use. SP reads a DTD to make sense of the markup you hand it, and it does a bang-up job. Many heavy-duty SGML and XML developers consider SP an important tool in their kit, so you might like it, too!

WebEQ v2.3.3

www.webeq.com/

WebEQ stands for Web Equations and consists of a 30-day trial evaluation copy of Geometry Technologies math viewer Web plug-in. For Internet Explorer and Netscape versions 4.0 and newer, this software provides a plug-in that supports MathML directly. Use it to add the capability to view MathML markup to standard HTML pages.

XML Pro v2.01

www.vervet.com

Vervet Logic's XML Pro is a low-cost ($99.95) but full-featured XML editor for Windows platforms that supports a variety of XML document design and creation functions. The version of XML Pro included on the CD is a complete version, but it won't allow you to save or print your work. It can give you a good idea of what the full version can do, so it's great for a test drive.

XSL Lint

http://nwalsh.com/xsl/xslint/xslint.html

XSL Lint, by Norman Walsh, is a syntax checker for XSL documents, otherwise known as style sheets. The term *Lint* has a long history in the UNIX community, where such utilities were introduced to parse code files and check for errors so that developers could make sure their files were syntactically correct before compiling them. Today, Lint utilities of many kinds abound and are used to check files for syntax errors as part of the development process. This freeware tool, even though it's an alpha version, makes building XSL style sheets much easier.

XT

www.jclark.com/xml/xt.html

XT is yet another fine tool from James Clark. It's a Java-based tool that implements XSLT (XSL Transformations) services as specified in the PR-xslt-19991008 specification from the W3C. It's a useful tool for those who want to experiment with using XSLT to translate XML markup into another form — often, HTML for Web delivery — to make XML-based data available online.

This freeware software tool is provided in Windows-only form on the CD, but the source code is available at Clark's Web site for those who want to compile it for use on other platforms.

Book-related CD Content

In addition to the many software packages mentioned in the previous sections, the CD also contains lots of information based on content that appears in the pages of the book itself.

The xmlfdum2 folder contains the majority of the *XML For Dummies* files, most of which are HTML documents. Here are the details:

- **default.htm:** The home page for the entire collection (start your exploration of the folder here). ***Note:*** The CD contains several files called default.htm; this home-page file is at the root of the xml4dum folder, at the same level as all the subfolders.
- **menu.htm:** A list of all files in the xml4dum folder, with hyperlinks and graphics.
- **contact.htm:** A list of e-mail links for the authors and the CD's Webmaster.
- **copy.htm:** Important copyright information.

The xmlfdum2/contents directory contains lists of the book's contents by chapter. Open the default.htm file and click Chapter Contents in this subfolder to view a hyperlinked listing of all chapter titles; then click on a chapter title to see a list of what that chapter covers.

You can go straight to a chapter by clicking the appropriate filename (the files are named chnncont.htm, where nn is the chapter number). You might find that this is a faster way to access a chapter's specific information.

The xmlfdum2/examples directory contains examples of all the XML code that appears in the book, sorted by chapter. Open the default.htm file in this subfolder to see a hyperlinked listing of all the chapter titles; then just click on a chapter title to see that chapter's examples. To return to the list of chapter titles, click on Chapter Examples from the bottom image map or text navigation menu.

Or you can go straight to a chapter by clicking on the appropriate filename (the files are named chnncont.htm, where nn is the two-digit chapter number) to see the examples from that chapter.

The xmlfdum2/extras directory contains information about XML online resources and applications, and includes a copy of all the DTDs that are used anywhere in the book. Open the default.htm file in this subfolder to see a hyperlinked table of contents for the folder; then click an item's name (Extras in this case) to view that item. To return to the list of titles in the Extras section, click Extras from the bottom image map or text navigation menu.

The `xmlfdum2/graphics` directory on the CD includes all the graphics files used on this CD. Likewise, the `xmlfdum2/urls` directory includes a hotlist of all URLs mentioned in the book. Open the `default.htm` file in this subfolder to see a hyperlinked listing of all the chapter titles; then just click on a chapter title to see the URLs cited in that chapter.

To return to the list of chapter titles, click Chapter URLs from the bottom image map or text navigation menu. Or to go straight to a chapter, click the appropriate filename (the files are named `chnncont.htm`, where nn is the two-digit chapter number) to see that chapter's URLs.

If You Have Problems of the CD Kind

We tried our best to compile programs that work on most computers with the minimum system requirements. Alas, your computer might differ, and some programs might not work properly for some reason.

The two likeliest problems are that your system doesn't have enough memory (RAM) for the programs you want to use, or other programs are affecting the installation or running of a program. If you get error messages such as `Not enough memory` or `Setup cannot continue`, try one or more of the following methods and then try using the software again:

- **Turn off any antivirus software that you have on your computer.** Installers sometimes mimic virus activity and might make your computer incorrectly believe that a virus is infecting it.

- **Close all running programs.** The more programs you're running, the less memory is available to other programs. Installers also typically update files and programs. So if you keep other programs running, installation might not work properly.

- **Have your local computer store add more RAM to your computer.** This is, admittedly, a drastic and somewhat expensive step. However, if you have a Windows 95 PC or newer or a Mac OS computer with a PowerPC chip or newer, adding more memory can help the speed of your computer and allow more programs to run at the same time.

If you still have trouble with installing the items from the CD, please call the Hungry Minds Customer Care phone number, 800-762-2974 (outside the United States, call 317-572-3993).

Glossary

active channel: In Microsoft Internet Explorer 4.0 and later, active channels are a collection of Web sites developed specifically for Internet Explorer that use Dynamic HTML to present their material.

ASCII (American Standard Code for Information Interchange): A coding method to translate characters, such as numbers, text, and symbols, into digital form. ASCII includes only 127 characters, and is only useful for English (okay, and Latin, but nothing else really).

attribute: In XML, a property associated with an XML tag that is a named characteristic of the tag. An attribute also provides additional data about an element.

attribute list declaration: Defines the name, data type, and default value (if any) of each attribute associated with an element.

CDF (Channel Definition Format): An XML-based file format, developed by Microsoft, for the description of channel information.

CGI (Common Gateway Interface): A standard that allows CGI programs of various types to interact with Web servers, usually to provide interactive response to user input from a browser.

channel: Information about organized content on an intranet or the Internet. Channels allow you to categorize and describe Web site content and make that data available to users on demand. Channels are specific to Internet Explorer.

character entity: A string of characters that represents other characters; for example, `&lt;` and `&Egrave;` show a string of characters (`lt` and `Egrave`) that stand for other characters (< and È).

character set: When referring to script, a character set represents a collection of values that maps to some specific symbol set or alphabet.

CML (Chemical Markup Language): An XML-compatible markup language with specific extensions for describing molecules and compounds.

content identifier: A token that can be used to uniquely identify any piece of data or content.

content model: Defines what components may make up a certain part of a document.

CSS (Cascading Style Sheets): A method of coding that allows users to define how certain HTML, DHTML, or XML structural elements, such as paragraphs and headings, should be displayed using style rules instead of additional markup. The versions of CSS are CSS1 and CSS2, with CSS2 being the most recent version.

DocBook: A heavy-duty DTD designed and implemented by HaL Computer Systems and O'Reilly & Associates in approximately 1991. It's used for authoring books, articles, and manuals, particularly those of a technical nature.

document type declaration: Tells the processor where the DTD is located and contains declarations for the particular document.

DOM (Document Object Model): A platform- and language-neutral programming interface that allows programs and scripts to access and update the content, structure, and style of documents in a standard way.

DOS (Disk Operating System): A widely used PC operating system. DOS has been largely supplanted by Windows on most desktops.

DSSSL (Document Style Semantics and Specification Language): A superset of XSL. DSSSL is a document style language used primarily with SGML (Standard Generalized Markup Language) files.

DTD (Document Type Definition): The statement of rules for an XML document that specify which elements (the markup tags) and attributes (values associated with specific tags) are allowed in your documents.

EDI (Electronic Data Interchange): A standard for the electronic exchange of basic business information.

e-commerce (electronic commerce): The exchange of money and goods over the Internet or some other public network.

element: A section of a document defined by start- and end-tags or an empty tag, including the content.

element content model: A way to include a specification regarding children in element declarations. For example, you can specify that an element may contain only child elements.

element type: A specific — or named — element, such as `<Book>` or `<Title>`.

element type declaration: Provides a description of an element type and its content within the DTD.

empty tag: A tag used in markup languages that does not require a closing tag. In XML, an empty tag must be identified with a slash (/) before the closing greater than sign (>). Occasionally called singleton tags.

entity: A character string that represents another string of characters.

entity declaration: Defines a named set of information that can be referenced by a name as an entity within a document or DTD.

external parameter entity references: Parameter entities that refer to information that's in a separate file than the DTD or document prolog in which they appear.

external subset: The portion of a DTD that's stored in an external file. Also called an *external DTD* and an *external DTD subset*.

FAQ (Frequently Asked Questions): A collection of questions and answers related to a specific topic. FAQs are most commonly found on Usenet newsgroups.

freeware: Software offered by companies at no charge.

FTP (File Transfer Protocol): An Internet file transfer service based on TCP/IP protocols. FTP provides a way to copy files to and from FTP servers elsewhere on a network.

GedML (Genealogical Markup Language): A set of XML tags that are used to describe genealogical data.

general entity: An entity created in the DTD but used in the XML document.

GUI (Graphical User Interface): A computer interface in which windows, graphics, and a mouse (or trackball) are used to interact with information instead of plain text at a command line.

HTML (HyperText Markup Language): One of the document-description markup languages used to create Web pages.

HTML syntax: The rules that govern the construction of intelligible HTML documents or markup fragments.

hypertext: A way of linking document locations such that clicking a particular element takes the user to another location within the same document or to another Web document.

inheritance: When an element (the child or sibling) takes on, or inherits, the characteristics assigned to a higher level element (the parent).

inline styles: A style that applies to an element within the XML document itself.

internal entity: An entity that contains the content directly within the declaration.

internal subset: The portion of the DTD that appears within the document. Also called an *internal DTD subset* or *internal DTD*.

intranet: A network within a company or organization that uses the same protocols as the Internet.

ISO (International Organization for Standardization): The most popular computing and communication standards organization. It is comprised of standards bodies from all over the world.

ISO-Latin-1: Also known as ISO 8859-1 (the numeric equivalent), it's the default character set used by XML and HTML.

Java: An object-oriented programming language used for Web application development. It was created by Sun Microsystems.

linking element: An element that contains a link. In HTML ⟨img⟩ and ⟨a⟩ elements are examples of linking elements. In XLink, ⟨simple⟩ elements are examples of linking elements.

locator: Data that identifies a resource to which you can link.

macro: A text or code script that performs an action when called, usually used to automate repetitive keystrokes, mouse click sequences, or both.

MathML (Mathematical Markup Language): An XML application that provides a way of representing mathematical and scientific content on the Web, especially where complex formulas or arcane notation are used.

metadata: Specially defined elements that describe a document's structure, content, or rendering, within the document itself or through external references. (Metadata literally means data about data.)

metalanguage: A language used to communicate information about language itself; many experts consider both SGML and XML to be metalanguages because they can be used to define markup languages.

MIME (Multipurpose Internet Mail Extension): Extensions that allow e-mail messages to carry multiple types of data (such as binary, audio, video, and graphics) as attachments. MIME types are also used to identify document types during transfers over the Web. XML documents are text/xml or application/xml.

mixed content: Allows your elements to contain character data or character data with child elements.

MSXML (Microsoft XML): The Microsoft Internet Explorer XML parser.

multimedia presentation: A presentation that involves two or more forms of media (text, audio, and video, for example).

namespace: See *XML namespace*.

newsgroups: A group of users who discuss issues related to a specific topic. Newsgroups are typically found on Usenet or other news servers.

node: Used in XML to denote a piece of the tree structure.

notation declaration: Associates a notation name with information that can help find an interpreter of information described by the notation.

numeric entity: A string of numbers that represents a character. These are identified by a pound sign (#) that follow an ampersand. For example, < and È show a string of numbers (60 and 200) that stand for characters (< and È). More commonly called *character references*.

occurrence indicator: A symbol, such as ?, *, and +, that's included in an element declaration to further provide structural guidance for your elements, such as how many times a portion of a content model may appear.

OFX (Open Financial Exchange): A specification that provides a standard way of describing financial data that banks, the Web, and your personal financial software can understand.

operating system: The underlying control program that makes the hardware run on a computer system. It also supports the execution of applications. Macintosh, Windows, UNIX, and DOS are common operating systems.

parameter entity: An entity created and used within a DTD.

PDF (Portable Document Format): A graphics file format created by Adobe Systems. To view a PDF file, you must download Adobe Acrobat Reader or have access to an Adobe application such as PageMaker or PhotoShop.

POST method: A means of returning information provided by a user through an HTML form to a server. Posted data returns to the server as directed by a CGI script. Often, such data is analyzed or processed in some way by an application that then returns a new Web page, often generated on-the-fly, to the user's browser.

processing instruction: Similar to a comment, but it provides a way to send instructions to computer programs or applications, not humans.

property: Another name for an attribute.

pull technology: A technique in which your browser retrieves information from a Web server.

push technology: A technique used to initiate delivery of material from a server to a properly equipped client. Also called *push publishing*.

PWS (Personal Web Server): A low-end version of IIS found on Windows 95/98. PWS allows your Windows 95/98 machine to act as a Web server.

remote resource: A document, an image, a sound file, or any other kind of resource located somewhere other than in the document that contains the link.

resource: Anything that can be retrieved over the Internet, for example, a document, an image, a sound file, or even a list generated automatically in response to a query.

root element: In XML, the element you create that is the equivalent of the `<html>` element in HTML. It's a single top-level tag. Also called a *document element*.

schema: A pattern that represents the data's model and defines the elements (or objects), their attributes (or properties), and the relationships between the different elements.

scripting: Lightweight programming within a Web page.

scripting language: A specialized language used to create scripts that, when inserted into a Web page, control various elements of the page, such as the user interface, styles, and HTML markup. JavaScript and VBScript are the primary scripting languages.

selector: In CSS, identifies the tag to which the style rule applies.

semantics: The science of describing what words mean; it's the opposite of syntax.

SGML (Standard Generalized Markup Language): A metalanguage used to construct markup languages, such as HTML and XML.

SGML declaration: Contains certain instructions, independent of a DTD, for an SGML parser.

SGML parser: A program that interprets SGML and passes the document structure and contents to another program.

SMIL (Synchronized Multimedia Integration Language): A language that allows the integration of a collection of multimedia objects that follow a schedule laid out by the developer.

SQL server: A database server that uses the Structured Query Language (SQL) to accept requests for data access. Also, the name of either of two database management products from Sybase and Microsoft.

style rule: A rule in an XML document that specifies a pattern and an action that the rule applies when the specified pattern is found. Such rules can result from the application of Cascading Style Sheets (CSS) or by the application of Extensible Stylesheet Language (XSL), which is also a dialect of XML.

style sheet: A file that holds the layout settings for a certain category of a document. Style sheets, like templates, contain settings for headers and footers, tabs, margins, fonts, columns, and more.

syntax: See *HTML syntax*.

template: The instructions in an XSLT style sheet that control how an element and its content should be converted. A template identifies which element in a document should be changed and then specifies how the element should be changed.

traversal: The act of using a link. By following a link, you traverse from one resource to another.

Unicode character set: A 16-bit character encoding scheme defined in ISO/IED 10646 that encompasses standard Roman and Greek alphabets, plus mathematical symbols, special punctuation, and non-Roman alphabets including Hebrew, Chinese, Arabic, Hangul, and other ideographic character sets.

UNIX: Designed by a hacker in 1969 as an interactive time-sharing operating system to play games on, it is now one of the most powerful multi-user operating systems around.

URI (Uniform Resource Identifier): A character string that identifies the type and location of an Internet resource.

valid: When an XML document adheres to a DTD.

validating parser: A software utility that compares your XML document to a declared DTD.

W3C (World Wide Web Consortium): The organization that develops standards for the Web.

well-formed document: An XML document that adheres to the rules that make an it easy for a computer to interpret.

white space: The area in a document created by spaces or paragraphs that do not contain text or graphics; in other words, the blank part of a page.

WIDL (Web Interface Definition Language): A relatively new, object-oriented, SGML-based markup language that helps designers create powerful, intuitive, Web-based user interfaces.

WYSIWYG (What You See Is What You Get) interface: An interface that allows users to enter and see information as it should appear in the final document, rather showing all the markup embedded with the text or other content.

XHTML (Extensible Hypertext Markup Language): The reformulation of HTML 4.0 as an application of XML 1.0.

XLink (XML Linking Language): In XML documents, it's a language that provides a simple set of instructions that describe the links among objects.

XML (Extensible Markup Language): A system for defining, validating, and sharing document formats.

XML declaration: The code at the very beginning of an XML document that specifies which version of XML the document is written in. (Currently, it must state XML 1.0 because that's the only version available.)

XML dialect: Any implementation of domain-specific XML notation governed by a standard DTD designed to support chemical markup (CML), mathematical markup (MathML), channel definitions (CDF), and so forth.

XML entity: A string of characters that lets a viewer display a symbol, yet not interpret it as markup. An entity often lets a viewer represent a larger range of characters than might otherwise be possible, yet keep character sets small.

XML namespace: A unique identifier (attached through a prefix) that links an XML markup element to a specific DTD.

XML notation: A form of XML markup designed to accomplish some specific objective; examples include the mathematical and chemical notations supported by the MathML and CML XML dialects, respectively.

XPath: A language that describes directions for how to get from one place in an XML document to another. XPath is used by XSLT and XPointer.

XPointer: Provides a method for getting to places inside a document even though you may not have edit privileges for that document.

XSL (Extensible Stylesheet Language): Defines the specification for an XML document's presentation and appearance. Both CSS and XSL provide a platform-independent method for specifying the document's presentation style.

XSLT (XSL Transformations): An XSL conversion tool that provides a set of rules to convert documents described by one set of tags to documents described by another set of tags.

Index

Notes

Notes

Not all software on the CD is governed by the license; see the CD for more info.

Hungry Minds, Inc.,
End-User License Agreement

READ THIS. You should carefully read these terms and conditions before opening the software packet(s) included with this book ("Book"). This is a license agreement ("Agreement") between you and Hungry Minds, Inc. ("HMI"). By opening the accompanying software packet(s), you acknowledge that you have read and accept the following terms and conditions. If you do not agree and do not want to be bound by such terms and conditions, promptly return the Book and the unopened software packet(s) to the place you obtained them for a full refund.

1. **License Grant.** HMI grants to you (either an individual or entity) a nonexclusive license to use one copy of the enclosed software program(s) (collectively, the "Software") solely for your own personal or business purposes on a single computer (whether a standard computer or a workstation component of a multi-user network). The Software is in use on a computer when it is loaded into temporary memory (RAM) or installed into permanent memory (hard disk, CD-ROM, or other storage device). HMI reserves all rights not expressly granted herein.

2. **Ownership.** HMI is the owner of all right, title, and interest, including copyright, in and to the compilation of the Software recorded on the disk(s) or CD-ROM ("Software Media"). Copyright to the individual programs recorded on the Software Media is owned by the author or other authorized copyright owner of each program. Ownership of the Software and all proprietary rights relating thereto remain with HMI and its licensers.

3. **Restrictions On Use and Transfer.**

   (a) You may only (i) make one copy of the Software for backup or archival purposes, or (ii) transfer the Software to a single hard disk, provided that you keep the original for backup or archival purposes. You may not (i) rent or lease the Software, (ii) copy or reproduce the Software through a LAN or other network system or through any computer subscriber system or bulletin-board system, or (iii) modify, adapt, or create derivative works based on the Software.

   (b) You may not reverse engineer, decompile, or disassemble the Software. You may transfer the Software and user documentation on a permanent basis, provided that the transferee agrees to accept the terms and conditions of this Agreement and you retain no copies. If the Software is an update or has been updated, any transfer must include the most recent update and all prior versions.

4. **Restrictions on Use of Individual Programs.** You must follow the individual requirements and restrictions detailed for each individual program in the "About the CD" appendix. These limitations are also contained in the individual license agreements recorded on the Software Media. These limitations may include a requirement that after using the program for a specified period of time, the user must pay a registration fee or discontinue use. By opening the Software packet(s), you will be agreeing to abide by the licenses and restrictions for these individual programs that are detailed in the "About the CD" appendix and on the Software Media. None of the material on this Software Media or listed in this Book may ever be redistributed, in original or modified form, for commercial purposes.

5. **Limited Warranty.**

   (a) HMI warrants that the Software and Software Media are free from defects in materials and workmanship under normal use for a period of sixty (60) days from the date of purchase of this Book. If HMI receives notification within the warranty period of defects in materials or workmanship, HMI will replace the defective Software Media.

   (b) HMI AND THE AUTHOR OF THE BOOK DISCLAIM ALL OTHER WARRANTIES, EXPRESS OR IMPLIED, INCLUDING WITHOUT LIMITATION IMPLIED WARRANTIES OF MERCHANTABILITY AND FITNESS FOR A PARTICULAR PURPOSE, WITH RESPECT TO THE SOFTWARE, THE PROGRAMS, THE SOURCE CODE CONTAINED THEREIN, AND/OR THE TECHNIQUES DESCRIBED IN THIS BOOK. HMI DOES NOT WARRANT THAT THE FUNCTIONS CONTAINED IN THE SOFTWARE WILL MEET YOUR REQUIREMENTS OR THAT THE OPERATION OF THE SOFTWARE WILL BE ERROR FREE.

   (c) This limited warranty gives you specific legal rights, and you may have other rights that vary from jurisdiction to jurisdiction.

6. **Remedies.**

   (a) HMI's entire liability and your exclusive remedy for defects in materials and workmanship shall be limited to replacement of the Software Media, which may be returned to HMI with a copy of your receipt at the following address: Software Media Fulfillment Department, Attn.: *XML For Dummies,* 2nd Edition, Hungry Minds, Inc., 10475 Crosspoint Blvd., Indianapolis, IN 46256, or call 1-800-762-2974. Please allow four to six weeks for delivery. This Limited Warranty is void if failure of the Software Media has resulted from accident, abuse, or misapplication. Any replacement Software Media will be warranted for the remainder of the original warranty period or thirty (30) days, whichever is longer.

   (b) In no event shall HMI or the author be liable for any damages whatsoever (including without limitation damages for loss of business profits, business interruption, loss of business information, or any other pecuniary loss) arising from the use of or inability to use the Book or the Software, even if HMI has been advised of the possibility of such damages.

   (c) Because some jurisdictions do not allow the exclusion or limitation of liability for consequential or incidental damages, the above limitation or exclusion may not apply to you.

7. **U.S. Government Restricted Rights.** Use, duplication, or disclosure of the Software for or on behalf of the United States of America, its agencies and/or instrumentalities (the "U.S. Government") is subject to restrictions as stated in paragraph (c)(1)(ii) of the Rights in Technical Data and Computer Software clause of DFARS 252.227-7013, and in subparagraphs (a) through (d) of the Commercial Computer–Restricted Rights clause at FAR 52.227-19, and in similar clauses in the NASA FAR supplement, when applicable.

8. **General.** This Agreement constitutes the entire understanding of the parties and revokes and supersedes all prior agreements, oral or written, between them and may not be modified or amended except in a writing signed by both parties hereto that specifically refers to this Agreement. This Agreement shall take precedence over any other documents that may be in conflict herewith. If any one or more provisions contained in this Agreement are held by any court or tribunal to be invalid, illegal, or otherwise unenforceable, each and every other provision shall remain in full force and effect.

Installation Instructions

The *XML For Dummies* CD offers valuable information that you won't want to miss. If you're running Windows 95, 98, NT, or 2000, follow these steps to install the items from the CD to your hard drive:

1. **Insert the CD into your computer's CD-ROM drive. When the light on your CD-ROM drive goes out, double-click the My Computer icon.**

2. **Double-click the icon for your CD-ROM drive.**

3. **Double-click the file called License.txt. When you've finished reading the license, close the program that displayed the file.**

4. **Double-click the file called Readme.txt.**

   This file contains instructions about installing the software from this CD.

5. **Double-click the folder for the software you're interested in.**

6. **Find the file called Setup.exe, Install.exe, or something similar (it varies depending on the software), and double-click that file.**

   The program's installer walks you through the process of setting up your new software.

If you're using the Mac OS, follow these steps to install the items from the CD to your hard drive:

1. **Insert the CD into your computer's CD-ROM drive. Then double-click the CD icon to show the CD's contents.**

2. **Double-click the Read Me First icon.**

   This text file contains information about the CD's programs and any last-minute instructions not covered in here.

3. **To install most programs, just drag the program's folder from the CD window and drop it on your hard drive icon.**

4. **Some programs come with installer programs; with those, you simply open the program's folder on the CD and double-click the Install or Installer icon.**

   After you've installed the programs you want, you can eject the CD. Carefully place it back in the plastic jacket of the book for safekeeping.

For more information, see the "About the CD" appendix.

FOR DUMMIES
BOOK REGISTRATION

Register This Book and Win!

We want to hear from you!

Visit **dummies.com** to register this ~~book~~ ~~and tell~~ us how you liked it!

✔ Get entered in our monthly prize giveaway.

✔ Give us feedback about this book — tell us what you like best, what you like least, or maybe what you'd like to ask the author and us to change!

✔ Let us know any other *For Dummies* topics that interest you.

Your feedback helps us determine what books to publish, tells us what coverage to add as we revise our books, and lets us know whether we're meeting your needs as a *For Dummies* reader. You're our most valuable resource, and what you have to say is important to us!

Not on the Web yet? It's easy to get started with *Dummies 101®: The Internet For Windows® 98* or *The Internet For Dummies®* at local retailers everywhere.

Or let us know what you think by sending us a letter at the following address:

For Dummies Book Registration
Dummies Press
10475 Crosspoint Blvd.
Indianapolis, IN 46256

™
...FOR DUMMIES

BESTSELLING BOOK SERIES